POLICY AND CHOICE

POLICY AND CHOICE

Public Finance through the Lens of Behavioral Economics

WILLIAM J. CONGDON

JEFFREY R. KLING

SENDHIL MULLAINATHAN

BROOKINGS INSTITUTION PRESS

Washington, D.C.

The Library of Congress has cataloged the hardcover edition as follows:
Congdon, William J.
    Policy and choice : public finance through the lens of behavioral economics / William
J. Congdon, Jeffrey R. Kling, and Sendhil Mullainathan.
        p.   cm.
    Includes bibliographical references and index.
    Summary: "Applies the psychological insights of behavioral economics to economic
concepts such as moral hazard, deadweight loss, and incidence. Explores how deviations
from the standard economic model of decisionmaking—imperfect optimization,
bounded self-control, and nonstandard preferences—might affect public finance policy
regarding externalities, information asymmetries, poverty, and taxes"—Provided by
publisher.
    ISBN 978-0-8157-0498-0 (hardcover : alk. paper)
    1. Finance, Public—Psychological aspects. 2. Economics—Psychological aspects. 3.
Finance, Public—Decision making. 4. Human behavior—Economic aspects. I. Kling,
Jeffrey R. II. Mullainathan, Sendhil. III. Title.
    HJ141.C65 2010
    336—dc22   2010050542
    ISBN 978-0-8157-2258-8 (pbk. : alk. paper)

Digital printing

Printed on acid-free paper

Typeset in Adobe Garamond

Composition by Cynthia Stock
Silver Spring, Maryland

Contents

Acknowledgments

We are grateful to the Smith Richardson Foundation, whose financial support made this book possible. We also are grateful to a host of individuals who read and commented on various drafts of this work, in whole or in part. We thank all of the people at ideas42 and the Brookings Institution whose ideas indirectly and directly contributed to the content here. We especially thank Hunt Allcott, Katherine Baicker, Rebecca Blank, John Friedman, Alex Gelber, Lisa Gennetian, Janet Holtzblatt, Lawrence Katz, Frank Sammartino, Benjamin Schoefer, Josh Schwartzstein, Dmitry Taubinsky, and Bruce Vavrichek for insightful suggestions that improved this work.

We also thank seminar participants at the Congressional Budget Office, the University of Pennsylvania, and the Center on Children and Families at the Brookings Institution as well as participants and panelists at the First Annual Conference in Behavioral Economics, at a panel of the National Tax Association 2009 Spring Symposium, and at a session of the 2010 American Economic Association's annual meeting for their helpful feedback.

Special thanks go to two anonymous reviewers who provided extensive comments on an earlier draft of this manuscript. Their comments on every aspect of the text, ranging from specific citations to the overall organization of the material, were in every instance thoughtful and constructive, and the final version of this work owes their attention and diligence a great debt.

We extend our appreciation to everyone in the Economic Studies program at the Brookings Institution who had a hand in helping us complete this project. We single out for special thanks Karen Dynan, both for her general support of this work and for her role in overseeing its review, and Linda Gianessi, who kept everything on track and who patiently answered all of our questions throughout the process.

Great thanks are due to everyone at the Brookings Press, which had the job of making this book a reality. Managing editor Janet Walker capably shepherded the book through the publishing process. Eileen Hughes, our editor, worked tirelessly and skillfully to improve the clarity and precision of our writing. Marketing director Chris Kelaher did an expert job of developing and coordinating messaging about the book and its themes.

Finally, note that despite the multitude of people whose help we received in preparing this text, the views expressed here, and of course any remaining errors, are those of the authors alone. In particular, the views expressed in this volume should not be interpreted as those of the Congressional Budget Office.

1

Introduction

When should the government intervene in the economy? When do markets fail? How do we craft policies that maximize social welfare? How do we design policies to minimize unintended consequences? Traditional public finance provides a powerful framework to tackle those questions. This framework, however, relies on an overly simple model of human behavior. This book revisits the core questions of public finance but with a psychologically richer perspective on human behavior. We do not merely apply psychology to economic problems; instead, we explore how psychological factors reshape core public finance concepts such as moral hazard, deadweight loss, and incidence.

The Promise

To build our case, we construct a single analytical framework that encompasses both traditional policy levers—taxes and subsidies—and psychologically informed ones—such as defaults and framing. Three examples—health insurance, taxes, and externalities—illustrate how this approach alters our understanding of basic policy problems.

Health Insurance

Models of health insurance emphasize moral hazard. Individuals choose care by comparing the price of care with its benefits. Since under insurance the price of care is often below its actual cost, people may overuse it. For example, because a consumer pays only a fraction of the full cost of an MRI, he or she may decide to get one even if it provides minor benefits. Insurance design seeks to balance the benefits of insurance against inefficient overuse, such as through copayments, health savings accounts, or consumer-directed health plans.[1] For our purposes, notice how the logic of overuse relies crucially on individuals making choices in a narrow, calculating fashion: it occurs because consumers make a trade-off between the price of care and its true benefit.

Medical studies, however, suggest that health care choices are significantly more complex.[2] Take the case of a diabetic who is prescribed medication. The cost-benefit calculus for taking the medication is clear cut. Diabetes is a serious disease, and insulin provides an important tool to manage it: the long-term health benefits drastically outweigh the monetary and "hassle" costs of buying and taking the medication. Human psychology can short-circuit that calculus. A patient focused on day-to-day concerns may simply forget to take his medication; another patient may simply "feel good" and decide that taking the medication is not worth it; and still another may decide to skip a dose simply because the benefits are in the future and not salient right now. Missing a single dose may not feel especially costly relative to the salient hassle costs ("I really don't feel like experiencing the pain of an injection right now"). Medication use by diabetics is not a unique example. Psychology affects decisions about nearly all types of medical care. In other words, the "psychic" cost-benefit calculus may be very different from the economic calculus.

For our purposes, we are particularly interested in how such deviations interact with traditional economic concepts, in this case moral hazard. We must now look beyond *overuse* of care. We must also consider the possibility of *underuse:* care that patients fail to use even when their benefits exceed the cost.[3] That has important implications for policy design. Take the case of copayments—the payments made by an insured person each time he or she uses a medical service. The usual policy logic dictates that we can use elasticity of demand for a category of care to set copayments. A high demand elasticity means that the care is of low value. If small changes in price (which bring it closer to true cost) dissuade many people, the value of that care must not have been very high: a high demand elasticity signals overuse. As a result, copayments should increase with the elasticity of demand.

That logic fails in a behaviorally augmented model. A high elasticity of demand no longer indicates overuse. When a copay increase reduces demand, we can no longer infer that the care is actually of low *social* value; perhaps people were underusing it and we are worsening the problem. When individuals do not choose optimally, a change in demand tells us only that people choose *as if* they do not value the care. Return to the case of insulin treatment for diabetes. A patient who was non-adhering on some days because he feels that medication is optional on days when he "feels good" will show price sensitivity: he will skip more doses on those days if prices are high. In effect, he feels that the care is optional. Increasing copays for such a patient on the basis of that elasticity would, however, be worsening a behavioral bias. In effect, psychology forces us to reinterpret empirical data on demand. Empirical studies can no longer simply use demand elasticities to measure moral hazard. We must understand more about the category of care where the elasticity appears. The demand elasticity is no longer sufficient for setting policy. The optimal amount of a copayment must be based on both knowledge of elasticity and an external assessment of the value of the treatment. In some cases, optimal copayments may even be negative—for example, in cases in which it is worthwhile to pay people to take their medication because of the positive spillover effects of doing so.

We can also examine nonprice levers. Consider the provision of "nudges," the label given by Richard Thaler and Cass Sunstein to psychologically astute interventions that influence behavior.[4] In the case of drug adherence, an example would be simple reminders to take medications. Once we recognize that nudges can affect use of care, we must examine insurance design more broadly. When will insurers nudge patients to use care? When will they nudge patients to reduce use of care? The answer depends on how profits align with health outcomes. Take again the case of drug adherence. Patients' failure to adhere to treatment regimes has long-term costs: hospital admissions, for example, will be higher. A long-term insurer will bear those costs; as a result, a profit-maximizing long-term private insurer will have incentives to devise and implement nudges to increase adherence. Investments in disease management—which many companies increasingly make—can be understood from that perspective. In contrast, a short-term insurer bears none of the costs of patients' non-adherence. They not only have zero incentives to provide nudges to improve adherence, they also have perverse incentives to find nudges that discourage use, even when use has high long-term benefits for the patient. For example, the short-term insurer can create costs by making it a hassle to schedule a doctor's appointment or to refill a prescription. The psychological perspective therefore can add to our understanding of why health insurance is structured in certain ways when provided in a private market.

A fuller integration of behavioral economics and public finance allows us to go beyond just suggesting specific psychologically astute policies to experiment with. It provides a different framework for understanding such traditional public finance levers as copayments and market structure.

Taxes

Governments must raise revenues to provide services. Traditional public finance has a well-developed framework for determining how to set taxes optimally. Models of incidence help us understand who bears the burden of taxes; models of efficiency help us understand how taxation can hinder economic activity. Together they offer practical insights for designing policy for taxes of all stripes: income, sales, and so on. For example, one broad insight is that efficient taxes are those that minimally distort consumer choices. Since individuals were choosing optimally in the absence of taxes, a change in the choices that they make represents a welfare cost. Concretely, one should raise revenues by, for example, taxing low-elasticity goods—taxes on, for example, cigarettes are often justified in part for this reason.

Behavioral economics complicates that logic. One recent study finds, for example, that individuals may fail to perceive sales taxes that are not included in the prices posted on store shelves but are computed at the register.[5] People may simply fail to attend to them—they are not salient at the time of choice. Applying traditional logic, tax non-salience represents an opportunity for governments: they can raise revenues without distorting behavior. That logic, however, is incomplete. Lack of response to a non-salient tax is not the same as lack of response to a salient tax. When people fail to respond to a non-salient tax, there is an error: they make consumption choices as if an item costs X, but in purchasing the item they actually spend $X + $Y. As a result, they have $Y less to spend in the future than they had planned.

How that affects all other consumption must now enter the welfare calculation. Consider two polar cases. The lost money could be treated as a pure income effect: individuals see that they have $Y less to spend on all other goods and adjust accordingly. That would, in effect, turn the non-salient tax into a lump-sum tax, and governments therefore should use non-salient taxes heavily. Alternatively, suppose that the $Y is taken out of a narrower mental account. For example, rather than thinking of their overall budget as depleted by $Y, individuals think of $Y as depleting their grocery budget specifically, and they may spend $Y less on their next trip to the grocery store. Or they may never change consumption and instead simply end up saving less. In such cases, the low demand response to non-salient taxes is misleading: though it does not generate distortions in the demand for the good being taxed, it is creating possibly higher distortions elsewhere. As a result, governments would need to take into account other potential distortions before using non-salient taxes.

In this case we also see that it is impossible to think about the implications of a nudge on tax salience—for example, excluding taxes from posted prices—in isolation from the public finance framework. The simple application of traditional logic suggests that one should always use nudges to reduce tax salience. In an integrated framework, that is no longer the case. The effects of reduced salience must include all the demand responses that it elicits.

Externalities

One of the triumphs of public finance is to provide a clear understanding of how to deal with external costs (externalities). Take the case of carbon emissions, which contribute to global warming, a typical negative externality. Individuals and firms do many things that affect carbon emissions, from driving automobiles to retrofitting factories; in making their choices, they impose costs on society. Traditional public finance provides an elegant solution to ensuring that those externalities are internalized in choice: individuals and firms must face the full costs of their carbon-emitting activities. The prices that they pay must include not only the marginal cost of the goods that they consume but also the cost of the carbon emissions that those goods produce. Put simply, we can achieve economic efficiency by placing a carbon tax on goods that is equal to the social cost of the carbon emissions produced by those goods. There are technical and political challenges in implementing such a tax, but the conceptual solution is clear.

As with the other examples, decisions involving carbon emissions may not be made in accordance with standard assumptions. For example, psychological studies suggest that social comparisons can drive behavior. Being told, for example, that "you used x kilowatt hours last month, but your neighbors used y kilowatt hours" can reduce a person's consumption of electricity. Based on that insight, a company called OPOWER has implemented a large-scale program that charges utilities to send social comparison reports to consumers. In randomized, controlled trials with hundreds of thousands of utility customers across the United States, the reports have been shown to reduce electricity consumption in the average household by about 2 percent.[6] Notice several interesting aspects of this example. First, even with a traditionally efficient carbon tax, there may be inefficiency if consumers do not choose their energy consumption levels optimally. Second, in addition to the role the prices play in affecting behavior, nudges or other interventions can play a powerful role. Third, and most important, in this case the private sector has generated a nudge—social comparison reporting—in order to affect energy consumption.

The last point is especially interesting because it suggests that policy levers besides carbon taxes and government-imposed nudges can be devised. Can the government somehow induce firms to nudge effectively? They have levers that can be used for that purpose. Consider decoupling for utilities, under which the profits of electricity retailers are no longer directly related only to the volume of electricity sold; they also receive revenues for *reducing* consumption. That type of lever, if it encourages utilities to nudge consumers toward reducing energy use (as it has in the case of OPOWER), is a powerful tool.

The logic here involves both economics and psychology. Psychology recognizes the power of nudges; economics recognizes the power (and peril) of markets. Firms may have nudges available to them that the government does not. So the government can do better than just implement its own nudges; it can look for policy levers such as decoupling that encourage firms to create and use nudges to improve consumer well-being.

These examples suggest that, first, psychological insights must be applied more deeply and broadly in public policy. They can be more than an added-on tweak at the end of a predetermined economic policy—they can alter the basic policy framework, from deadweight loss to moral hazard. Second, many of the policy suggestions based on behavioral insights are not especially behavioral. Decoupling is a traditional economic policy lever, but the behavioral approach enriches our understanding of its impacts. Finally, these examples illustrate that the law of unintended consequences continues to be important: policy changes (nudges or otherwise) must continue to be analyzed within the broader system in which they operate.

The Pitfalls

While integrating the psychological insights of behavioral economics into public finance policy holds great promise, as illustrated above, doing so also introduces a set of potential stumbling blocks for analysis and policy design. The approach described in this book overcomes or at least alleviates two of the major challenges.

Can the number of potential psychological factors be made manageable?
Psychology is, naturally, a very rich discipline, full of insights. That richness creates an overload of information. For any policy problem, it seems that an endless array of psychological phenomena could be relevant. The length of unemployment spells could be influenced by cognitive dissonance, hyperbolic discounting, anchoring, overconfidence, and loss aversion, to cite just a few examples. How do we handle such a vast array of possibilities?

We believe that the answer lies in abstraction. Knowing the specific psychological factor that drives a behavior is important in designing nudges. For example, job seekers may procrastinate in searching for jobs for a variety of reasons. Some activities (going out with friends, watching TV) may be enjoyable and therefore hard to resist. On the other hand, unemployment can sap a person's motivation, making it hard to exercise the self-control needed to engage in day-to-day activities such as sending out resumes. Those factors suggest different interventions: should we reduce procrastination by offering people a chance to commit themselves to searching for work in the future, or by finding a way to remotivate the unemployed?

Our insight is that despite the differences in those two examples, they have much in common: in both, the unemployed individuals recognize the future benefits of searching for a job; in both, they would like to and plan to search for a job; in both, they are unable to implement their desires because, at the moment, something (a tempting activity, lack of motivation) intervenes. We can lump those factors and other phenomena into a particular category labeled *bounded self-control*—the category of psychological factors that reflect a general tendency whereby people would like to take an action with future benefits but fail to do so. Categorizing helps us to craft policy principles. For example, when bounded self-control is a problem, we would argue that one must be very careful about the structure of incentives. Giving a person a bonus to leave unemployment will have weak effects if the benefits are realized far in the future. Those with bounded self-control already recognize and would like to capitalize on the future benefits of searching for a job. Their problem is implementing their desires; adding a modest bonus to those future benefits will not help much.

More generally, we create three categories of deviations from the standard economic model of decisionmaking: imperfect optimization, bounded self-control, and nonstandard preferences. These categories capture much of the psychological evidence that is both robust (supported by a vast majority of evidence) and important across a broad range of policy applications. Different psychological factors are considered similar if they call for the use of similar kinds of public policy levers: taxes, eligibility rules, and so on. Even when the focus is on the creation of nudges, categorization helps us see the general psychological force on which a nudge ought to operate. Our categorization is by no means perfect; there inevitably will be important psychological factors that are hard to categorize. Nor is it a magic bullet. But we do feel that categorization greatly simplifies addressing policy problems and in several important cases allows us to make significant progress with little reference to specific psychological factors.

The first category, *imperfect optimization,* captures errors: mistakes that people make in choosing among alternatives. For example, overconfidence or misunderstanding risks could lead people to under-demand insurance. Imperfect optimization means that people may have desires that do not match hedonic utility and may make choices that do not match their desires. The second category is *bounded self-control,* discussed above. Bounded self-control means that people, even when they are accurate in what they want, often are unable to implement their wants. The third category is *nonstandard preferences*: what individuals want is not what we presume. Even when people are accurate in their wants and they are able to choose in accordance with their wants, those wants may be different from the standard model. Their preferences include components or take a shape that the standard model usually assumes away.

Does imperfect optimization make welfare economics impossible?
Even if the myriad psychological phenomena can be made generally accessible to policymakers and economists, can we implement welfare economics if we incorporate them? Welfare analysis is built on the assumption that choice reveals preference, with social welfare reflecting an aggregation of the utility functions thus revealed. In the behavioral model, choices no longer reveal preference. Take the case of cigarettes. A behavioral approach emphasizes a conflict of preferences here. On one hand, people do not want to consume them; they would like to quit. On the other hand, they would like to quit in the future; right now, they would like a cigarette. That generates a preference inconsistency.

If we take the stated desire to quit seriously, we might use taxes to make it harder for people to smoke. Research in fact finds that cigarette taxes can be shown to assist individuals who have problems with self-control to do better for themselves.[7] But should we have such taxes? Ultimately, who is to say that individuals should smoke fewer cigarettes? Notice that we can no longer assume that choices reveal people's preferences because people may reveal multiple preferences. The failure of revealed preference deprives public sector economics of a clean analytical foundation for assessing the welfare impact of policies. When individuals behave in inconsistent ways, what actions should public finance economists take to reflect welfare?

We focus on two complementary ways to solve that problem. First, we observe a practical reality. In the vast majority of cases, public finance economists (behavioral or otherwise) are not asked to make such judgment calls. Instead, policymakers and societies more broadly typically make those judgments. Policies already reflect a decision to discourage smoking, encourage saving, and ensure adherence to some drug treatment regimes. Instead, the role of most public finance economists is to design policies that take such welfare functions as given. That is similar in some ways to how, in traditional public finance, we do not expect economic theory to resolve *interpersonal* preference conflicts. When, for example, economic polices will have distributional consequences, public finance does not in general offer a way to compare the losses of one group against the benefits to another. We take as given the weights that the social planner gives to different people.

Leaving it to society to resolve *intrapersonal* preference conflicts is not too different. Of course, for economics as a field, it is important to make progress on the fundamental question of inferring hedonics in a world of behavioral agents. The most complete work to date on this fundamental question has been done by Douglas Bernheim and Antonio Rangel, who rigorously draw out the serious challenges of making such inferences.[8] Overcoming this problem will be a key challenge for behavioral public finance. In this book, we sidestep the question by examining the design of policy when the policymaker has already made such inferences.

Second, we observe a misleading aspect of the cigarette example. In that example, the only reason for government to intervene is to solve a *behavioral* problem—to "fix" smokers' mistake in smoking. In sharp contrast, most policies aim to solve *nonbehavioral* problems. Social programs aim to redistribute social benefits, taxes aim to raise revenues or address externalities, Social Security and health insurance policies aim to solve market failures, and so on. With those problems, policies already have been implemented to solve other market failures. As a result, the issue of welfare, while not disappearing, becomes secondary. In those cases, there are first-order consequences of individuals' behavior to *society*, independent of the consequences for their own welfare. For example, if decision-making biases lead individuals to systematically disfavor fuel-efficient vehicles, one can debate what their true utility function is. But the carbon externality that they impose in making their choice is clear. In most of what we do, we focus on how behavioral economics changes policies in areas in which government already plays a traditional role.

The Payoff

Integrating behavioral economics into public finance results in a new set of principles for both understanding the role of government in the economy and informing policy design. This approach to public finance reveals deep insights for policymakers—for how incentives operate, for how markets work and fail, and for the role of information—which yield a variety of results.

Perceived prices drive behavior.
Standard public finance emphasizes the use of price changes, through taxes and subsidies, for example, to attain efficiency. Behavioral public finance recognizes that psychology mediates consumers' responses to prices. For example, individuals with limited attention and limited computational capacity respond not to actual prices but to the prices that they *perceive*. Similarly, responses to prices may not reflect *intended* responses because of an individual's imperfect capacity for self-control. As a result, prices will not always be effective levers for changing behavior, especially when prices are not salient or when the targeted behaviors already are the result of imperfectly optimal behavior.

For example, complicated subsidies may prove ineffective. Take the case of the Saver's Credit, a policy that subsidizes retirement saving. In part because the credit is somewhat obscure and difficult to understand, its effectiveness in actually increasing retirement saving among targeted individuals appears to be limited. The evidence suggests that, dollar for dollar, a subsidy structured in a more straightforward way, such as a savings match, might have a greater impact on saving behavior.[9] That is emblematic of a behavioral policy error: the presumption that the objective price (the extent of the Saver's Credit) matches the subjective price (the perceived subsidy in the Saver's Credit).

Nudges have social as well as private effects.
The success of automatic enrollment in increasing the contribution rates to savings plans begs its application to other contexts. Many have suggested that if the application process for means-tested programs such as Temporary Assistance to Needy Families (TANF) or Medicaid were simplified so that benefits were easier to claim, the benefits would reach more qualifying individuals. There is some evidence that simplifying application procedures also works, for example, for college financial aid.[10] But is that a good idea? Public finance demands that we integrate the psychological approach closely with the original rationale for intervention. In these cases, government is attempting to redistribute income or assist those with low incomes. But while we want everyone to do at least some saving for retirement, we do not want to redistribute equally to everyone. In fact, creating hurdles to claiming public benefits could screen out those who need them least. Automatic enrollment could subvert a screening process that is actually economically efficient. The behavioral public finance framework suggests that it is necessary to answer empirically the question of who is screened out of programs by enrollment procedures in order to understand the impact of simplification of these programs on social welfare.

Take another example, the Medicare prescription drug program, also known as Medicare Part D. Medicare Part D provides prescription drug insurance for seniors, who must choose among private plans. Evidence demonstrates that the choice among plans is difficult for individuals and that they make mistakes in choosing.[11] Intelligent assignment, automatically enrolling individuals in low-cost plans, is one possible way to structure this policy—in fact, some states did so for their low-income participants—and one that would be suggested by the automatic enrollment experience. But allowing for individuals to make those mistakes—or randomly assigning low-income participants to plans, as other states did—might have had beneficial effects in terms of risk pooling.

Nudges cannot be assessed by whether they help individuals. One must understand how nudges interact with the market failures that motivated the nudge policy and evaluate them within the broader social welfare function.

The social welfare function has psychological aspects.
Without looking through the behavioral lens, we may also misunderstand the social welfare function. Take Social Security. To understand its role, economists look for a market failure. As we age, we face the risk of outliving our resources. While annuities could solve that problem, adverse selection makes annuities very expensive or unavailable for some. Social Security exists to solve that market

failure. This story has some truth—longevity risk is a genuine problem—but it seems incomplete. Surely Social Security was motivated in part by a belief that people will fail to save effectively for retirement. Bounded self-control in the face of day-to-day consumption demands and temptations makes it hard to implement one's saving preferences. Imperfect optimization makes retirement planning difficult and error prone (How much to save? Where?). From a behavioral perspective, one of the primary *purposes* of Social Security is to reduce the demands on willpower and the complexity of saving for retirement. That understanding affects the form and design of Social Security policy. It also reinforces the earlier point about how the welfare problem is solved in practice: policymakers and society have, as in other cases, already adjudicated intrapersonal conflicts. They have sided with the self that wants to save more over the one that fails to save. They have decided that some choices, such as paying high fees for an index fund, are simply errors.

Unintended behavioral responses to policies do not necessarily represent moral hazard. Economics often uses behavioral responses to make important inferences, but psychological factors can change what those inferences can or should be. We saw this in the example of health insurance, taxes, and externalities, but it operates more generally. Consider unemployment. We might attribute a person's disinclination to look for a job to moral hazard: knowing that they get unemployment benefits, people enjoy their leisure until they exhaust those benefits. Alternatively, unemployment may undermine the willpower needed to search for work. Misunderstanding the original problem can lead to faulty policies. Long-term incentives work if the behavior is driven by moral hazard, but they work poorly if it is driven by lack of willpower or procrastination. That may help us understand, for example, why some experiments with creating incentives to counteract moral hazard have proven disappointing.[12]

Selection effects reflect both incentives and psychology.
Much of public finance emphasizes the role that prices, incentives, and information play in screening or generating selection effects. But behavioral economics emphasizes that individuals can respond to incentives in nonstandard ways that can undo or reverse selection effects. That might be true both in markets with asymmetric information, where the standard approach might identify adverse selection, and in cases where public policy wants screening in order to generate efficient outcomes.

An example of a screening problem in which behavioral tendencies may pose a design challenge is when the government seeks to induce efficient screening, which arises, as noted above, in targeted transfer programs. Traditional economic logic suggests that barriers to program take-up, such as application cost or waiting time, can serve as an effective way to screen the needy from those who simply seek to exploit the program. However, if people fail to participate because of human frailties—procrastinating in filing the application form, being put off by the tediousness or hassle of completing it, or failing to understand program rules—screening may not be efficient. Nonparticipants then are not those who value the program the least but those who understand the rules the least or who have the biggest procrastination problem. In some cases, such as transfer programs, those individuals might be the very population targeted by the program.

Similar forces might operate to affect outcomes in markets with asymmetric information. For example, in health insurance markets, individuals are thought to have an informational advantage (asymmetric information) with respect to their own health status, which is believed to lead to adverse selection, which in turns undermines the efficient operation of such markets. However, the extent to which individuals correctly perceive and act on any such information may be mediated by psychological factors that affect their demand for health insurance.

Government intervention is more effective when attuned to the market's choice architecture.

A final insight involves markets. Regulations, taxes, or subsidies that better align firm profits with *true utility* mean that markets can be used to solve behavioral biases, as in the case of OPOWER described previously. That mirrors one of the innovations of modern public finance: even in cases of market failure, clever policies can harness market forces to resolve the original market failures (as in the case of tradable pollution permits). Similarly here, careful policy can harness market forces to resolve behavioral biases.

That also means that when creating markets, governments must be careful to minimize choice errors. A recent example of this lesson is the case of Medicare Part D, which was designed as a marketplace in which seniors could choose subsidized coverage from private providers. The hoped-for gains from competition, however, may have been dissipated by choice errors. Part D choice is rife with complexity: participants choose from dozens of plans that are differentiated in ways that make it hard to value them. For example, each plan has a unique schedule of benefits, so different drugs are covered differently by each plan. And subsequent empirical research has shown that the program's complexity has had quantitatively large consequences: seniors make errors in plan choice that, on average, cost them hundreds of dollars a year.[13] Similar difficulties have been observed in markets established by policymakers to provide, for example, education.[14] When individuals choose badly, firms compete to cater to their bad choices, leaving little hope for maximizing welfare.

Organization of the Book

In the chapters that follow, we develop our insights more systematically and in greater detail. The rest of the book proceeds in two parts.

In part 1, we set the stage for integrating behavioral economics into public finance by interpreting the evidence from psychological studies and developing a framework for applying it to questions in public finance. Chapter 2 presents and organizes the evidence from the psychology and behavioral economics literatures, abstracting from the specific results in a manner that will make the results useful for economic analysis. Chapter 3 introduces and develops our framework for integrating behavioral economics into public finance on a conceptual level.

In part 2, we apply that framework to topics in public finance. Chapter 4 considers problems and policies stemming from asymmetries of information, with an emphasis on social insurance, including old-age insurance, health insurance, and unemployment insurance. Chapter 5 treats externalities and public goods, with a focus on applications to environmental externalities, public health externalities, and education. Chapter 6 applies behavioral insights to issues related to income support and redistribution. Chapter 7 explores the behavioral dimensions of the economics of taxation and revenue.

Part

I

Psychology and the Foundations of Public Finance

In part 1, we cover some basic lessons of behavioral economics before applying those lessons to topics in public finance in part 2. First, we review what the lessons of behavioral economics are, examining some of the main findings from psychology and behavioral economics, and what they imply for our understanding of preferences and choice. Second, we develop a conceptual framework for integrating behavioral economics and public finance that will pay dividends when we go to apply those findings to topics in public finance.

In chapter 2, "Psychology and Economics," we discuss the range and nature of deviations from the standard economic model of decisionmaking that psychologists and behavioral economists have identified. We focus on the deviations that are most relevant to the topic of public finance and classify them at a level of abstraction amenable to economic analysis. We emphasize three key deviations: imperfect optimization, bounded self-control, and nonstandard preferences.

In chapter 3, "Behavioral Economics and Public Finance," we develop a framework for analyzing the implications of deviations from the standard assumptions on choice and decisionmaking for the methods and conclusions of public finance. We consider the implications of such behavioral tendencies for three sets of challenges that concern public finance: understanding market failures and other sources of welfare loss; assessing the nature and terms of trade-offs involved in setting policy; and designing appropriate and effective policy responses. For each, we identify the general principles of a behavioral approach, which we then apply to the topics of public finance in part 2.

2

Psychology and Economics

W hat do people want? Do they even know? How do they make choices, big and small? Answers to questions like these—how individuals form preferences, how they make decisions—guide how economists think about the world. No matter how far removed the immediate questions of study in any particular field—macroeconomics, finance, trade—may seem from matters of individual choice, scratch the surface and the analysis nearly always depends in some part on assumptions or observations regarding how individuals choose and behave. They may be hidden or implicit, they may be ad hoc or unexamined, but there they are.

Public finance is no exception. While it is easy to think of public finance mainly in terms of more aggregate units of analysis—how markets fail, how they can be repaired—its conclusions are undergirded everywhere by a theory of individual choice. The occurrence and the consequences of market failures depend on elements of individual decisionmaking just as much as they do on the role of market structure. For example, the implication of negative externalities in the consumption of polluting forms of energy—like gasoline for cars—is a joint outcome of the failure of prices to reflect those external costs and the behavioral response of individuals to that pricing failure. Similarly, conclusions about whether and how the government should intervene in response to market outcomes turn on how we believe people will respond to those policies. A corrective tax on gasoline, for example, is presumed to be effective because of the way that it will enter the choice calculus of those who must pay it.

If the usual approach of public finance is to elide any serious discussion of how people form preferences and make choices, it is not, then, because such questions are irrelevant. Rather, it is because they are treated, for most practical purposes, as settled. In the standard economic analysis, our answers primarily follow from the assumption that individuals optimize perfectly, by which we mean, roughly speaking, that individuals are good at choosing among the options that different market structures or different policy environments present them with. People know what makes them happy. They hold preferences that are complete, stable, and well specified. They make plans to maximize their well-being, and their choices reflect those plans. Many times we go further, making simplifying assumptions about what people want, as well—for example, that people are purely self-interested, or nearly so.

Even as public finance economists employ such assumptions, they recognize their limitations. Of course people make mistakes, of course they give in to temptations that they later regret, and of course they can be altruistic. Despite such violations of economic assumptions, the standard model remains a durable feature of public finance. Even if it is not completely true, it is useful. It gives clear guidance on how to set policies—everything from how to set a tax to correct an externality to how to structure social insurance in the face of adverse selection. In short, the standard model survives because it is presumed to be a reasonable approximation of reality for many problems and because there is no obvious alternative that is as concrete and useful.

Increasingly, however, the evidence suggests that deviations from the standard model are more the rule than the exception and that they have consequences in the aggregate and for policy responses. Psychology has demonstrated that violations of the standard economic assumptions about preference and choice are pervasive. Behavioral economics has identified a number of contexts in which deviations have consequences for market or policy outcomes. Centrally, that evidence suggests that when people deviate from the standard assumptions, they do so in predictable ways. Thus behavioral economics does not just question the validity of old assumptions; it replaces them with new ones.

In this chapter, we catalog evidence from psychology and behavioral economics of behaviors that are inconsistent with the standard assumptions, and we classify those specific findings into a set of broad behavioral tendencies. The core challenge for incorporating the results from psychology and behavioral economics into public finance is simply making sense of them. The literature on psychology is vast, providing deep and wide-ranging insights across a variety of phenomena of the mind. To economists, a first reaction to this literature can be to view it merely as a collection of isolated observations with an obscure taxonomy: Mental accounting. Asymmetric dominance. Choice overload. And so on.

By themselves these results seem both too specific and too diverse to be immediately useful for drawing general conclusions about how they relate to economic activity. From this large pool, however, only a small set of abstract insights about behavior—insights that crudely capture many different psychological phenomena in a few broad behavioral tendencies—is sufficient for economic analysis. Obviously such a distillation results in a tremendous loss of rich insights for understanding the mind. But for understanding how to set policy and regulatory levers, that richness is neither necessary nor desirable. In general, the goals of economic policy are not to understand or correct the behavior of individuals but to affect behavior in the aggregate or on the margin.

So, for example, consider the specific findings mentioned above: mental accounting, asymmetric dominance, and choice overload. They refer to very particular and very different behaviors. Mental accounting refers, roughly speaking, to the tendency of individuals to fail to treat income or wealth as fungible across sources or uses. Asymmetric dominance refers to the tendency of individuals to allow their preferences to be swayed by the introduction of irrelevant alternatives. And choice overload describes the tendency of individuals to be put off from making a choice as alternatives proliferate. But all three can also be viewed as examples of a more general finding that people are not unbounded in their ability to consistently consider and respond to all of the features of complex choices. Therefore, these and similar findings can be categorized under a more general psychological tendency that might be referred to as limited computational capacity.

The other way in which public finance can abstract from psychology is to determine which results from psychology are important to incorporate into economics and which can be safely ignored. The test here is whether the psychological principle is likely to have much bearing on the validity of the standard assumptions about economic agents. So psychological results about decisionmaking errors (which bear on assumptions about the ability of economic agents to optimize perfectly) or other-regarding preferences (which relate directly to standard assumptions about the form of preferences) must be incorporated in some way. On the other hand, psychological results that do not relate directly to those assumptions—such as, say, the tendency to obey authority—though obviously not without economic consequences on some level, are largely beyond the scope of public finance.

We should be clear up front that while there are benefits to doing this type of selective aggregation and creating a broader taxonomy of behavioral tendencies, there also are costs. For example, while it is useful for many purposes to think of asymmetric dominance and mental accounting as manifestations of a broader tendency toward limited computational capacity, there will be instances in public finance in which the specific features of those behaviors and the distinctions between them remain important. In designing policy responses, for instance, asymmetric dominance may argue for restricting choice sets while mental accounting may argue for framing choices differently. Similarly, aspects of psychology that we will largely ignore, such as the tendency to obey authority, will be in some instances important for public finance, and by excluding them we do lose some power for understanding and designing policy.

Below, we describe our classification scheme for results from psychology and behavioral economics, which organizes findings around three basic deviations from standard assumptions:

—*Imperfect optimization.* The classical model assumes that individuals are capable maximizers of their own utility—that is, that they know what they want and what will make them happy and that their choices and preferences are consistent. Behavioral economics, however, finds that individuals are imperfect in their ability to maximize their own welfare and that their choices are often inconsistent—that is, that individuals have more difficulty knowing what they want than the standard model assumes.

—*Bounded self-control.* Even when individuals accurately perceive their own interests, they can have difficulty realizing their intentions. The classical model allows for no such difficulty, and it assumes time consistency in preferences. Behavioral economics recognizes forces such as temptation and procrastination as real and meaningful phenomena—that is, that individuals have more difficulty doing what they want than the standard model assumes.

—*Nonstandard preferences.* Finally, the standard model also makes some weak assumptions about the shape of individual preferences. Behavioral economics finds two important cases in which those assumptions appear inaccurate: First, preferences appear to be set over changes in status rather than over end states. Second, the assumption of pure self-interest is often a bad assumption, in that individuals routinely hold preferences that are other-regarding—that is, that what people want is different from what we usually assume.

For each deviation, we describe some of the available empirical evidence. We relegate to appendix A a brief discussion of how to incorporate these deviations into economic models of choice and welfare in a slightly more formal way. Finally, note again that we make no attempt here to do a thorough review or complete summary of behavioral economics but seek instead to highlight features that will be important for public finance. Good reviews and summaries are available in the literature.[1]

Imperfect Optimization

Economists famously assume that individuals are optimal decisionmakers. Technically, optimality in choice is a matter of adherence to a set of assumptions that impose both a degree of accuracy on choices—that choices reflect all of the relevant, available information, for example—and a logical consistency on choices—for example, that choices are independent of irrelevant alternatives. Less formally, optimality in choice amounts to an assumption that individuals are basically good at making choices that maximize their own welfare: individuals know what they want, and they make choices that realize their desires.

However, psychology and behavioral economics have amassed a growing collection of findings suggesting that according to those criteria, individuals are, in practice, flawed decisionmakers. Consider one well-known case relating to choice behavior in the face of an increase in the number of alternatives. Standard assumptions of optimization imply that increasing the number of elements in a choice set should leave individuals at least as likely to choose from the set of increased choices as to choose from the original set. At worst, individuals will continue to select as they did from the original options, and at best they will make new selections from among the new options. But an experiment in which shoppers in a grocery store were given coupons for jam after being randomly offered samples of either a few selected varieties of jam or a wider assortment of jams found evidence that contradicted that prediction.[2] While 30 percent of subjects offered the smaller set of samples ultimately purchased jam, only 3 percent of subjects offered the wider set went on to purchase jam. Researchers interpreted that finding to mean that individuals offered the larger set of samples were actually put off from choosing by the difficulty of selecting from the greater number of options. Moreover, results of this type are not limited to psychology experiments. There is, for example, some evidence that individuals are less likely to participate in their employer's retirement plan as the number of investment alternatives increases.[3]

Such results are part of a large set of findings in the psychology of judgment and decisionmaking that suggest that, in fact, individuals are not always good at making choices.[4] They make choices that appear to ignore or misconstrue available information or that exhibit the types of logical inconsistencies disallowed by full optimality. The full catalog of particular deviations is long, and it can be organized in different ways. For the purpose of working through their implications for public finance, we will group the deviations into three categories according to the general feature of decisionmaking that drives the deviation: *limited attention, limited computational capacity,* and *biased reasoning.* Limited attention captures deviations from optimality that appear to be due to the fact that there are limits to the bandwidth of the human brain in processing stimuli—that individuals cannot notice and attend to all of the features of choice simultaneously. Limited computational capacity captures deviations that are due to the limits of the processing power of the human brain—that even when individuals are capable of attending to the relevant features of a choice, making some choices simply is complex or otherwise intrinsically difficult. Biased reasoning captures deviations from optimality that are due to a set of persistent biases in the way that the human brain appears to subjectively evaluate alternatives, especially those involving probabilities or statistics.

Limited Attention

Optimal choice generally requires actively considering the properties of multiple alternatives along multiple dimensions. Unfortunately for human decisionmakers, psychologists have observed that individuals have a limited capacity to attend to multiple features of choice simultaneously.[5] The mind appears able to attend to only a small fraction of the stimuli that it perceives, and that attention is focused in a way that is neither random nor entirely conscious. As a result, individuals can focus on, or attend to, only a few of the many features of their choice environment at once. As a result, choice becomes sensitive to the way in which attention is allocated or directed. That can cause individuals to ignore some features of choice and to be excessively sensitive to others, depending on the extent to which those features attract attention. It can also lead individuals to construe their choices in artificially narrow terms as they direct their attention across the features of choices, leading to locally rather than globally optimal choice. Following the psychology literature, we refer to this feature of decisionmaking as limited attention.

Limited attention is responsible for several features of observed choice behavior that are either broadly inconsistent with optimal choice or at least puzzling from the standard perspective. Two that are important for public finance are *salience effects* and *local construal*.

SALIENCE EFFECTS

Because individuals cannot attend to everything at once, salient features of their environment will command their attention and can influence behavior and choice. An illustrative finding from psychology is that while individuals are generally unable to simultaneously process a second set of words that they hear while paying attention to a first, an exception occurs when the second set includes a person's own name—literally an attention-grabbing word for most individuals.[6] This result is sometimes labeled the cocktail party effect because of the way that it mirrors the familiar experience of overhearing, but not following, chatter at a cocktail party until someone speaks your name, which you immediately recognize. The relative salience of different features of choice directs attention in a similar way, and in doing so guides choice. Cues that direct attention toward or away from particular options or that highlight or conceal specific characteristics of alternatives can affect behavior even when the underlying choice set is preserved. For example, items in grocery stores sell better on shelves at eye level, where consumers' attention is focused by default, than at other shelf heights.[7]

In general, more salient features of choice get access to the limited attention of decisionmakers, while less salient features do not. That seems to be true in policy contexts, as well. For example, there is evidence that raising or lowering the salience of taxes or fees, without changing their level, affects behavior.[8] Another consequence of salience effects is that individuals can have trouble ignoring salient information even when they want to—told not to think of a white bear, many people will immediately conjure an image of a white bear.[9] That can be economically significant when, for example, it would benefit individuals who have an informational advantage to be able to predict the behavior of those who do not— they may be unable to bring themselves to ignore their private information.[10]

LOCAL CONSTRUAL

The other set of effects of limited attention on choice comes about because individuals with limited attention can direct that attention. The ability of individuals to direct their limited attention is powerful. Psychological research that asks individuals to pay attention to one part of an image or video often finds that those individuals fail to notice even unusual or striking images when their attention is focused on the part that they were instructed to observe. In perhaps the most famous such example, when asked to count the number of passes made in a video of people playing with a basketball, many observers failed to notice an individual walking across the frame in a gorilla suit.[11] The result of focusing attention for choice is that it can lead to choice processes that result in what are local, rather than global, optimization patterns. For example, individuals may engage in elimination by aspects—whereby they consider aspects of available alternatives one at a time, eliminating options that are undesirable according to each aspect in sequence—or in similar choice behaviors.[12] Another type of local optimization that may be driven to some extent by limited attention is choice that narrowly construes not the choice set, but the hedonic consequences of choice. In particular, individuals may focus on immediate or salient outcomes rather than the full range and path of outcomes.[13]

Limited Computational Capacity

While limits to attention underlie many of the specific decisionmaking errors and biases that psychologists and others have observed, other anomalous behaviors appear to reflect a deeper set of cognitive limitations. Even when individuals are not constrained in terms of attention, they can find some choices hard to make because of the complexity of evaluating the alternatives and because they are not unbounded in their capacity to think and reason. Individuals appear to have difficulty thinking and reasoning accurately or consistently about choices and preferences. They hold subjective valuations that are inconsistent or arbitrary. They have difficulty penetrating opaque pricing schedules. They exhibit evidence of an inability to integrate decisionmaking across domains. And their decisions can be influenced by spurious features of the choice environment. In general, we group findings of this type from the psychology and behavioral economics literatures as evidence of limited computational capacity.

The main implication of limited computational capacity for economic behavior is that optimization generally is only approximate, not accurate or precise. We collect a variety of specific classes of choice anomalies under this broad heading: *decisional conflict, inconsistent subjective valuation, "schmeduling,"* and *mental accounting and choice bracketing.*

DECISIONAL CONFLICT

The clearest demonstration of how individual choice is affected by the processing limitations of the human brain is the direct evidence that individuals appear to find the process of choosing itself to be difficult under some conditions. In the jam example above, the proliferation of choices appeared to inhibit choosing any alternative at all, a condition sometimes labeled choice overload.[14] That is an extreme example of a more general finding that individuals sometimes seek to avoid making choices. More specifically, there is evidence that what individuals seek to avoid are difficult choices. When individuals face choices among options with no clearly dominant alternative, they are more likely to look for ways to avoid choosing, such as seeking additional alternatives or deferring choice, than when a dominant option is available.[15]

INCONSISTENT SUBJECTIVE VALUATION

An essential element of optimal choice is that it is based on an underlying set of consistent preferences. A range of evidence from behavioral economics suggests that individuals in fact have a difficult time forming consistent subjective valuations. Valuations instead appear malleable and arbitrary, as demonstrated in contexts in which alternatives have attributes that are not easily valued or that vary along multiple dimensions. For example, individuals often reverse their stated preferences when they are given choice attributes jointly instead of separately.[16] Valuations of positive and negative attributes of alternatives differ depending on whether individuals are selecting or rejecting alternatives.[17] And the attributes that individuals base their valuations on can be difficult to view as the result of perfect optimization. In one example, individuals tasting wines were found to peg their valuations of different wines—as indicated through brain imaging—to the price of the wine rather than the taste.[18]

Perhaps most dramatically, other results suggest that individuals' preferences can be influenced by external cues that have no plausible connection to subjective value. For example, experiments have shown that reminding individuals of the last two digits of their Social Security number affects how they value goods—individuals with higher numbers will tend to value goods more highly than those with low numbers, even while being reminded of the arbitrariness of their Social

Security number.[19] Finally, preferences appear to be very sensitive to the way in which choices are structured. The addition or subtraction of alternatives, even irrelevant alternatives, can also lead to preference reversals. For example, individuals often are influenced by the introduction of asymmetrically dominated alternatives, whereby adding a third alternative causes individuals to switch their preference over an initial pair.[20] In a similar manner, the existence of extreme alternatives can promote the selection of intermediate options.[21]

SCHMEDULING

If one cornerstone of optimal choice is the presumption that individuals can form and access consistent subjective valuations of choice alternatives, the other is that individuals correctly perceive their cost. Schmeduling is a label, coined by economists Jeffrey Liebman and Richard Zeckhauser, for behaviors that appear to be a result of difficulties that individuals may have with understanding price schedules—that is, with knowing what they are paying. It refers to a tendency of individuals to hold and act on only approximate mental representations of price schedules.[22] Individuals are thought to be susceptible to two types of errors in particular, which are to incorrectly smooth price schedules, such as by mistaking average for marginal prices, and to incorrectly respond to local prices when the full schedule of prices is relevant for decisionmaking. Findings from psychology, such as those on the tendency of individuals to respond to incentives in a way that is attractive piecewise but suboptimal in the aggregate, suggest the susceptibility of individuals to such tendencies.[23]

However, the bulk of the evidence for this difficulty comes from choices that individuals make in economic settings that are consistent with the hypothesis that individuals respond to complex price schedules in ways that are hard to square with perfect optimization. For example, the failure of incomes to bunch around the points in the income tax schedule where tax rates change discretely (kink points) is consistent with individuals responding to average rather than marginal tax rates.[24] Individuals are thought to face similar difficulties when the price schedules of consumer goods are complex.[25] Evidence suggests that individuals choosing prescription drug plans in Medicare Part D had difficulty choosing the least costly plan, a result due in part to the complexity of the price schedules involved.[26]

MENTAL ACCOUNTING AND CHOICE BRACKETING

A further important set of deviations from perfect optimization is captured by the concepts of mental accounting and choice bracketing. Mental accounting is the tendency of individuals to evaluate choices with respect to discrete, notional accounts rather than general measures of financial status, such as overall wealth, total income, or total spending.[27] The clearest cases of mental accounting come from household budgeting behavior, wherein individuals routinely treat income from different sources as flowing to, or spending for different purposes as drawing down, distinct mental accounts. For example, individuals spend money differently—usually more frivolously—when they perceive it as having been won or found rather than having been earned.[28] Individuals can also be more or less willing to take actions depending on the mental account to which they post—credits or debits.[29] In one well-known study, individuals were more willing to drive twenty minutes in order to save $5 on a $15 calculator than to save $5 on a $125 jacket, apparently because they evaluated the $5 discount relative not to their overall wealth but to a mental account out of which they were spending $15 in one case and $125 in another.[30]

Such behavior may explain similar relationships between the source and disposition of funds that we observe in policy contexts. For example, tax benefits seem to be more likely to lead to increased spending on children simply by virtue of being labeled child credits, possibly by affecting the mental accounting of the benefit.[31] Mental accounting can also affect how individuals make choices about the time path of consumption, payment, and debt, depending on how individuals form the respective accounts.[32] The process of structuring and balancing mental accounts is closely related to another dimension, sometimes known as choice bracketing, in which limits to computational capacity can affect choice.[33] Individuals can choose to use broader or narrower brackets, and the bracket used will have an impact on choice. For example, individuals may be more inclined to commit to making small, recurring payments, such as to a charity, because they bracket the choice narrowly—comparing the payments to other small, frequent expenses rather than considering the aggregate expense.[34]

Biased Reasoning

A final category of behavioral tendencies that are broadly inconsistent with optimal choice has to do with statistical reasoning and judgments of probability. These deviations take the form of biases that individuals exhibit when assessing the probabilities associated with risky choice or when making judgments about their own place in the distribution of possible outcomes. These deviations are slightly different from those above in that they appear to reflect not limits to processing capacity but a set of persistent biases in the way that the human brain processes probabilities. Put another way, if limited attention and limited computational capacity are for the most part a result of the imprecision of the human brain as a decisionmaking organ, these deviations are about its inaccuracy. We group this set of behaviors into a category we call biased reasoning. Biased reasoning of this sort is manifested in two broad categories, *probabilistic reasoning* and *motivational biases*.

PROBABILISTIC REASONING

Individuals appear to have difficulty making correct or consistent decisions under uncertainty.[35] For example, individuals appear to employ an availability heuristic, in which they assess an event or outcome as more or less likely depending on how easily it can be thought of or imagined.[36] Similarly, individuals appear to employ a representativeness heuristic, in which they tend to ignore the relative frequency of alternatives in probability judgments.[37] In addition, individuals appear to systematically overweight low probabilities and underweight high probabilities in decisionmaking.[38] That is, they make decisions treating very unlikely events as more likely to occur than they are and likely events as less likely to occur than they are. They mistake randomness for patterns.[39] These biases also are consistent with behavior outside the lab. The same availability heuristic that leads to deviations in controlled settings is seen in the behavior of individuals who purchase flood insurance after being hit by a flood rather than before.[40] The underlying probability of being flooded in any given year is unlikely to change; what changes is that the flood itself causes individuals to appreciate the risk differently.

MOTIVATIONAL BIASES

Related but slightly different are biases in probability assessments related to individuals' chances of success in their own endeavors, what are sometimes referred to as motivational biases. One such result is overconfidence. Individuals are found to be routinely overconfident about their own abilities.[41] For instance, the majority of drivers believe themselves to be better-than-average drivers.[42] Overconfidence also appears to be related to some economic behaviors, like risk taking by entrepreneurs.[43] A related but distinct bias is a tendency toward over-optimism, of which there also is evidence.[44] For example, unemployed workers appear to be excessively optimistic about their chances of finding work, which appears to affect their search effort.[45] Individuals also appear to possess a self-serving bias, a tendency to consider their own self-interested judgments as fair; that tendency has been shown to lead to difficulties in negotiations.[46]

Summary

Taken together, limited attention, limited computational capacity, and biased reasoning have broadly similar consequences in that they allow for the possibility that individuals make systematic errors in attempting to maximize their own utility. They lead individuals to make decisions based on heuristics and biases. They suggest that rather than the kind of deliberate choice that the standard model envisions, individuals more often use shortcuts or crude rules of thumb that can be incorrect. They each, in their own way, show how making good decisions is hard—much harder than the standard model emphasizes. They are, broadly speaking, manifestations of imperfect optimization.

Finally, it is worth noting before moving on that none of these limitations—limited attention, limited computational capacity, or biased reasoning—is tantamount to limited intelligence. They reflect decisionmaking as practiced, not capability. Moreover, they appear to be nearly universal features of decisionmaking. Students at MIT give intuitive but incorrect answers to questions designed to prey on cognitive biases, just as anyone else does.[47] Even professionals such as physicians demonstrate these biases within their areas of expertise.[48] So these limitations are not related to intelligence, or even expertise. They simply appear to be properties of the way that the human brain forms judgments and makes decisions most of the time. There is even some reason to think that such errors and biases may be adaptive. Some evidence indicates that in certain contexts people are more satisfied with their choices when they neglect conscious deliberation and rely on heuristics instead.[49]

Bounded Self-Control

In addition to assuming that individuals are good at knowing what to choose, economists further assume that individuals are good at implementing their choices—in particular, that they possess what can be broadly termed self-control, that they do not face any tension between what they intend to do and how they act. Slightly more formally, we might say that the standard economic model is one in which choices display time consistency. When choices are time consistent, consumption patterns observed ex post are consistent with consumption plans made ex ante.

But just as psychologists and economists have found that individuals can have difficulty knowing what they want, in the case of imperfect optimization, behavioral economists have uncovered evidence that individuals have difficulty doing what they want. In addition to failures of reason, individuals also often suffer from failures of self-control. Individuals choose and act in ways that are time-inconsistent, and they often display a bias for present over future consumption. Consider, for example, the finding that individuals' preferences often are inconsistent over delayed rewards.[50] Individuals often prefer to receive a larger delayed reward later in the future, but a smaller more immediate reward today: for example, they prefer to receive $110 in thirty-one days rather than $100 in thirty days, but they prefer to receive $100 today rather than $110 tomorrow. This behavior is time inconsistent: if both choices were executed, on day thirty the individual would find that she had committed to a path that she no longer found optimal.

Similar conflicts are evident in real-world behaviors. For example, individuals have been found to face a similar choice when selecting pricing plans for gym membership. Expensive monthly plans make sense only if individuals intend to go to the gym a sufficient number of times over the month to make the average daily cost of the monthly plan less than the price of a day pass. Research finds that in fact individuals who choose the monthly pass attend the gym too few times during the month to make it worthwhile.[51] Time-inconsistent individuals decide months or weeks in advance that on some fraction of future days they will want to go to the gym but then, when many of those days actually arrive, they decide that they would rather not go.

The failure of individuals to display time-consistent preferences is an example of a general tendency that we label bounded self-control. A multitude of findings from psychology and behavioral economics indicate that individuals make choices over time in ways that are broadly inconsistent with the standard model.[52] In general, translating intention into action seems to involve difficulties that the standard model does not allow for and results in behaviors that it does not predict and cannot easily accommodate. People sometimes do things that they really do not want to do or fail to do things that they wish they had done. They can be influenced toward or away from actions by minor inducements or inconveniences. And so on. Among the many manifestations of this general tendency, important classes of behavior include *procrastination and temptation, channel factors, state and affect,* and *addiction.*

Procrastination and Temptation

One major consequence of bounded self-control is the gap that it can create between intention and action. As in the case of gym membership and exercising, individuals may engage in procrastination, failing to take actions that they intended to take. Conversely, it can lead individuals to succumb to temptation, taking actions from which they intended to refrain. For example, when choosing for immediate consumption, individuals prefer junk food and trashy movies, even while stating a preference for healthy food and high-brow films when making plans for later.[53] One important source of evidence that individuals are subject to temptation is their demand for and behavior in the presence of commitment devices—for example, deadlines can be shown to improve student outcomes.[54] Similarly, the willingness of individuals to engage in illiquid forms of savings even in the absence of higher expected returns, apparently to avoid the temptation of consuming out of savings, is another consistent piece of evidence.[55] The role of commitment devices also serves to highlight the fact that while individuals have only bounded self-control, that does not imply that they are necessarily naïve about their lack of self-control.[56]

CHANNEL FACTORS

One of the most striking results in psychology is that allowing for a gap between intention and action, research finds that only very minor features of choice can serve to widen or narrow that gap. Psychologists have labeled those features of choice channel factors.[57] Channel factors can explain the tendency of individuals to be steered toward or away from choices by ostensibly quite minor barriers or inducements. One classic study in psychology finds, for example, that a message to receive an immunization was many times more likely to result in an individual following up and receiving the shot if the initial message was accompanied by a map to the health clinic and a request that the person decide on a time to get the shot.[58] Moreover, individuals often can be unaware of the influence of these factors on their own intentions—in one study in which minor cues such as reminders were found to influence behavior, those cues did not affect self-predictions about behavior.[59] Effects consistent with channel factors also are observed in many real-world contexts. The dramatic results of automatic or simplified enrollment procedures in social programs, such as college financial aid programs or employment benefit programs such as 401(k) plans, are likely due in part to channel factors.[60]

STATE AND AFFECT

Another important aspect of bounded self-control is that the ability of individuals to exhibit self-control depends not just on the context of choice but also on the state of the decisionmaker. There are at least two ways in which state and affect can influence the ability of individuals to take actions that match their intentions. First, when individuals find it difficult to exert self-control, other aspects of their mental state can modulate their ability to overcome that difficulty. For example, stress and cognitive load may cause individuals to act impatiently—something as simple as asking people to hold a long string of digits in their head can make them more likely to select a more tempting, less healthy snack.[61] Outside the lab, episodes of stress have been found to have a similar effect on the ability of quitters to refrain from smoking.[62] Similar effects may result from other visceral states, such as hunger or fear.[63]

Second, state and affect can play a role in time-inconsistent behavior to the extent that the inconsistency comes about because of the difficulty that individuals have in predicting their hedonic state, or forecasting their affect, at the time of forming their intentions. In particular, individuals tend to display what has been labeled projection bias—a tendency to project their current preferences onto their future selves.[64] So, for example, individuals will elect to receive more or less healthy snacks one week from now depending on whether they are hungry now.[65] Similar effects have been observed with catalog orders, when individuals were more likely to return orders for cold weather gear when orders were placed on unusually cold days, suggesting that at the time of placing the order, individuals were projecting a desire for such gear that did not persist when the order arrived and the weather had improved.[66]

ADDICTION

Finally, at the extreme, individuals may lose self-control outright due to addiction, which is a behavioral tendency worth separating from the others. Tobacco use and smoking—and substance use more generally—is the common case, but other behaviors, such as gambling, also have properties of addiction. Standard economic analysis can accommodate even models of addictive behavior.[67] But evidence suggests that characterizing addiction as a process by which individuals lose the ability to maintain self-control may fit the data better.[68] Recent models of addiction, which are more grounded in the physiology of the brain, argue that addiction is a matter of substances or behaviors leading to a direct interference with the ability of the brain to forecast hedonic states.[69] Those models capture common features of addiction, such as a stated preference for quitting in the face of the oftentimes practical inability to do so.

Summary

Before moving on it is worth commenting on a feature of our aggregation and classification of psychological findings into behavioral tendencies that is especially evident in our discussion of bounded self-control. We are categorizing behaviors according to how they operate and in a way that will be useful for thinking about their consequences for public finance. Consequently, from the perspective of psychology or behavioral economics, the categorizations may be somewhat loose with respect to both the underlying nature of the behaviors and some related terminology. With respect to the underlying psychology of failures of self-control, for example, there are alternative models and hypotheses that we subsume in our discussion. Failures of self-control can be thought of as a result of present-biased preferences due to quasi-hyperbolic discounting.[70] They can also be thought of as a result of conflict between the mental processes by which individuals plan and those by which they act.[71] Alternatively, they might be thought of as a result of a decisionmaking process in which self-control demands willpower and willpower is costly to exercise.[72] They also can be thought of as a result of individuals construing the time dimension of choice in some nonstandard way.[73] In part as a result of the variety of processes that might in fact generate such behaviors, it is somewhat imprecise to label all of the behaviors described here as features of bounded self-control. That loss of precision at this stage is deliberate—it is the cost of having a convenient shorthand for referring to classes

Box 2-1. *Bounded Rationality*

The integration of findings from psychological research and economic analysis described here owes much to the behavioral economics literature of recent decades that follows the work of Daniel Kahneman and Amos Tversky.[a] This literature stresses the way that the human brain ordinarily approaches decisionmaking. It highlights the shortcuts, the heuristics and biases, that individuals commonly employ and the ways in which they lead to decisionmaking patterns that are at odds with the patterns that a model of fully optimal decisionmaking would predict.

Before applying a behavioral approach to public finance, it is worth pausing to note that there is an older strain of research, going back to the work of Herbert Simon, that describes a slightly different approach to thinking about the implications of psychological realities for decisionmaking and economic analysis.[b] This alternative line of research also acknowledges the limits of the human brain as a decisionmaking organ and recognizes that there are costs to thinking and deciding. But this approach preserves the possibility of what is referred to as bounded rationality: that individuals make optimal decisions subject to those constraints. That is, rather than limits to attention or computational capacity leading directly to imperfect decisionmaking, in this model individuals optimally allocate attention and computational capacity. Individuals remain limited in their capacity to choose optimally and consistently, but they can be savvy about how they manage those limits.

Which model is correct, in the sense that it best describes how individuals make decisions and why we observe behavior that violates standard assumptions, is ultimately an empirical question. The answer is surely a mix of both. Moreover, it is important not to fashion out of the distinction a false dichotomy: the two approaches are clearly related. That said, we tend to take the approach described in this chapter—of stressing imperfections in decisionmaking rather than the bounds on rationality—and we do so for several reasons.

of behavioral tendencies when we move on to our central goal of reviewing public finance through this lens.

That said, our approach to considering these behavioral tendencies does make one substantial but implicit assumption about the decisionmaking process that generates these tendencies. In particular, we follow recent developments in behavioral economics in taking the view here that both imperfect optimization and bounded self-control, in general, derive from an underlying psychology of judgment and decisionmaking that leads individuals to act in ways that are inconsistent or even erroneous, not from a considered judgment on the part of individuals about how to deploy limited cognitive resources or manage limited reserves of willpower. For more on this distinction, see box 2-1.

First, this is the direction in which psychological research has trended in recent decades. Many of the pieces of individual evidence described here are difficult to view as consistent with bounded rationality. For example, the evidence on the importance of context and situational factors, whereby extremely minor or apparently irrelevant features of the choice environment affect behavior, seems more of a piece with a model in which individuals are simply imperfect decisionmakers.

Second, in other contexts that suggest direct tests of imperfect decisionmaking models against cost-of-thinking models, we view the evidence as favoring imperfect optimization or bounded self-control. The payoffs to decisions such as electing to participate in 401(k) plans or choosing prescription drug plans optimally in Medicare Part D are so large compared with the costs that they are a poor fit for models of bounded rationality. That is, a decisionmaker who was optimally allocating her scarce attention or computational resources would almost surely have devoted it to making such high-return decisions in an optimal manner.

Finally, to the extent that the different models matter for policy design, the imperfect decisionmaking model has in some ways done a better job at identifying opportunities ex ante than models of bounded rationality. Even if, ex post, costs of thinking or processing information can explain outcomes such as the failure of qualified individuals to apply for college financial aid, the hypothesis that application assistance could be important came out of an imperfect decisionmaking model. Even without settling the question, for the narrow purposes of this book, that is a substantial practical advantage of the imperfect decisionmaking approach.

a. Daniel Kahneman and Amos Tversky, "Prospect Theory: An Analysis of Decision under Risk," *Econometrica*, vol. 47 (March 1979), pp. 263–91.

b. Herbert Simon, "A Behavioral Model of Rational Choice," *Quarterly Journal of Economics*, vol. 69, no. 1 (1955), pp. 99–118.

Nonstandard Preferences

Usual economic assumptions about choice include some weak assumptions about the shape and content of preferences. Two, in particular, are relevant here. First, economists typically assume that individual utility is a function of end states—that is, how individuals value an outcome usually does not depend on the path taken to realize it or on the position of the outcome relative to other possible outcomes, but simply on the outcome itself. Second, economists commonly assume that individuals are purely self-interested. It should be noted that in neither case are those assumptions essential features of the standard model of choice; they are instead standard simplifying assumptions.

Psychology and behavioral economics have produced findings that suggest that in many cases those assumptions are a poor fit with the preferences exhibited by many decisionmakers. Take, for example, the results of a study investigating how individuals form valuations in markets.[74] In that experiment, the authors first randomly distributed coffee mugs to half of the participants, leaving the remaining participants empty handed. They then asked each participant with a mug to indicate the price at which he or she would be willing to sell the mug and each participant without a mug to indicate the price that he or she would be willing to pay to acquire a mug. Using that information, the researchers set a market-clearing price and executed the trades indicated at that price. Because the mugs had been allocated randomly, the expectation was that about half of the participants would trade mugs in that market arrangement. But, in fact, very few trades occurred—only about one-tenth of the mugs were traded. What happened? Against expectations that valuations would be randomly distributed throughout the class, the mugs came to be systematically valued more highly by those to whom they were initially allocated than by those to whom they were not. Those given mugs were, on average, unwilling to sell them for less than about $5, while those who initially did not receive mugs were, on average, willing to offer only about $3 for a mug. Merely assigning ownership of the mug appeared to affect how much participants came to value it. Preferences were formed with respect to the initial allocation—people put a value on giving up the mug or on acquiring the mug—not with respect to an abstract valuation of the mug. Similar results have been observed in the field. For example, homeowners and homebuyers sometimes display similar preferences.[75]

This result, an example of what is known as the endowment effect, is a consequence of reference-dependent preferences, a violation of the assumption that individuals' preferences are over end states. Reference-dependent preferences are one type of nonstandard preferences that is especially important for public finance. Other-regarding preferences—a violation of the assumption of pure, or nearly pure, self-interest—is another.

Reference-Dependent Preferences

Choice theory in economics typically assumes for the sake of simplicity that goods enter individual utility functions in absolute terms. That is, goods have an intrinsic value that does not depend on how they compare with alternatives. In many instances however, individuals appear to evaluate many choices in relative terms, in particular in comparison with some reference point.[76] Preferences over alternatives might depend on whether an alternative represents a gain or a loss relative to expectations or to prior experiences. They may depend on whether individuals are valuing a good to sell it or to buy it. Or they may depend on their relationship to the status quo. These results are manifestations of what behavioral economists refer to generally as reference-dependent preferences.

Among the catalog of choice anomalies observed by behavioral economists, several important examples are arguably a result, at least in part, of reference-dependent preferences. They include the *endowment effect*, *loss aversion*, and *status quo bias*.

Endowment Effect

The endowment effect is described above in the coffee mug experiment. The general finding is that where individuals start from, in terms of their endowment, matters for choice because it creates a reference point that affects how they value outcomes. The authors interpret the findings in the coffee mug example as evidence that individuals think of, and subjectively value, the experience of acquiring a good differently from the experience of giving one up. Parting with an item that individuals think of as their own seems to hurt them more than acquiring the same item benefits those who do not own it. As a consequence, owners required more compensation to give up the mugs than non-owners were willing to pay to obtain them. More generally, the endowment effect may result from individuals setting reference points around expectations—evaluating outcomes relative to those expectations.[77] That interpretation can also incorporate apparent rejections of the endowment effect, as exceptions that prove the rule: where experimental conditions mitigate expectations of continued ownership, the endowment effect will not manifest.[78] One important consequence of the endowment effect is that willingness-to-pay valuations may not match willingness-to-accept valuations.

Loss Aversion

Another reference point around which individuals tend to form preferences is zero; that is, individuals do not value or experience losses and gains symmetrically. This result is known as loss aversion, because of the consistent finding that individuals perceive losses more intensely than gains.[79] That is, to give someone with loss aversion some amount of money and then take it back would not leave the individual's welfare unchanged, as in the standard model—rather, the individual would feel worse off, because paying the money back would reduce his or her welfare by more than the original gift increased it. That effect has been demonstrated in a number of contexts, including policy-relevant ones. For example, experimental work suggests that the tendency of individuals to spend out of a tax cut might be sensitive to whether the cut is framed as a tax rebate or a bonus because one is perceived as repayment of a loss and the other as a gain.[80]

One important consequence of loss aversion is that individuals can express what appear to be odd preferences with respect to risk. In particular, individuals can make choices that reveal an extreme aversion to risk.[81] What looks like extreme aversion to risk may be driven in part by an aversion to the possibility of loss (combined with the tendency of individuals to overweight small probabilities, as described above). That has some real-world consequences. Loss aversion may be behind why individuals insure against very small risks or choose to have very low deductibles.[82] Loss aversion also has the effect of making individuals risk averse with respect to gains, as standard assumptions predict, but possibly risk loving with respect to losses—that is, individuals may be willing to accept risk in order to avoid greater losses. One important demonstration and implication of the effects of loss aversion is that whether choices are framed as losses or gains can have a measurable effect on choice.[83]

STATUS QUO BIAS

Another consequence of reference-dependence is status quo bias, the tendency of people to stick with what they have. It was originally noted in the tendency of individuals to stick with their health insurance plan and retirement options over time.[84] Similar results have been found in other contexts as well, such as individuals' preferences with respect to service options from utility providers.[85] This effect operates at least partly in conjunction with other tendencies—such as procrastination—but it also seems to be partly a function of using one's current situation as a reference point in evaluating alternatives. The effectiveness of defaults in promoting enrollment in employment benefits and social programs, noted above as consistent with the effect of channel factors, is also reinforced by status quo bias.

Other-Regarding Preferences

One final assumption of the standard model that leads economists and policy-makers astray is the assumption that people are purely self-interested. While it is only a simplifying assumption on the part of the standard model, it is central to a number of specific results, including results in public finance. Findings from psychology and behavioral economics suggest that preferences and choices are interdependent in a wide variety of ways. People care about the outcomes realized by others, or at least they act as if they do. They care about the outcomes for groups and how those outcomes are generated. They care about how their choices compare with those of others and how they are viewed by others. And so on. In general, we categorize the ways in which individual preferences are related to the choices and outcomes of others as demonstrations of what we label other-regarding preferences. There are several facets to other-regarding preferences that are relevant to the economics of the public sector. They include *altruism, fairness, social norms,* and *interpersonal preferences.*

ALTRUISM

Evidence from multiple domains supports a view of human nature that is less dim than what economists typically suppose. Rather than pursuing narrow conceptions of self-interest alone, people frequently act as though they care about the outcomes of others, either individually or as a group.[86] Many results from laboratory experiments, for example, are inconsistent with strong forms of self-interest. Consider the results of the "ultimatum game," which has been repeated many times in many different contexts: There are two players, one of whom proposes a certain split of a pool of money. The other player can either accept the proposed split—in which case it is realized—or reject it, in which case neither player receives a payout. Were the game played by purely selfish individuals, a bare minimum offer should be made and accepted. In fact, when this game is played, offers tend to be around 40 percent of the pool.[87] In addition, the consistency of this behavior suggests that rather than being an artifact that might result from imperfect optimization, findings of this sort reveal preferences for altruism.[88]

One important consequence of this behavior for public finance is that individuals may engage in what amounts to voluntary redistribution. Indeed, an important piece of real-world evidence for altruism comes from donations to charities, which are substantial and difficult to explain if individuals are purely selfish.[89] Another important consequence for public finance is that this behavior may lead to voluntary contributions to public goods. Evidence from laboratory experiments suggests that individuals tend to contribute to public goods in excess of what an assumption of pure self-interest would predict.[90] There also is some evidence from the field that voluntary contributions are made to public goods such as public radio stations and schools that are difficult to reconcile with pure self-interest.[91]

FAIRNESS

A related finding but one that has distinct consequences is that individuals have preferences with respect to the process that generates outcomes, as well as the outcomes themselves.[92] That is, there is evidence that individuals have preferences for fairness. Survey responses, for example, indicate that individuals value fairness in price and wage setting.[93] Behaviors in experimental settings also are consistent with preferences for fairness. For example, individuals appear to value cooperation and more generally to act in accordance with reciprocity.[94] Those behaviors are in many ways more consistent with a taste for fairness than strategic behavior.[95]

SOCIAL NORMS

Individuals are influenced by the behavior of others and by the way that others expect them to act to an extent that is surprising in the standard model.

Individuals will often behave in a way that conforms to community norms.[96] For instance, results suggest that in addition to an intrinsic preference for fairness, a desire to be perceived as fair by others—in particular, by following the norm of splitting rewards evenly—partly drives such results in laboratory games.[97] Field experiments confirm that social norms influence behavior. For example, individuals given a flyer are less likely to dispose of it by littering in environments that have been manipulated to be relatively free of litter.[98] Direct messages that indicate to people that most other people behave a certain way have been found to promote conformity to that behavior.[99] In one striking set of findings, showing individuals how their consumption of residential energy use compared with that of their neighbors and framing above-average energy use as undesirable was found to reduce energy consumption.[100]

INTERPERSONAL PREFERENCES

A final set of interrelationships among the choices that individuals make arises from the fact that people care how they are viewed by and how they are positioned relative to others. For instance, in a set of results that combines reference-dependent preferences and other-regarding preferences, individuals often are found to have positional preferences.[101] That is, their utility is a function of their outcomes relative to the outcomes of others. For example, in one study, individuals were found to be less happy when their neighbors had higher earnings.[102] Another result of interpersonal preferences is that individual choices have been found to depend to some extent on how individuals identify socially.[103] For instance, individuals exhibit preferences that depend on which of their multiple social identities—for example, student, employee, spouse, American—is salient at the time of choice.[104]

Summary

What these findings on reference-dependent and other-regarding preferences indicate, ultimately, is that results in public finance that are sensitive to assumptions about the form and content of preferences require review. For example, as noted above, the levels of private contributions to public goods, such as public schools, are sometimes higher than predicted by the standard model, a result that can be explained in part by the existence and nature of other-regarding preferences. Conclusions about the efficient level of public provision of public goods such as these, derived under assumptions of perfect self-interest, will need to be revisited in light of empirical evidence with respect to other-regarding preferences.

What the results on nonstandard preferences should not be interpreted to mean is that they have taken down a straw man. Pure selfishness and reference-independent preferences are not central features of the standard model of deci-sionmaking; they are merely simplifying assumptions that have been convenient to use in economic analysis. The issue becomes one of whether, for example, self-interest or altruism is the more appropriate operating assumption for how economic agents interact with the world. Are expressions of altruism unim-portant or rare deviations, or are they common, widespread, and important for understanding behavior? Questions such as these are an empirical matter. A similar caveat, in fact, applies not just to the findings on nonstandard prefer-ences but to all of the findings described in this chapter—the standard model is a set of assumptions, and the issue is not whether those assumptions ever fail, but whether they fail so regularly that they are worse operating assumptions than the alternatives.

Ultimately, the important question for public finance, in all cases, is whether allowing for these key behavioral deviations from the usual assumptions—imper-fect optimization, bounded self-control, and nonstandard preferences—matters. They seem on their face to create the possibility that results in public finance may change if revised assumptions about individual decisionmaking are incorporated. But do they? Do choice errors matter in the aggregate or in equilibrium? Do individual decisionmaking failures matter for market failures? And so on.

The answers are not obvious. For one, it may be that individuals exhibit these behaviors in experimental settings but not in real life, where the stakes are higher and the influence of experience and learning may be more substantial.[105] There is some evidence that behavioral tendencies that stand out in the lab can be attenu-ated in the field or in agents with greater experience or strong financial incentives. For example, the endowment effect can be less pronounced among individuals with more experience in relevant markets.[106] However, given evidence from the field, this is clearly not always true, as in the case of automatic enrollment in retirement saving plans. Separately, it may be the case that markets operate in a way that neutralizes the effects of individual decisionmaking errors on aggregate outcomes. That is theoretically possible;[107] however, so is the converse.[108] Tests under market conditions, including the evidence from the field and simulated markets, suggest that markets are not always sufficient to enforce the outcomes predicted by the standard model.[109]

To understand the true implications of behavioral economics for public finance, then, we cannot simply apply findings from psychology directly to issues in public finance piecemeal. It is necessary instead to integrate findings on behavioral tendencies into the economic framework of public finance—into the analysis of externalities and asymmetries of information, and so on—and work through their implications for the role of government and for the design of public policy.

3

Behavioral Economics and Public Finance

E ven with the simplifying assumptions that economics usually makes about how individuals form preferences and make choices—perfect optimization, self-interest, and so on—the rigorous analysis of public policy questions is a challenging endeavor. Frame questions too narrowly, such as by asking whether a particular policy works or not, and the analysis can miss larger issues, such as whether the policy was a good idea to start with. Fail to anticipate the ways that individuals will respond to the incentives that policies create or to anticipate the ways that markets will adjust, and policy design will suffer. And so on. Considering the full implications of policies and the conditions that make them necessary requires a comprehensive analytical approach.

Public finance provides such an approach. Public finance begins with a theory of when public policy can be productive, identifying conditions under which unregulated markets lead to inefficient or undesirable outcomes. From that understanding, it develops guidelines for designing policies that address those conditions. The power of modern public finance lies in its ability to identify a core set of economic forces (adverse selection, externalities, and so on) and to use those forces both to ascertain the need for policy responses on a wide array of topics—unemployment, environmental policy, and so on—and to generate those responses.

In the standard case, public finance does all of that under the assumption that individuals are perfect optimizers, have unbounded self-control, and, usually, have standard preferences. Behavioral economics finds that those assumptions frequently are a poor match for reality. Moreover, we are beginning to discover that those assumptions fail in ways that matter for policy outcomes. For example, in the well-known case of enrollment in retirement saving plans, behavioral economics has shown how default rules—whether individuals must actively enroll or are automatically enrolled, with the ability to opt out—can have surprisingly substantial effects on participation and saving. The standard approach to public finance—which emphasizes the tax subsidy to such plans as the key incentive for participation—did not suggest such an effect and struggles to explain it. Such findings have raised the possibility that the usual conclusions of public finance, by failing to adopt a behavioral approach, may be missing something about how policy—and the world—works.

In this chapter, we outline our framework for integrating insights from behavioral economics into the general public finance approach. What is that approach? The study of public finance casts economists in a role similar to that of medical doctors. Much as doctors work with patients to understand what is wrong when they are sick and how to use medicine to improve their lives, public finance economists work to understand what is wrong with the economy when markets fail and how to use the apparatus of the state to improve social outcomes. Much as the analytical process that a doctor follows progresses from diagnosing a problem to advising judgments on how to proceed to prescribing a course of action, so does the process that a public finance economist follows.

Psychology and behavioral economics are like a new technology now available to economists and policymakers. Just as a new medical technology such as advanced imaging techniques can improve the accuracy of diagnoses, change judgment calls, and lead to new prescriptions, so can behavioral economics change the way that public finance treats policy problems at each stage of the analytical process. The new model of behavior introduced by psychology can affect our understanding of how markets do or do not fail. It can change the terms and nature of the trade-offs that policymakers face in setting policy. And it can lead to a new set of tools for achieving policy goals as well as refine our understanding of how the old ones work.

Below we expand on the ways in which the standard conclusions of public finance are subject to revision when individuals exhibit behavioral tendencies. We review how and why those conclusions can change when policymakers undertake the following three tasks:

—*Diagnosing policy problems.* The first and fundamental issue in public finance is understanding when and how markets fail to maximize social welfare; traditionally, this occurs when markets fail to generate efficient outcomes due to market failure or when market outcomes are in conflict with other social goals, such as equality. A behavioral approach shows how standard public finance sometimes misdiagnoses the ways in which market failures translate into welfare losses, misstates the welfare costs of outcomes like inequality, and entirely misses other opportunities to improve social welfare.

—*Judging policy objectives.* Given an appreciation for the welfare costs of market failures or other sources of welfare loss, public finance can inform the question of how to weigh competing policy objectives and social goals. While it is ultimately up to policymakers and society—not economists—to make the judgments that such trade-offs require, public finance can shed light on the nature and the terms of the trade-offs. Allowing for behavioral tendencies can alter the terms of long-standing trade-offs as well as introduce new trade-offs.

—*Prescribing policy responses.* Finally, public finance can suggest appropriate designs for policy responses that reflect judgments about policy objectives. Public finance generates a set of principles for policy design—such as how to set taxes or subsidies—that already derive in large part from consideration of how individuals respond to the incentives that they are offered. Behavioral findings, by changing our expectations regarding individuals' responses to policy, can generate an updated set of principles for policy design.

For each stage, we discuss ways in which behavioral economics may change the standard analysis. In appendix B, we offer a slightly more formal way of thinking about the implications of a behavioral perspective on choice and welfare for policy. Finally, note that just as the prior chapter was not intended to be a comprehensive review of behavioral economics, this chapter does not attempt a comprehensive review of public finance; standard undergraduate public finance textbooks can provide a suitable reference.[1]

Diagnosing Policy Problems

Public finance starts with identifying a set of problems that require a policy solution. Traditional public finance considers essentially two classes of policy interventions to be welfare improving: corrective policies that address market failures and redistributive policies that seek to improve social welfare. When markets fail due to externalities or asymmetries of information, unregulated outcomes are no longer presumptively efficient, and government policies that correct for those failures can increase efficiency. When market outcomes are efficient but undesirable, due, for example, to unmet preferences for equity, the government can intervene to improve social welfare by redistributing income. Somewhat separately, public finance recognizes that governments face the problem of raising revenue in an efficient manner to support those and other functions of government.

Behavioral economics modifies the approach to these problems in two ways. First, behavioral tendencies may change the way that policy problems related to both market efficiency and economic equity translate into welfare outcomes. For example, asymmetric information is usually thought to create a policy problem because of the way that individuals respond to informational advantages or disadvantages—in particular, that they do so in ways that lead to outcomes like adverse selection, which in turn operate to undermine market efficiency. But when individuals are behavioral, the mere fact of informational asymmetries may not generate such outcomes—for example, such individuals may not recognize or otherwise be able to fully act on an informational advantage, thereby mitigating or possibly even overturning the standard set of consequences for market outcomes and welfare. Similarly, by changing assumptions about, for example, the form of individual utility functions or how they aggregate, behavioral economics can also change how poverty and inequality translate into lost social welfare.

Second, behavioral tendencies may also in some cases create the underlying conditions of a market failure directly. For example, imperfect optimization might create asymmetries of information in some markets where they would not otherwise exist. Or other-regarding preferences might create interdependencies in welfare that allow new types of externalities to arise.

Market Failures

The central theoretical result in welfare economics is that markets, when they are perfectly competitive and otherwise well functioning, result in a level of economic efficiency on which government policy cannot improve. In practice, that result holds only when markets exhibit certain characteristics, such as common information. When the standard assumptions fail to hold, markets fail, and government intervention may improve market outcomes. There are a number of conditions under which markets can fail. Two are of central interest for the study of public finance: asymmetries of information, which occur when relevant information is not common among all market participants, and externalities, which occur when the welfare of some individuals is interrelated with that of others through channels that are not mediated by the price system. (A third, market power, is less central to public finance and is briefly discussed in box 3-1 on pages 48–49.) In each case, public finance provides a standard approach to describing the nature of the problems that those conditions present for policy. And behavioral economics, by updating the assumptions of individual preference and choice on which that approach to some extent depends, can modify the standard conclusions.

ASYMMETRIES OF INFORMATION

Asymmetries of information occur when some market participants have more complete information than others about relevant market features. Markets characterized by asymmetries of information can fail to operate efficiently, in particular because such asymmetries can lead to adverse selection. Adverse selection arises when buyers or sellers with private information self-select into or out of transactions based on that information in ways that ultimately undermine the market. A classic example of asymmetric information is thought to occur in health insurance markets, in which individuals are likely to have private information about the status of their own health. Selection can arise in such a market because health insurance will be more valuable to individuals who know themselves to be less healthy—as a result, those individuals will be more likely to purchase health insurance. The selection is adverse because health care costs for those individuals are higher—offering the insurance can become unprofitable at the original price. Such markets are fragile and in the extreme can fail to exist at all. In the case of health insurance, for example, the market can enter a death spiral, in which adverse selection leads to increases in insurance premiums, which lead to further adverse selection, which leads to further premium increases, and so on until insurance can no longer be profitably offered. In response, the government may be motivated to regulate or participate in such markets in order to ensure their smooth operation. The perceived likelihood of asymmetries of information in health insurance markets, for example, motivates in part the public insurance programs in the United States, such as Medicare and Medicaid, as well as the extensive regulation of private health insurance.

The key to seeing how behavioral economics is likely to modify some of the usual conclusions about asymmetries of information is to recognize that the standard model of when and how adverse selection operates is premised on the assumption that individuals choose optimally according to their private information—for example, that individuals have the computational capacity to understand the implications of their private information. That is why, in the example above, unhealthy individuals may be disproportionately attracted to health insurance products.

However, if individuals have difficulty translating their private information into optimal decisions and actions, then asymmetries of information will not necessarily generate adverse selection according to the usual model. If, for example, unhealthy individuals can assess the implications of health risks only in an approximate way, or with error, that may modulate the extent to which they find health insurance attractive. Such a result is not only possible but also plausible. Note, for instance, that the types of insurance markets in which asymmetries of information are likely to arise tend to require the type of complex judgments over which individuals are especially likely to display behavioral tendencies. By the nature of insurance, for example, judgments involve probabilistic reasoning, which individuals generally tend to do in error and with biases. Motivational biases can also play a role—if individuals are overly optimistic about health outcomes, then health insurance may be perceived as less valuable even by the less healthy. Other behavioral tendencies, such as failure of self-control and the ways that individuals trade off outcomes across time, also matter, as do reference-dependence and especially loss aversion. All are likely to be important in how individuals view both the costs and benefits of insurance and how they make decisions about coverage.

As a result of the interaction between asymmetric information and behavioral tendencies, the consequences of asymmetric information for market outcomes and the nature of the resulting policy problem become much less certain. If individuals in a position to exploit an informational advantage that would, in the standard model, lead to adverse selection fail to understand that advantage or are unable or unwilling to act on that information, there may be less adverse selection than the standard model would predict. The extent of the market failure—and the corresponding welfare losses—would be diminished. In extreme cases, it seems possible that such tendencies could even change the sign of selection effects. For example, if leading an unhealthy lifestyle is strongly correlated with the same types of decisionmaking errors that lead individuals to fail to appreciate the risks of being uninsured, that could lead to advantageous selection, whereby unhealthy individuals are disproportionately less likely to purchase health insurance than healthy individuals. Under such an outcome, unregulated markets remain robust.

Finally, note that in principle the effects of this interaction could go in either direction: behavioral tendencies could mitigate or exacerbate selection in insurance markets. Just as failure to act on private information could hold health insurance markets together, the failure, say, to assess risk probabilities correctly could accelerate adverse selection and market unraveling. Understanding the extent of the adverse selection caused by asymmetric information when individuals exhibit behavioral tendencies becomes a much more empirical exercise.

Another way in which behavioral tendencies can interact with asymmetries of information is by creating them outright. In the standard model, asymmetries of information are typically assumed to follow from the features or structure of the market—that, for example, health status is simply impossible or infeasible to monitor accurately—but not from differences in the capacity of market participants to attend to or process information. Behavioral tendencies, however, raise the possibility that asymmetries of information could arise from such differences—for example, when individuals in their role as consumers are constrained by limited attention or computational capacity in a way that firms in their role as suppliers are not.

Behavioral economics also allows us to reinterpret the relative importance of possible alternative sources of some policy problems generally thought to relate to asymmetric information. For example, policies like Social Security and the suite of government programs that relate to retirement security more broadly often are understood in the standard approach as, at least in part, a response to a failure in the market for annuities due to adverse selection with respect to longevity risk. In that view, the government provides annuities through Social Security so that all can benefit from the mandated pooling of longevity risk, which markets cannot achieve. While that story has some truth—longevity risk is a genuine problem—it also seems incomplete. Behavioral economics invites a reappraisal of the importance of other forces—for example, how government programs to enhance savings (or to mitigate the consequences of failing to save) can be a welfare-improving response to the tendency of time-inconsistent individuals to fail to save adequately for retirement.

Here and elsewhere, asymmetries of information operate alongside behavioral tendencies that may have direct costs in terms of social welfare. Identifying behavioral effects, of course, raises profound issues about how or even if economic analysis should consider them in defining a policy problem. We defer a full discussion about how public finance should deal with such matters to the section below on judging policy objectives, which judgments such policies necessarily reflect. We note here only that, first, welfare loss (under some conception of welfare) may be caused by such behavior, and second, that policy problems may in some cases be reinterpreted as addressing behavioral tendencies.

EXTERNALITIES AND PUBLIC GOODS

Externalities occur when some element of an individual's welfare function is determined in whole or in part by the action of some other agent that does not take that fact into account in determining its own behavior. The classic example of an externality is pollution. Take the case of air pollution caused by a firm in the course of production, which affects the air quality for some individual. The pollution harms the individual, but in general there is no reason for the firm to consider that cost to social welfare when determining how much to produce and pollute. Because that cost is unpriced to the firm, the market fails, and unregulated levels of pollution will be inefficiently high, leading to a loss of welfare relative to the social optimum. Note that in general externalities can be negative or positive and can result from either production or consumption. Finally, note that a special case of an externality, called a public good, is of particular interest in public finance. A public good is an externality that enters each individual's utility function at its aggregate level. National defense is a classic example. Simply by living within a country's borders, one benefits from the aggregate level of defense protection that the country offers. In general, public goods, like all goods that generate positive externalities in production, will be underproduced by the market.

The standard models of how externalities form and how they lead to inefficient outcomes, as with asymmetries of information, depend closely on how individuals behave and how they respond to those externalities. So, for example, the excess consumption of fossil fuels like gasoline that the standard model predicts in the face of negative externalities in their consumption—in the form of pollution or their contribution to global warming—comes about because of the way in which individuals are assumed to respond to the artificially low price of gasoline.

The psychology at work in deciding how to consume energy and in what form, however, might cause individuals to make different choices. Individuals with other-regarding preferences may internalize those externalities voluntarily, leading to efficient outcomes even in the presence of the externality. In the example of gasoline consumption, a sensitivity to pro-environmental social norms may lead individuals to partially internalize the externalities involved and, say, change their commuting patterns or purchase a different type of car.

As a result, when individuals exhibit behavioral tendencies, the ways in which the unpriced interrelation between the actions of one agent and the welfare of another translate into inefficient quantities of some good or service being produced or consumed depend on how individuals respond to the mispricing. In general, the welfare costs of externalities may be either mitigated or exacerbated by the presence of behavioral tendencies. So for instance, other-regarding preferences may lead individuals toward voluntary internalization or provision of public goods, which tends to reduce the magnitude of welfare losses associated with the externality. To the extent that individuals voluntarily elect to engage in green behaviors that benefit the environment out of concern for others or due to the influence of social norms, there is less scope for policy. But, for example, to the extent that time-inconsistent preferences make individuals more likely to purchase fuel-inefficient cars, the magnitude of the problem is that much larger.

In addition, behavioral tendencies may sometimes lead directly to new types of externalities or outcomes that mimic externalities. That can result when, for example, imperfectly optimizing behavior has consequences for others. For example, errors by individuals in making choices that affect, say, public health outcomes have external consequences. Another potential behavioral source of externalities is due to the fact that behavioral tendencies can create an interdependence between the actions of one agent and the welfare of another where they are not assumed to exist in the standard model. In particular, behavioral tendencies such as other-regarding preferences or bounded self-control may lead actions and utilities to be linked across individuals in ways that the standard model downplays. So, for instance, activities like eating junk food or smoking cigarettes in the presence of individuals who have only bounded self-control can impose negative externalities to the extent that those activities raise the costs to those individuals of exercising self-control or cause their self-control to fail entirely.

In thinking through the implications of behavioral economics for understanding how markets fail and what the consequences are, one key point is that behavioral economics does not in every case justify more government intervention—in many cases it may actually call for less. That result can be counterintuitive. At first glance, it may seem that the integration of behavioral economics with public finance will lead only to the discovery of additional cases in which government intervention can theoretically improve market outcomes. However,

---

Box 3-1. *Market Power*

Markets also can fail when firms have market power, that is, when they are no longer price takers. When firms have market power, they are able to restrict supply and sell their goods and services at prices above marginal cost, which is inefficient and leads to a loss of welfare relative to the social optimum. While market power is a form of market failure and thus fits with this discussion, it often is not treated as a topic in public finance but left to the separate field of industrial organization. We follow that practice and therefore do not give a detailed treatment of market power in the text.

It is worth noting, however, that just as the conclusions in public finance about the sources and effects of information asymmetries and externalities depend in part on assumptions about how individuals choose and behave, so too can the economic analysis of market power be sensitive to the findings of behavioral economics. The most notable potential effect is that firms may be able to take advantage of behavioral tendencies on the part of consumers in order to gain or manipulate the extent of their market power—for example, by taking advantage of limited attention in order to develop or sustain pockets of market power or exploiting tendencies to bounded self-control in order to affect the elasticity of the demand curve that they sell along.

There is, in fact, an important and growing line of research in what is sometimes called behavioral industrial organization that considers such effects.[a] This research explores whether and how behavioral forces can create monopoly power or mediate existing monopoly powers. For example, one line of work shows how, in theory, imperfectly optimizing consumers can create market conditions under

---

identifying an additional layer of deviations from the standard model—adding decisionmaking failures to market failures—does not simply add to the occasions on which government intervention can improve social welfare. The two forces interact. The impact of that interaction on the magnitude of the policy problem—and thus the scope for policy—is in many cases theoretically ambiguous. For example, imperfect optimization may either increase or decrease the potential for adverse selection in insurance markets. Other-regarding preferences might create new opportunities for externalities on one hand but lead to an increase in the potential for voluntary internalization on the other. In general, the impact of behavioral tendencies on the depth of the policy problem—that is, the magnitude of the welfare loss—due to market failures often is in practice an empirical question whose answer is determined by the interaction of a specific deviation from perfect competition and a specific deviation from standard assumptions about choice.

which firms can charge markups over competitive pricing on goods in such a way that neither the presence of competing firms nor information disclosure will lead profits to be competed away.[b] That result follows from the inability of some individuals to accurately perceive and respond to complex price schedules. Other deviations from standard assumptions can have corresponding effects. For example, other research shows how individuals with self-control problems who are naïve about those problems can lead firms to set price schedules in ways that exploit that tendency, leading in turn to reductions in consumer welfare even when markets are otherwise perfectly competitive.[c]

Important as those results are, a full consideration of these effects would take a treatment of behavioral public finance too far afield. The relationship between behavioral tendencies, the conditions leading to market power, and the welfare consequences of market power are left to be treated with behavioral industrial organization in general as a separate topic of study.

a. Glenn Ellison, "Bounded Rationality in Industrial Organization," in *Advances in Economics and Econometrics: Theory and Applications, Ninth World Congress*, vol. 3, edited by Richard Blundell, Whitney K. Newey, and Torsten Persson (Cambridge University Press, 2006), pp. 142–74.

b. Xavier Gabaix and David Laibson, "Shrouded Attributes, Consumer Myopia, and Information Suppression in Competitive Markets," *Quarterly Journal of Economics*, vol. 121, no. 2 (2006), pp. 505–40.

c. Stefano DellaVigna and Ulrike Malmendier, "Contract Design and Self-Control: Theory and Evidence," *Quarterly Journal of Economics*, vol. 119, no. 2 (2004), pp. 353–402.

Poverty and Inequality

Another class of policy problems considered by public finance arises from the failure of market outcomes to maximize social welfare even when markets operate efficiently. These policy problems reflect the fact that not all efficient outcomes are equally desirable from the perspective of society. In such cases, government policy can be used to potentially improve market outcomes by improving some conception of social welfare. The predominant reason that public finance considers some market outcomes socially undesirable is the presence of poverty and inequality. Even when market outcomes are efficient, they can leave wide dispersions in income or other economic outcomes. Depending on how individuals form preferences over relevant outcomes and how society aggregates those preferences, outcomes with lower levels of poverty and inequality can often lead to a higher level of social welfare.

The analysis of the policy problems in this class begins with some conception of social welfare, where social welfare is an aggregation of individual utilities. The welfare costs of one distribution of income relative to another are then due to the shape of those individual preferences and the manner in which they are aggregated. For example, when an individual has a welfare function with a declining marginal utility of income and when social welfare is additive, then, other things being equal, higher-inequality distributions lead to lower levels of social welfare than do lower-inequality distributions. As a result, income support and redistribution policies can, holding all else constant, improve social welfare over the free market outcome.

Improving social welfare through policies of this type clearly depends on the ways in which individuals form preferences and make choices. Because behavioral economics allows for and emphasizes nonstandard preferences, a behavioral approach to the problems of poverty and inequality is likely to alter those conclusions. Nonstandard preferences, in general, and other-regarding preferences, in particular, change both the presumed shape of individual preferences as well as the arguments that enter the utility function, and they may even have implications for how preferences are aggregated.

As a result, welfare losses due to inequality or poverty may be larger or smaller due to behavioral tendencies. The extent to which inequality is a source of welfare loss is, in particular, sensitive to assumptions about preferences. The way in which inequality translates into welfare costs is explicitly a function of preferences. For example, to the extent that individuals have other-regarding preferences, the social welfare implications of inequality may be magnified. Similarly, preferences that individuals may have over the process generating the income distribution, such as preferences for fairness, may affect the social welfare costs of inequality. Individuals may even have preferences for features of the income distribution directly. Other-regarding preferences might manifest as a generalized distaste (or taste) for overall levels of inequality. Alternatively, individuals may hold preferences about their relative place in the income distribution, such as explicit preferences to inhabit favorable positions in the distribution, independent of their level of income or wealth. All of those factors affect how inequality affects social welfare.

The nature and magnitude of the policy problem posed by poverty are likely to depend on behavioral tendencies in special ways. Here, the important behavioral issues are less likely to be nonstandard preferences than imperfect optimization and bounded self-control. On one hand, behavioral tendencies can inform our understanding of the causes of poverty, which may alter how poverty matters for social welfare. In general, behavioral tendencies such as, say, failing to save adequately due to failure of self-control or failure to attend to expenses that are not salient can have outsized effects on those in or near poverty. The poor have small margins for error, so that even small mistakes can have large consequences. Such effects could, depending on the formulation of social welfare, alter the social costs of poverty. On the other hand, behavioral insights can help to inform our understanding of the consequences of poverty, which can also have implications for social welfare. For example, the stresses associated with poverty might reinforce the effects of behavioral tendencies, by, for example, making it more difficult for poor individuals to exert self-control. Such stresses could directly magnify the social consequences of poverty.

Taxation and Revenue

A third category of policy problem in public finance concerns the problem of taxation and raising revenue. The various functions of government require funding, including the redistribution of income implied by the social welfare costs of inequality and the corrective activity indicated by the market failures described above (such as those resulting from asymmetries of information and externalities, including public goods) as well as government activities not concerned with issues related to public finance. That leads the government to raise revenue, through some combination of taxation, borrowing, and other funding instruments.

The government must, therefore, set tax and revenue policies in order to meet its budget requirement. That requirement does not depend in any direct way on how individuals form preferences or make choices; consequently, behavioral economics does not actually change the underlying problem that taxation and revenue have to solve. That said, while there is no behavioral component to the matter of *why* the government seeks to raise revenue, there is an important behavioral dimension to *what* the government should do in response. Raising revenue optimally involves setting the level and structure of taxes in a way that must address key trade-offs, such as weighing the efficiency costs of taxation against the benefits of raising revenue, and the terms of the trade-offs depend on how individuals respond to taxes. As a result, regardless of whether or how behavioral economics changes the nature of policy problems, it can inform and clarify the terms of the trade-offs that policymakers face in setting and meeting policy objectives. We turn to this issue—of how behavioral economics can inform policy judgments and trade-offs—below.

Judging Policy Objectives

Between identifying and realizing opportunities to improve welfare, policy must often make reference to social goals in some form. Traditionally, public finance views policy objectives in terms of social welfare. In practice, that often requires subjective judgments on the part of society and policymakers regarding how to navigate trade-offs in choosing among alternative policies as well as how to weight the welfare of different individuals relative to each other. For example, determining the level of social insurance to provide may require society to decide where to locate along an equity-efficiency frontier, trading off insurance value for moral hazard. Similarly, setting redistribution policy may require deciding how to weight the welfare of individuals in different parts of the income distribution.

Of course, setting such policy objectives is an exercise that is largely outside the scope of public finance—and even economics. But that does not mean that there is no role for public finance at this stage of analysis. Public finance can identify the judgments required and the terms of the trade-offs that they reflect, even if it cannot ultimately make those judgments. For example, while the methods of public finance cannot determine how much efficiency loss, such as that due to the creation of moral hazard, society is willing to tolerate in the name of providing social insurance, it can build a theoretical model of how one trades off against the other and specify empirical tests of what those trade-offs are in practice. That is, economics can describe the equity-efficiency frontier, even if it cannot specify where society should locate on it. The principle extends to other trade-offs that policies require.

Behavioral economics also introduces an important new dimension in policy trade-offs. First, in considering the terms of policy trade-offs, policymakers must consider the possible role of behavioral tendencies. Imperfect optimization, bounded self-control, and nonstandard preferences all may modify the effects of policy and the way in which alternative policy regimes are traded off for one another. For example, to the extent that moral hazard in social insurance policies is mitigated or exacerbated by, say, self-control, the trade-offs between equity and efficiency in providing social insurance will be different. Second, in addition to balancing the competing interests of different individuals (that is, assigning welfare weights, if only implicitly, to individuals), policymakers must make judgments about how to weigh the various conflicting preferences that inconsistent decisionmakers appear to hold. So, for example, when individuals exhibit time-inconsistent preferences, policymakers must choose whether policy will favor the short- or long-run interests of the individual.

Finally, it is worth noting before proceeding that while a behavioral approach clarifies and makes explicit such types of judgments, it does not create them—such judgments already are an inherent part of the policy process. The policy environment will reflect such judgments, one way or the other, either explicitly or implicitly; that is, in practice, policymakers' choices already address the challenges presented by behavioral tendencies. Consider again the problem of social insurance and moral hazard, as in the case of unemployment insurance muting the incentives of unemployed individuals to return to work. Social insurance policies reflect the belief that the unemployed do not search for work with optimal intensity of their own accord. While that is due in part to the fact that the motivation to return to work is blunted by the moral hazard created by unemployment insurance and related programs, it may also be due to a tendency on the part of workers to procrastinate in searching for a job. To that extent, then, policy to encourage reemployment must choose how to balance the long-run preferences of the individual, which are consistent with wishing to return to work, against his or her short-run preferences, which reflect a desire to put off returning to work. The key point is that given such behavior on the part of the unemployed individual, policy will necessarily reflect a judgment about which preferences to favor, whether or not that judgment is made explicit by taking a behavioral approach. Policies that seek to explicitly combat procrastination reflect a judgment about which set of preferences to favor, and so do policies that ignore that tendency. Behavioral economics can thus add precision to the understanding of which such judgments policy should properly consider and can make explicit and systematic some considerations that policymakers already address in a more informal way.

Policy Trade-Offs

The solutions to many of the policy problems described above have both costs and benefits. Many of the trade-offs that policymakers face are specific manifestations of a general, pervasive trade-off in public finance between equity and efficiency. For example, social insurance provides income-smoothing benefits but can induce costly moral hazard. Alternative tax policies can have competing properties of equity and efficiency. Policymakers must make judgments about what benefits are worth what costs in these situations, such as how much moral hazard to tolerate in achieving the goals of social insurance or what mix of equity and efficiency is optimal in tax policy.

Behavioral economics can lead the terms of these trade-offs to differ from those in the standard model. The equity gains or the efficiency costs of policy may be greater or lesser depending on how individuals perceive the incentives created by the policy and how they respond to it. Because behavioral tendencies—including imperfect optimization, bounded self-control, and nonstandard preferences—affect behavioral response, findings from behavioral economics are of consequence in understanding costs and benefits. For example, the efficiency costs of redistribution and transfer policy come largely in the form of the disincentives that those policies create, such as those with respect to working or to thriftiness, in terms of both the moral hazard that they create for recipients and the distortions created by the taxes levied to fund the policies.

Both of those effects depend closely on behavioral response. If the behavioral response to either the diminished incentive to work or the taxes is less than in the standard model, due, say, to limited computational capacity as applied to complex benefit reduction schedules or to limited attention to taxes that are not salient, then the efficiency costs of such a policy may be less than under the standard model. In general, the direction of the effects will be ambiguous and will depend on the interaction of specific behavioral tendencies and the policy trade-offs in question. In principle, behavioral tendencies could increase or decrease either costs or benefits.

Among the many specific trade-offs that policy judgments must reflect, two stand out as being both especially important and especially sensitive to the possibility of behavioral tendencies: the moral hazard costs that weigh against the benefits of social insurance and redistribution and the efficiency costs that weigh against the revenue raised through taxation.

Moral Hazard

Moral hazard arises when individuals protected by policy from the full negative consequences of some adverse state—unemployment, for example, or poverty—face diminished incentives to avoid such conditions or to escape them. The effect is to create efficiency costs for the policies because of the way that they can lead to a lower labor supply or less saving and investment. Policy then must determine how much moral hazard society is willing to tolerate for the insurance value or for the social welfare improvement through redistribution. But the extent and nature of moral hazard in any given program are likely to be highly sensitive to behavioral dimensions of preference and choice.

The effect of behavioral tendencies may be to either mitigate or exacerbate moral hazard. For example, moral hazard may be diminished, or even fail to exist, if individuals cannot accurately perceive the incentives created by the programs. Individuals may perceive the difference between the incentives created by a program and the incentives that they face in the absence of a program as being smaller than it really is, creating a situation in which imperfectly optimizing behavior mitigates the prospects of moral hazard. For example, if workers are shortsighted when it comes to planning for retirement, then programs like Social Security need not be overly concerned with moral hazard—individuals would likely fail to save adequately in any event. Similarly, while traditional moral hazard suggests that people overconsume prescription drugs or doctor visits when they have health insurance, self-control problems related to adherence to a drug treatment regime or doctor visits might work against that.

In other circumstances, behavioral tendencies might reinforce moral hazard. In providing benefits to workers while they are unemployed, unemployment insurance undermines incentives to search for and return to work. It also seems possible that unemployment insurance contributes to diminishing the willpower necessary to search for work. In this case the behavioral tendency, procrastinating in searching for a job, works in the same direction as moral hazard. Note that in such cases as these, the problem of and costs imposed by moral hazard are transformed in a fundamental way, wherein the interests of policymakers in discouraging moral hazard actually align with at least one conception of the individual's welfare, his or her long-run preferences. In cases like these, behavioral economics may not just affect the slope of the trade-off between equity and efficiency but may in fact indicate that ignoring those factors leaves policy inside the frontier. That is, that there is scope for policy innovations that are both more efficient, in that they reduce moral hazard, and more equitable, in that they benefit the individual.

OPTIMAL TAXATION

The other set of trade-offs of particular interest and importance is the one embodied in determining optimal taxation. Raising revenue through taxation creates distortions in the markets that they affect that come at a cost to economic efficiency. Because taxes affect the relative prices of goods and services, working and leisure, saving and consumption, and so on, they move economic outcomes away from optimal levels and allocations. So, for example, implementing a commodity tax will, ordinarily, raise the price of the affected good, forestalling transactions that would have been welfare improving in the absence of the tax. That comes at a cost to economic efficiency. In addition, taxes have distributional effects. In the case of the commodity tax, the tax itself along with the forgone surplus will be distributed in some way between buyers and sellers of the good. Tax policy therefore must reflect judgments about what efficiency consequences of taxation are worthwhile and how to equitably distribute the burden of taxation.

Both the equity and efficiency consequences of taxation are a function of the way in which individuals respond to taxes, and behavioral tendencies such as imperfect optimization affect the response to taxes in many ways. Individuals respond to taxes only as they perceive them, which may be in error. Their response may deviate from their intentions due to failure of self-control and so on. For example, if individuals fail to attend to taxes that are not salient, such as commodity taxes not posted in prices, and so do not change their behavior in response to the tax, that may have consequences both for the distortions created by the tax and for who ultimately faces the incidence of such a tax. In the traditional model, lack of response to a tax is indicative of an insensitive demand curve and marks a good as a prime candidate for efficient taxation. In a behavioral model, however, lack of response may also indicate failure to respond due to, for example, errors born of limited attention, which create their own welfare costs. As a result, the welfare implications of insensitivity to taxes may be different when allowing for behavioral tendencies. Similar consequences are possible if, for example, individuals respond to complicated income tax schedules in error due to limited computational capacity (such as by responding to average rather than marginal rates) or if individuals do not make the connection between linked taxes and benefits (such as Social Security taxes and benefits). Such effects require a reevaluation of the terms of the optimal taxation problem.

Finally, before proceeding it is worth considering a common objection to a behavioral approach to policy that, while ever present, is perhaps most salient here. It is that behavioral economics creates something of a paradox in requiring more of policymakers—such as new judgments about identifying and distinguishing behavioral tendencies—while suggesting that policymakers' capacity to make such judgments may be impaired to the extent that they too are behavioral agents. On one hand, policymakers as individuals are human beings and are certainly subject to the same biases, heuristics, and bounds as other individuals. On the other hand, policymakers in their role as agents in a deliberative process are protected to some extent from committing such errors in an unchecked fashion. Ultimately, understanding the consequences of this apparent paradox is a matter more for the study of political economy. Here and throughout we largely set aside questions regarding the ability of government to implement what economic analysis suggests in order to focus on the implications of psychology for the economic conclusions of public finance.

Welfare Weights

In addition to changing the terms of existing policy judgments, behavioral economics also identifies new ones. How should policy address the possibility that individuals make choices that are in error, that represent a failure of self-control, or that are inconsistent? If individuals do not necessarily make stable or consistent choices in their own self-interest then, rather than take choice as a revelation of true preferences, policymakers must judge whether and how to balance the interests of different revealed preferences or stated preferences or preferences inferred by other means. That is, policy must reflect judgments about which preferences to favor and to what degree.

There is no agreed-on analytical framework within economics for translating choice inconsistencies into a judgment call about preferences. Moreover, it remains far from clear that economics as a discipline is especially well-equipped to recover preferences when they are not revealed by choice or to choose among inconsistent preferences. That is not, however, an entirely unfamiliar position for public finance. For example, traditional public finance allows that redistribution among individuals can improve social welfare without claiming privileged knowledge regarding the optimal level of redistribution. Similarly, behavioral public finance can recognize that policies favoring one set of preferences over another—for example, stated preferences for saving over revealed preferences for consuming—can improve welfare without having to specify definitively which preferences we should favor when and to what degree. It seems clearly the case that behavioral economics and psychology often are in a position to inform such debates even when they cannot resolve them.

The specific approach that we follow here is to treat the preferences revealed by any particular choice to be only one of a set of preferences that policymakers can choose to respect; they then can decide what weight to give different preferences in the same way that redistributive policy decides the weight to give different individuals in the social welfare function. That is, that the problem of making judgments about intrapersonal preference conflicts is structurally similar to making judgments about interpersonal preferences. And that, just as public finance can engage in debates about redistribution that it cannot ultimately resolve, so too can public finance evaluate the structure of competing claims about choice and preference even when it cannot ultimately evaluate their content. In this way, dispensing with revealed preference need not open a Pandora's box of policy conclusions, any and all of which can be supported by whatever assumptions about behavior are convenient. Instead, a behavioral approach to public finance can look essentially like business as usual for public finance economists, although one based on updated assumptions about individual behavior that are, in fact, specific, limited, and empirically identified. This perspective allows us to move past debates about identifying true utility and focus (as with traditional public finance) on the consequences for policy design, taking as given some judgment about welfare weights.

The policy judgments introduced by behavioral economics in this case involve setting policy in ways that resolve intrapersonal preference conflicts. Policy must reflect, for example, judgments about distinguishing what look like choice errors from what are simply unusual preferences. Similarly, policy must also reflect judgments about how to balance competing short- and long-run interests when individuals exhibit what appear to be time-inconsistent preferences. And policy must finally reflect judgments about how to balance the varying preferences that might be revealed when choice is otherwise inconsistent, as it can be due to reference-dependence or framing effects.

For example, when it appears that individuals fail to save optimally for retirement, policy must reflect a judgment of how to weight the choices of individuals in the short run (to consume while working) relative to what policymakers may have reason to believe are the long-run interests of individuals (to have saved when they reach retirement). In the standard economic analysis, in which choices reflect preferences, policy should place a weight of one on individual choice and zero on what policymakers, psychologists, or economists believe to be in the long-run interests of the individual. The behavioral approach simply recognizes that policy may in practice reflect some convex combination of those weights.

Finally, a key point here is that, in practice, policy will tend to reflect such judgments, perhaps implicitly, whether or not they are considered as an explicit component of public finance. Even the approach of standard economics, to always respect choice, reflects a judgment about how to weight alternative conceptions of preferences. Such judgments ultimately cannot be avoided, in much the same way that advocating against redistributive policies is not neutral about welfare weights across individuals but reflects a judgment to respect the welfare weights of the market. Moreover, policymakers are in many cases already making such trade-offs informally. The approach outlined here is simply a way to make judgments explicit, systematic, and informed by the relevant psychological insights. But economics is far from having achieved consensus on how to address this challenge; other approaches are described in box 3-2.

Prescribing Policy Responses

Opportunities for improving welfare having been identified and policy objectives established, public finance goes on to draw conclusions for policy design. For example, in the case of goods with negative externalities, the question is how to discourage their consumption. Traditional public finance offers a menu of principles for policy design. In general, when government seeks to discourage an activity it uses taxes, but it might instead set regulations to limit production and consumption of such goods. It also can establish fees on the externalities directly, create markets for setting prices on the unpriced activity, and so on.

The principles of program design that come out of public finance are to a large degree a matter of anticipating and managing the behavioral response to programs. Correcting externalities is commonly a matter of either encouraging or discouraging behaviors associated with those externalities. The implementation of social insurance and transfer programs frequently is concerned both with creating incentives among eligible individuals to screen themselves into programs efficiently and with managing the behavior of covered individuals in response to the moral hazard that the programs can create. Designing efficient and equitable tax systems is a matter of considering the ways in which individuals respond to taxes.

Relaxing the standard assumptions about behavior calls into question many standard conclusions about policy design. Broadly speaking, there are three classes of insights that behavioral economics brings to policy design. The first has to do with using prices and incentives to affect and manage behavior. Standard economic analysis suggests a relationship between incentives and level effects—for example, that corrective taxes can reduce the level of carbon emissions. Behavioral tendencies change the way in which prices affect behavior and allow for the impact of nonprice levers. The second has to do with the ability of policy to manage and use private information to achieve policy goals. That is, standard analysis posits a relationship between incentives and selection effects—for example, that tagging in social programs screens the right groups in and out on the basis of self-selection. But how individuals react to incentives when either advantaged or disadvantaged by private information is determined, in part, by behavioral tendencies. The third class of insights has to do with the use of markets and choice architecture to achieve policy goals in general equilibrium—such as by establishing a market to achieve policy goals or setting policy to elicit or inhibit responses from firms or other actors in markets in order to achieve those goals. For example, in the case of policies such as school choice that rely on market forces, the standard analysis has straightforward predictions for how markets operate and the outcomes that they generate. The outcome of such market processes, however, depends at least in part on the behavioral tendencies of market participants.

Prices and Incentives

Perhaps the fundamental design rule of public finance is that when policymakers seek to change market outcomes, they can change prices. As a general rule, in the standard model, when the objective of policy is to encourage behavior, policymakers can employ subsidies, and when the objective of policy is to discourage behavior, they can impose taxes. So, for example, when market outcomes are inefficient due to the existence of externalities, policy can manipulate the level of production and consumption to achieve efficient levels through taxes and subsidies or equivalent policies.

A behavioral approach to policy design suggests a less straightforward relationship between prices and behavior. This approach notes that how individuals respond to prices is mediated by behavioral tendencies. For example, individuals with limited attention and computational capacity respond not to actual prices but to the prices that they perceive. Similarly, responses to prices may not reflect intended responses due to an imperfect capacity for self-control. As a result, prices will not always be effective levers for changing behavior, especially when prices fail to be salient or when the targeted behaviors already are the result of behavioral tendencies. Behavioral economics also suggests that nonprice levers (or nudges, to use the terminology popularized by Thaler and Sunstein) can be effective in changing behavior. Nudges are features of policy that operate directly through the behavioral tendencies that individuals exhibit in order to elicit a response. Nudges allow policymakers to effect changes in behavior without changing prices in some circumstances, such as with automatic enrollment in retirement plans. Ultimately, prices and nudges interact to determine the level of behavioral response to policy parameters.

RESPONSE TO PRICES

Behavioral tendencies such as imperfect optimization or bounded self-control mean that individuals will not necessarily respond to prices in a straightforward

Box 3-2. *Behavioral Welfare Economics*

How to treat welfare considerations when choice cannot be assumed to reveal preference is one of the thorniest issues for behavioral economics and policy and one
to which a consensus approach has not been developed. The approach that we
describe in the text is only one possible way of dealing with the challenges posed
by behavioral economics for understanding welfare and setting policy. Some other
approaches that have been described elsewhere include the following:

Libertarian paternalism. This approach argues that policy should fundamentally
respect choice while engaging in choice-preserving interventions that target the
behavioral tendencies of individuals.[a] Libertarian paternalism supports policies
such as automatic enrollment in retirement saving plans, which address behavioral
tendencies in order to encourage saving (the paternalistic feature) but ultimately
leave individuals free to choose and opt out (the libertarian feature). Such policies
by definition do not affect individuals when they are behaving according to standard assumptions.

Optimal paternalism. Another approach is to explicitly weigh the costs to individuals who choose well of policies aimed at improving outcomes for individuals who
exhibit imperfect decisionmaking. This approach is exemplified by the case of taxes
on goods such as cigarettes.[b] Cigarette consumption is possibly optimal, but it also
is consistent with bounded self-control. The fundamental observation here is that
a tax on cigarettes would have a large benefit for individuals whose consumption
is due to failure of self-control but only a relatively small cost to individuals whose
consumption is in fact optimal. As a result, there is an argument that, on net, such
a policy is worthwhile even when it negatively affects some individuals. A similar
example shows how with imperfect optimization, social welfare can be improved
by restricting choice sets, balancing the costs to individuals who are forced into a
suboptimal alternative against the reduction in errors by people who would have
chosen badly in the larger choice set.[c]

Recovering preferences. This approach takes choice as revealing preferences when
there is no reason to believe otherwise, such as when individuals' choices are consistent, and then looks to nonchoice evidence for an indication of which preferences to favor when choices are not consistent.[d] Nonchoice evidence might include
either empirical psychological or economic evidence or even results from neuroscience. For example, under this approach, policy toward cigarettes takes the fact that

individuals have chosen to smoke as one piece of evidence that smoking makes them better off, but it is considered only one of several pieces of evidence and not necessarily determinative. Policymakers would further consider evidence based on the psychology and biology of addiction that suggests that the choice to smoke is suspect. With that evidence in hand and in conjunction with a model of decisionmaking and addiction, policymakers could then decide what truly maximizes individual welfare and set policy accordingly—in this case, to discourage smoking. Such evidence, along with models of behavior, may (or may not) also lead to judgments about what functional form the resulting policy should take—say, a sin tax instead of a ban.

Respecting choice. Finally, a perfectly valid and sometimes advocated position is that economists should simply stick with revealed preference. One argument along these lines simply emphasizes that going beyond choice is not the province of economics.[e] Another stresses the reasons to think that neither economists nor policymakers are likely to do very well at weighing the evidence and making these kinds of judgments.[f]

a. Richard Thaler and Cass Sunstein, "Libertarian Paternalism," *American Economic Review,* vol. 93, no. 2 (2003), pp. 175–79; Colin Camerer and others, "Regulation for Conservatives: Behavioral Economics and the Case for 'Asymmetric Paternalism,'" *University of Pennsylvania Law Review,* vol. 151, no. 3 (2003), pp. 1211–54.

b. Ted O'Donoghue and Matthew Rabin, "Studying Optimal Paternalism, Illustrated by a Model of Sin Taxes," *American Economic Review,* vol. 93, no. 2 (2003), pp. 186–191; Ted O'Donoghue and Matthew Rabin, "Optimal Sin Taxes," *Journal of Public Economics,* vol. 90, no. 10–11 (2006), pp. 1825–49.

c. Eytan Sheshinski, "Optimal Policy to Influence Individual Choice Probabilities," unpublished working paper, 2010.

d. B. Douglas Bernheim and Antonio Rangel, "Behavioral Public Economics: Welfare and Policy Analysis with Nonstandard Decision-Makers," in *Behavioral Economics and Its Applications,* edited by Peter Diamond and Hannu Vartianen (Princeton University Press, 2007); B. Douglas Bernheim and Antonio Rangel, "Beyond Revealed Preference: Choice-Theoretic Foundations for Behavioral Welfare Economics," *Quarterly Journal of Economics,* vol. 124, no. 1 (February 2009), pp. 51–104.

e. Faruk Gul and Wolfgang Pesendorfer, "The Case for Mindless Economics," in *The Foundations of Positive and Normative Economics,* edited by Andrew Caplin and Andrew Shotter (Oxford University Press, 2008).

f. Edward L. Glaeser, "Paternalism and Psychology," *University of Chicago Law Review,* vol. 73, no. 1 (2006), pp. 133–56.

way. Individuals possessing only limited attention or computational capacity will respond not to prices but to their own, error-prone construal of prices. So, for example, when price schedules are complex or the link between consumer behavior and marginal costs is opaque, adjustments to prices are possibly blunt instruments for policy. Moreover, individuals with bounded self-control may not respond to prices in predictable ways. When policies intend to encourage or discourage activities that involve self-control or willpower, prices may be weak policy levers.

In general, psychological forces tend to mean that prices will not be as uniformly effective in driving behavior as presumed in the standard case. In many cases, that creates a new set of challenges for policy. For example, in the face of behavioral tendencies, the subsidization of behaviors like retirement saving through the tax code may be too complicated or too indirectly related to the behavior that it is intended to encourage; consequently, its effectiveness may be compromised. Or it may be too hard for individuals to see the marginal costs of residential energy use or to calculate the relationship of those costs to their behavior to allow energy taxes to generate the desired response in combating environmental externalities. Note that in other situations, however, policymakers may be able to use insensitivity to prices to their advantage. For example, if eligible individuals perceive the work incentives of programs like the earned income tax credit (EITC) only in an approximate way—and in particular as being generally pro-work, without distinguishing between features of the EITC that reward work and features that do not—then such programs may fail to generate undesirable incentives to reduce labor supply.

NONPRICE LEVERS

The same behavioral tendencies that blunt the old tools can create new ones. Although behavioral tendencies mean that prices will not always be effective in achieving policy objectives, effective levers besides prices exist for generating a behavioral response to a policy. That is, policymakers can exploit behavioral tendencies even as they attempt to correct for their consequences. So, for example, in the case of automatic enrollment in retirement plans, the effect of default rules obtains only because the policy design uses the tendency of individuals to adhere to defaults. If individuals responded optimally to the small costs associated with enrolling in or leaving such programs or understood their optimal savings strategy so perfectly that the default did not influence their perception of what their behavior should be, then defaults would presumably be ineffective as policy levers. Note that a common and important feature of nudges is that they frequently are very cheap to implement relative to price levers. The price-based incentives for retirement savings—primarily the tax advantages—cost the government billions of dollars each year in tax expenditures. Encouraging automatic enrollment, on the other hand, is all but costless to the government.

Nudges can take many forms, and in general they derive their power from the way in which they interact with specific behavioral tendencies. For example, defaults take advantage of the fact that individuals tend to procrastinate in making changes, among other factors. Other behavioral tendencies lead to other nudges. For example, the influence of social norms creates a channel by which the nudge of telling individuals how their residential energy use compares with their neighbors' use can lead individuals to reduce their energy consumption.

Note finally that prices and nudges generally do not operate in isolation but are instead interdependent. For example, policy can employ nudges to increase the salience of prices or highlight the link between marginal prices and behavior in order to overcome insensitivity of behavior to prices. For example, the nudge of requiring merchants to post tax-inclusive prices might strengthen the behavioral response to a corrective tax. Similarly, the nudge of employing devices that clarify complex price schedules, such as home thermostats that make the costs of marginal changes in energy consumption more salient, might also increase responsiveness to a corrective tax. Sometimes policymakers can also use prices to effect nudges. For example, the striking effectiveness in some jurisdictions of small taxes on plastic grocery bags in reducing their use is consistent with a model in which the tax, in addition to changing relative prices, also effected a shift in social norms.

Information and Screening

Another set of results for program design in public finance has to do not with the level effect of program parameters on behavioral response but with their screening effect—that is, whom incentives impact and what the mix of responses is rather than their overall impact. In the standard model, which assumes that individuals correctly understand their own circumstances, that essentially collapses into a question of understanding and designing policy around the appropriate elasticities. For instance, when policymakers implement cost-sharing measures, such as co-pays for doctor visits, in an effort to prevent moral hazard from leading to excess use of health care in a social insurance program, that will discourage some individuals from going to the doctor. And the standard model assumes that because individuals have knowledge of their type—in this example, whether they are sick or healthy—that leads to efficient screening: only sick individuals will be willing to pay a small amount for the visit, while healthy individuals will stay away.

A behavioral approach complicates the relationship between incentives and selection substantially. In the presence of choice errors, self-control failures, and nonstandard preferences, prices and other incentives cannot be assumed to influence those whom they objectively benefit or cost the most. In particular, prices and nudges can work against each other to create inefficient selection. That is, while price changes create incentives for individuals to act according to type, nudges can lead individuals to respond irrespective of type or even perversely by type. In the example of co-pays and doctors visits, price incentives should discourage healthy individuals from going to the doctor. But individuals may not be able to accurately understand their type (whether they are sick or healthy) due to factors like limited computational capacity. Or co-pays might reinforce procrastination in going to the doctor, the tendency toward which may even be correlated with health status in such a way that co-pays discourage the relatively unhealthy. Overall, the result of such factors is that in the behavioral model, prices and incentives do not necessarily affect individuals in the way that they would in the standard model.

Another example of a screening problem in which behavioral tendencies may pose a design challenge occurs when the government seeks to induce efficient screening in targeted transfer programs. Traditional economic logic suggests that barriers to program take-up, such as application costs or waiting times, can serve as an effective way to screen the needy from those who simply seek to exploit the program. However, if people fail to participate because of behavioral tendencies—procrastinating in filling out the form, being put off by the tediousness or hassle of completing it, or failing to understand program rules—screening may not be efficient. Nonparticipants then are not those who value the program the least but those who understand the rules the least or who have the biggest procrastination problem. In some cases, such as transfer programs, those people might be the very target population.

This result is in some ways even more general, in that standard policy results count on behavior conforming to standard assumptions to ensure important screening effects of policies even when information is not a central feature of either the underlying policy problem or the policy solution. Consider, for example, the welfare consequences of a corrective tax in the case of a negative externality. The reason that we believe this tax to be an efficient policy response in the standard model is that we presume not only that the increase in the price leads to the correct level of reduction in consumption of the good, but also that it discourages the right mix of people—namely, those who derived the smallest amount of consumer surplus from consuming the good prior to the imposition of the tax. This policy is then efficient, in the sense that the private welfare lost by consumers is minimized. When individuals are imperfect optimizers, we can no longer assume that policies such as a corrective tax are discouraging the right mix of people, because this screening feature of prices may no longer operate in that fashion. As a result, policy generally has to more carefully consider whether the mix of nudges and prices that it employs to generate a response is creating desirable or undesirable selection effects.

Finally, the interaction of behavioral tendencies with selection effects can sometimes create opportunities for policy, in addition to challenges. Policy might under some conditions be able to use nudges to induce the desired selection effects. For example, policymakers might be able to take advantage of confusion on the part of consumers to ensure the existence of pooling equilibria in insurance markets. If, for example, people who fail to opt into a health care program tend to be individuals who are unhealthy but tend to procrastinate rather than people who are healthy, the program may not suffer from the adverse selection that the standard model might lead policymakers to fear.

Markets and Choice Architecture

A final issue for policy design in public finance has to do with structuring and taking advantage of markets in order to achieve policy goals. The general idea is that policy can harness the general equilibrium properties of markets to ensure desirable outcomes by taking advantage of the choice that markets offer and the competitive pressure that can generate efficient outcomes. Policies sometimes establish markets directly, as in the case of school choice or the Medicare prescription drug benefit. Other times, policies seek to influence the outcomes of established markets, such as by setting energy efficiency standards for appliances in order to encourage competition along that dimension. In the standard model, people choose optimally, production responds, and efficient outcomes result.

In the behavioral model, however, people may not choose optimally, and that has consequences for market outcomes. The key insight from behavioral economics is that markets give people what they think they want at the time of choosing—not necessarily what actually makes them best off. Individuals can choose badly in markets, because they make mistakes or exhibit failures of self-control. So, while competition will ensure that markets efficiently deliver the goods and services that people choose, those choices do not necessarily correspond to optimal outcomes. Moreover, that individuals may choose badly in markets matters both for the individuals themselves and the market outcome as a whole. Obviously individuals who choose badly will be made worse off directly. But what is possibly more problematic for public policy is that their choices also have consequences for overall market outcomes. When individuals are choosing badly in markets, the result will be to mute the competitive pressures in those markets to deliver the outcomes that policymakers intend.

One implication is that building and structuring markets to get policy results is a harder problem than it is usually taken to be. The establishment of markets will not always have the intended effect. While harnessing the power of markets can be an efficient policy solution in principle, in practice markets work as predicted by the standard model only if they are set up so that imperfectly optimizing individuals can appreciate the price signals that they create. For example, in the case of the Medicare prescription drug benefit, individuals appear to fail to respond to the costs of drug plans by switching to low-cost providers, in part because of the complexity of the price schedules involved. That leads to welfare costs to participants who fail to choose the lowest-cost plan, and, perhaps more important, it inhibits the ability of participants to enforce the market discipline that policymakers were counting on to ensure the efficient provision of benefits in this market.

Another example of markets failing to operate as expected due to behavioral constraints is seen with school choice. Some evidence suggests that parents may have difficulty choosing schools optimally. Over and above the consequences that that difficulty has for the static quality of their children's education, it also presumably blunts the hoped-for competitive pressure for schools to dynamically improve along relevant dimensions. In both cases, the implication seems to be that policymakers may have to do more to structure choice for individuals and to pay more attention to the complete "choice architecture" of markets—to borrow another term from Thaler and Sunstein—in order to ensure the types of outcomes that the markets are intended to generate. For example, providing market participants with individualized information about alternatives and the consequences of choice may improve outcomes.

Another implication is that markets do not necessarily respond to policies intended to change market outcomes in the way that the standard model predicts. In particular, firms and other market participants may respond in a way that mediates the impact of, or even offsets, policy parameters. Firms can undo nudges or even set their own nudges. For example, in order to address environmental externalities, policy can regulate features of the car-buying decision, such as mandating the disclosure of automobile mileage. But sellers of cars control to some extent how salient that information is made to buyers, as well as how to frame that information. For that reason, policy must attend more fully to the complete choice architecture that develops in markets where firms or other actors also participate. That suggests that realigning the incentives of firms so that they do not offset policy—or so that they even work to actively reinforce it—can be a powerful policy lever. The government can take steps to set the choice architecture for a market as a whole, or it can work to change the dimensions along which firms compete and respond to policy.

Part II

Behavioral Economics and Public Finance in Practice

Having extracted the relevant elements from psychological research and developed a framework for behavioral analysis in part 1, we can now examine topics in public finance through the lens of behavioral economics. Our examination focuses on the policy problems usually considered in traditional public finance. First we address market failures due to both information asymmetries and externalities including public goods. Then we tackle issues in poverty and inequality. Finally we address a set of questions related to taxation and revenue. For each, we consider the implications of a behavioral approach for the diagnosis of policy problems, the description of policy objectives, and the design of policy responses.

In chapter 4, "Asymmetric Information," we discuss the implications of behavioral economics for policy problems that, in the standard view, stem from asymmetries of information. We show how behavioral tendencies both interact with adverse selection and moral hazard and also operate alongside them to create new challenges for policy questions related to old-age insurance, health insurance, and unemployment insurance, and for each we derive implications for policy design.

In chapter 5, "Externalities and Public Goods," we focus on the implications of behavioral economics for our understanding of policy problems that arise due to externalities. We show how behavioral tendencies can interact with classic externalities and how they can lead directly to new types of externalities. To illustrate the former, we use an extended example of environmental externalities in the case of energy consumption; to illustrate the latter we use an example of externalities related to public health. We separate out some of the behavioral implications particular to the issue of public goods. And we give a brief treatment to some special implications of behavioral economics for public education.

In chapter 6, "Poverty and Inequality," we take up the analysis of the social welfare costs associated with poverty and inequality and the concomitant policy response. We discuss how behavioral economics changes how we think about some of the welfare consequences of inequality as well as how behavioral economics changes our thinking about the costs and consequences of poverty. We develop implications for the design of transfer policies, focusing on the targeting and delivery of benefits, the relationship between program benefits and participant outcomes, and the consequences of benefits for work incentives.

Finally, in chapter 7, "Taxation and Revenue," we address the implications of behavioral economics for the design of policies intended to raise revenue in an efficient and equitable manner. We consider first how behavioral tendencies mediate how people perceive and respond to taxes and then explore what that means for understanding both the efficiency costs of taxes as well as their incidence. We derive some implications for tax policy, which we apply to issues in the design of commodity taxes, income and other labor taxes, and capital taxes.

4

Asymmetric Information

The U.S. government has been described, with tongue only slightly in cheek, as "an insurance company with an army."[1] In terms of dollars spent, that description is not far off. In recent years Social Security, Medicare, and Medicaid alone have accounted for about 40 percent of all federal government spending, and while those programs are far and away the largest social insurance programs, they are not the only ones. Unemployment insurance, for example, protects workers against precipitous declines in income and consumption between jobs. Nor is the federal government the exclusive provider of social insurance. States both finance portions of social insurance programs such as Medicaid and regulate and mandate others, such as workers' compensation, which insures workers against injuries sustained while on the job. When all the various programs are considered, providing social insurance is by some measures the single largest economic function of the modern state.

Why is government in the insurance business? Different answers come from different quarters. There are arguments from the perspective of justice, which hold that some forms of insurance are a right that the government should guarantee, health insurance in particular. Others argue for insurance programs as a way to address poverty and inequality. The old-age portion of Social Security, for example, pays retirement benefits that are a progressive function of earnings. And there are arguments from political economy—for example, that Social Security is necessary because society cannot credibly commit to allowing individuals to face the full consequences of failing to prepare adequately for retirement.

Public finance focuses on the possibility that unregulated markets for insurance have properties that make them susceptible to failure. When market-relevant information is common knowledge, other things being equal, markets work efficiently. But especially in markets for insurance, information may be private rather than public. That can lead insurance markets to fail to operate efficiently or to fail to exist altogether. In particular, private information in those markets can lead to adverse selection. Health insurance, for example, is more attractive to individuals who believe themselves to be sick or at risk of illness. When consumers have private information about their health status that insurers do not, the resulting selection effect in consumption can cause the market to unwind. Policymakers set objectives and design responses accordingly. In the case of health insurance, for example, they can encourage or even force risk pooling in response to adverse selection in health insurance markets through regulation of and subsidies to private insurance markets, or they can provide fully public insurance.

Those results, however, rest on assumptions about how individuals respond to private information. Specifically, they rely on the assumption that individuals react to information asymmetries according to standard assumptions. Allowing for behavioral tendencies—that individuals may be imperfect optimizers or may hold nonstandard preferences—may change the results. For instance, individuals may not press information advantages that they would seek to exploit under standard assumptions; they may not even accurately perceive that they have private information to begin with. Moreover, behavioral tendencies can drive results that work in conjunction with asymmetries of information to lead directly to inefficient outcomes. The same behavioral tendencies that might mitigate adverse selection might also lead to decisionmaking errors that themselves lead to a loss of welfare.

In general, behavioral economics identifies a set of forces that both interact with and operate alongside of information asymmetries to determine outcomes in insurance markets. In this chapter, we consider how behavioral tendencies interact with information asymmetries, and we draw out the implications for policy for three types of insurance that receive considerable policy attention— old-age insurance, health insurance, and unemployment insurance.

—*Old-age insurance.* The old-age component of Social Security, in addition to having an important redistributive element, can be seen as solving a failure in the market to insure against longevity risk. A behavioral approach emphasizes the role of imperfect decisionmaking in undermining demand for annuity products. In addition, it recognizes that individuals are not very good at saving and planning for their own retirement: they save too little, they invest in the wrong assets, and so on. Behaviorally informed policy thus reconceptualizes the role of Social Security and highlights other ways of assisting individuals with life-cycle saving.

—*Health insurance.* In the standard model, health insurance markets are understood to be fragile because of the information advantage that individuals are presumed to enjoy with respect to their own health status. Decisionmaking errors such as overconfidence, difficulty in evaluating risks and making judg-ments under uncertainty, and so on mean that the private information associated with health status may not necessarily translate into the sort of adverse selection predicted by the traditional model. Policy responses to increase access to health insurance therefore might succeed or fail in part depending on how they address issues related to individual choice.

—*Unemployment insurance.* In the case of unemployment insurance, informa-tion asymmetries likely remain severe, but behavioral economics adds a richer understanding of the psychology of job loss that identifies new challenges for policy. It recognizes that behavior under coverage that looks much like standard moral hazard may in fact be a result of behavioral tendencies such as failure of self-control or reference-dependent preferences. In seeking to provide benefits to the unemployed while maintaining incentives to return to work, policy design may have to consider these features of decisionmaking.

We consider these three topics in turn. For each, we discuss how behav-ioral insights change our understanding of the diagnosis of market conditions, the judgments required in assessing alternative possible outcomes, and policy prescriptions.

Old-Age Insurance

The U.S. government sponsors numerous programs that are massive in scope in the name of supporting the consumption of retired workers. Policies to encour-age and subsidize retirement savings through tax incentives such as IRAs and 401(k)s amount to tax expenditures on the order of $100 billion annually.[2] Poli-cies support the functioning of markets for financial products such as reverse mortgages that assist individuals with drawing down their assets in retirement. Most prominent, policy provides, through the old-age insurance component of Social Security, a series of transfers directly from workers to retirees. The old-age portion of Social Security alone provides more than $350 billion in benefits to more than 30 million retired workers each year.[3]

A literal application of the standard model to such policies treats at least their elements that are distinct from pure redistribution as social insurance. So, for instance, Social Security can be viewed as a response to failures in annuity mar-kets that may stem from asymmetries of information. Similarly, products such as reverse mortgages may not flourish in unregulated markets.

Other elements of this set of policies, such as the subsidies to private savings, are not as clear a fit with the standard model. Individuals should, after all, find it in their own best interests to save adequately for retirement without govern-ment assistance. Even standard treatments in public finance commonly allow that policies to encourage saving or protect against the consequences of failing to save may be a response, in part, to error or shortsightedness on the part of workers and retirees—that is, to behavioral tendencies. Such an approach emphasizes the fact that the old-age insurance component of Social Security inhabits a larger policy space from which it is inextricable, namely, that of life-cycle saving and consumption planning.

But while public finance increasingly recognizes the role of behavioral forces in savings and retirement policy, application of behavioral insights remains largely informal and idiosyncratic. A behavioral analysis of the role of government considers the full implications of behavioral tendencies for the broader challenge of life-cycle saving and consumption planning. It examines behavioral forces that both operate alongside and interact with the traditional information problems in this market to create a new set of policy problems. It identifies new judgments about policy trade-offs, such as how to weigh possibly conflicting short- and long-run preferences, and revises the terms of old trade-offs such as moral hazard. Finally, it offers direct implications for policy design, both for Social Security as well as policies that directly assist individuals in first accumulating assets and later in drawing them down.

Behavioral Dimensions of Life-Cycle Saving

The central problem for savings and retirement policy is, ultimately, whether individuals have access to the resources necessary to maintain consumption in retirement. In perfectly functioning markets, with perfectly optimizing participants, individuals solve this problem privately by engaging in life-cycle saving. Where barriers exist to the ability of workers to efficiently accumulate assets during their working years or draw them down once retired, there is room for policy to improve welfare.

The traditional analysis of the problem begins with the markets that individuals avail themselves of in order to save, invest, and draw down their assets. The main threat of market failure in this domain lies in the potential for asymmetric information to undermine the annuity market. Individuals face longevity risk— the risk of outliving their assets—which could in principle be pooled through insurance products such as annuities. When individuals have private information about their likely longevity, however, it can lead to adverse selection that may cause private markets for annuities to fail. Social Security, which provides benefits in a form that mimics an annuity, can be seen in part as a response to that problem.

A behavioral approach to retirement and saving policy considers the ways in which behavioral tendencies contribute to the problems associated with ensuring adequate resources for consumption in retirement. It identifies two primary channels. The first is that behavioral tendencies operate alongside traditional market failures to create separate challenges for policy. Even when markets function properly, private life-cycle saving will fail to be efficient if individuals do not have the psychological resources—the willpower or the computational capacity—to form and execute optimal life-cycle saving plans. The second is that these behaviors interact with any information problems that do arise in markets and as a consequence influence the nature of the resulting market failure.

SAVING AND INVESTING

The primary dimension along which behavioral tendencies create new challenges for policy is that of saving and investing for retirement, which is hard for individuals to do optimally. Determining how much to save for retirement and how best to invest retirement savings is a vastly complex problem. Accumulating a portfolio of assets requires not just the self-control to delay consumption in order to save but also the willpower to resist the temptation to draw down those assets prior to retirement.

The complexity of optimal life-cycle saving is self-evident. Setting an optimal saving rate while working requires, at a minimum, the ability to project one's future earnings profile, estimate portfolio returns and variances over the same period, and forecast consumption preferences for the rest of one's life. Allocating investments optimally requires at least a working knowledge of the characteristics of alternative vehicles and assets, to say nothing of additional complicating factors such as the tax environment. Even for individuals who have that working knowledge, those are daunting tasks—the relevant economic literature itself has failed to reach a consensus on what constitutes an adequate level of life-cycle saving.[4] When the complexity of the task intersects with behavioral tendencies such as limited attention and limited computational capacity, it becomes all but impossible to perform without error.[5]

The evidence that the complexity of the choice environment leads individuals to imperfect or inconsistent saving behavior comes in many forms. For example, the high degree of variation in wealth holdings across households in otherwise similar economic circumstances suggests the use of rules of thumb, mental accounting, or other shortcuts rather than a fully optimal approach to life-cycle saving.[6] Another type of evidence comes from the sensitivity of retirement saving to the presentation of opportunities to save. For example, individuals participate in tax-preferred saving at higher rates when a retirement savings tax credit is presented as a match instead of as a credit.[7] They also participate in employer-sponsored plans at higher rates when enrollment in the plan is automatic.[8] When choices of investments in retirement plans proliferate, individuals are sometimes less likely to invest at all.[9] Such results are consistent with the interpretation that individuals see complexity as a barrier to determining their optimal level of retirement saving. Finally, there is evidence that saving may suffer in part simply because the act of saving has to compete for individuals' limited attention—experiments find that reminders to save can, by themselves, increase saving.[10]

The problem of accumulating sufficient wealth is made more complicated still by the fact that, in addition to determining the proper level of retirement saving, individuals also must determine how to save. That is, individuals must make choices about their investments and manage their wealth. Management involves choices that are complex on a number of levels, from the choice of vehicles (for example, Roth IRAs versus traditional IRAs), to the choice of ways to diversify over asset classes (for example, stocks versus bonds), to the choice of specific assets. Evidence abounds that individuals make what can only be classified as elementary investing mistakes.[11] For example, individuals hold what appears to be an excessive amount of retirement wealth in the stock of their employer.[12] They also appear to make investment decisions without respect to the fees associated with, for example, mutual funds.[13] Individuals commonly pursue diversification strategies that appear to follow simple heuristics, such as dividing their savings evenly among available assets or funds.[14] They also are sensitive to defaults and presentation effects in setting allocations.[15] Results showing peer effects in saving and investing are consistent with social preferences and indicate that individuals may make investment decisions based on rules of thumb and the type of rough guidelines that may be transmitted through neighbors and colleagues.[16]

In addition to being complicated, saving for retirement requires individuals to exercise self-control. Saving for retirement while working means forgoing current consumption in favor of consumption years or even decades later, and accumulating sufficient assets requires resisting the temptation to draw them down before reaching retirement. Evidence that individuals hold preferences for current consumption that are present-biased comes from many quarters, and those findings apply nowhere with such force as to life-cycle saving.[17] Laboratory experiments show a relationship between willpower and saving.[18] Field experiments show that individuals demand illiquid saving vehicles that offer no premium, possibly as a commitment device.[19] Consistent with a behavioral model, individuals who fail to plan accumulate less wealth.[20] Finally, present-biased preferences might affect not only the level of retirement savings but also investment decisions about vehicles and asset classes. For example, impatience might steer individuals toward traditional IRAs, which provide tax benefits in the near term, and away from Roth IRAs, which provide back-loaded tax benefits.

CONSUMING IN RETIREMENT

The second phase of life-cycle saving, drawing down assets and consuming in retirement, presents another set of challenges for individuals. In particular, the problem of how to optimally transform a lump sum of retirement wealth into a stream of consumption is a complicated one. Doing that on one's own would involve complex calculations involving forecasts of consumption needs to determine when to begin drawing down assets, at what rate, and how to adjust investment strategies in order to maximize welfare while minimizing the chance of outliving one's wealth.

Here, behavioral challenges also interact with a potential market failure. A simple and, given actuarially fair prices, optimal way to draw down wealth in retirement would be to purchase an annuity. The fact that retirement annuities are relatively uncommon, despite their clear insurance value and consumption-smoothing benefits, is usually attributed to adverse selection.[21] But simulations still suggest that at prevailing prices, which reflect those selection effects, many individuals would be better off annuitizing their retirement wealth.[22] Moreover, available results suggest that even when annuities are available at actuarially fair prices, individuals do not find them to be a subjectively attractive product.[23]

Behavioral tendencies may interact with information asymmetries in the annuity market to explain a double puzzle—why adverse selection is not so severe as to undermine the market and why individuals fail to purchase annuities regardless.[24] First, behavioral limitations may prevent individuals from fully appreciating or being able to act on any private information that they have. That is, people might have private information about how long they expect to live, but they may not recognize the value of that information or may be otherwise unable to capitalize on it, due to, for example, limited computational capacity. In this way, behavioral economics may mitigate against adverse selection in this market.

Second, behavioral tendencies such as limited computational capacity could easily lead people to incorrectly estimate the value of annuitization—for example, by making the problem of comparing lump-sum wealth to a stream of income difficult. Or reference-dependence could make individuals reluctant to part with lump-sum wealth. There is some evidence that such behavioral tendencies affect the demand for annuities. In one survey, individuals found products with the properties of annuities more or less attractive depending on whether they were framed as reflecting consumption or investment decisions.[25] Evidence from a lab experiment is consistent with reference-dependence and biases in risk assessment playing a role in depressing demand for annuities.[26]

New Challenges for Saving and Retirement Policy

While the welfare analysis suggests that support for life-cycle saving can in principle improve outcomes, practically speaking the implementation of such policies raises questions that can be resolved only through the policymaking process— such as how to weigh the competing interests of providing social insurance and encouraging private saving and how to balance conflicting short- and long-run preferences for saving. As in many policy areas, often there are no clear right or wrong answers.

In the traditional analysis, the main trade-offs that policymakers have to juggle have to do with Social Security. The old-age insurance component of Social Security, like any social insurance policy, raises questions of how to trade off support for beneficiaries and moral hazard. By providing for consumption in old age, Social Security cannot help but dull the incentives for private saving to some extent. The question for policymakers and society is how to weigh the benefits of old-age insurance against the costs of the moral hazard, specifically in the form of reduced private saving, that it creates.

From a behavioral perspective, the trade-off between old-age insurance and private retirement savings looks quite different. If people generally are not going to save adequately, even in the absence of old-age insurance, due to failures of self-control or as a response to the complexity of the problem, there presumably is less scope for old-age insurance to discourage saving. That is, the standard analysis may be overstating the impact of Social Security on reducing private saving because it overstates the likelihood that individuals save adequately in its absence. That may make old-age insurance a relatively more attractive policy option. It suggests that, in practice, moral hazard may not be as important a factor as the traditional model suggests.

Whether and to what extent behavioral modifications to the standard understanding of Social Security and moral hazard might matter are largely unresolved issues. Estimates of the effect of Social Security on saving are in fact usually negative, although results are variable.[27] Increases over time in Social Security benefits are related to reduction in poverty among the elderly, which is consistent with the behavioral model though amenable to other explanations.[28] Theoretical assessments of Social Security and welfare find that under some assumptions, allowing for time-inconsistent preferences can improve the trade-offs in favor of Social Security, as the net impact on saving is diminished.[29]

While the behavioral problems with life-cycle saving suggest that there may be value in reexamining the role of moral hazard in Social Security, they also create an entirely new set of challenges for policymakers. Given the possibility that life-cycle saving may be at suboptimal levels due to choice errors or failures of self-control, policy has to reflect some judgment about these matters. With respect to errors, policy must reflect a judgment about when observed behavior reflects errors and when it simply expresses unusual preferences. So, for example, when individuals hold large amounts of their employer's stock in their retirement portfolio, it may look like a mistake, but it can be rationalized by, say, an individual's preference for being known as a company booster.[30] A policy response to such behavior, or even no policy response at all, reflects some judgment on this dimension.

With respect to time-inconsistent preferences—as, for example, when young earners fail to save and ultimately become retirees who regret past choices—policy must reflect some weighting of individuals' competing short- and long-run preferences. To fail to intervene in such cases is to implicitly favor the short-run self over the long-run self. Assisting with commitment or obviating the need for it favors the long-run self. There is no obviously right answer to how best to set the relative weights, but policy reflects a position on the issue, intentionally or not.

Crafting Savings and Retirement Policy

Regardless of the conception of the savings and retirement problem and the position that society and policymakers take on the judgments required to address it, insights from psychology can inform the design of policy responses. A behavioral approach can address not only the behavioral but also the traditional challenges to optimal life-cycle saving, and behavioral principles can help to encourage saving and assist consumption planning in retirement directly. They also bear directly on the design of Social Security.

SAVINGS POLICY

Taking as given that social policy places some weight on individuals' long-run preferences, policy can help to ensure adequate levels of consumption in old age by assisting individuals with accumulating adequate wealth during their working years. Behavioral economics offers new perspectives on how to effectively accomplish that.[31] If low levels of saving are simply a function of saving being unattractive relative to consumption, then subsidization, such as through existing tax incentives, is sufficient. But if low levels reflect choice errors or a failure of self-control, subsidies may be neither sufficient nor necessary.

The key implication for policy of behavioral findings indicating that individuals can find it hard to save is that if policy seeks to encourage more saving, it can do so by making it easier to save. The evidence from the effects of automatic enrollment in 401(k) plans is clearest: making it easy for individuals to enroll in retirement saving plans leads people to save more.[32] Enrollment need not even be fully automatic to increase enrollment; forcing individuals to choose or dramatically simplifying the enrollment process also increases participation and saving.[33] Simplifying the process of opening and contributing to other types of retirement accounts, such as IRAs, could have similar effects.[34] A proposal for an automatic IRA for workers whose employer does not otherwise offer a retirement plan was included in the Obama administration's 2011 budget.[35]

A corollary is that transparent subsidies can be more effective than complex subsidies. Simplifying not just the enrollment process but also the terms of saving programs can encourage saving. For example, a tax benefit for retirement savings may be more effectively delivered as a match to private savings than as a tax credit, because even when the effective subsidy rate is the same, a match may be easier to understand than a credit.[36] The administration's 2011 budget proposed replacing the Saver's Credit, which currently offers a tax credit for retirement savings to low-income households, with a match.[37] Another implication of this is that the existing alphabet soup of tax-preferred saving plans may be less effective at encouraging saving than a single or a few salient saving-related tax provisions. Finally, note that in an environment in which individuals struggle with managing information, even innocuous-seeming program parameters may convey information about desirable levels of saving. Individuals who would otherwise have difficulty determining how much to put away each year may take the annual contribution limit on, say, 401(k) plans as an endorsement of such a level of savings as being adequate.

A related policy option is to take advantage of moments when opportunities to save are salient to encourage saving. For example, individuals might be encouraged to route tax refunds into accounts where they are likely to be saved rather than spent.[38] One recent policy innovation to encourage such behavior has been the advent of split tax refunds. Since 2007, individuals have been able to split their tax refunds across multiple accounts, including savings accounts and IRAs; since 2010 they have been able to use refunds to purchase savings bonds. Evidence suggests that this policy might work to encourage saving.[39]

Likewise, the key to encouraging better saving among individuals who find saving and investing complicated is to make it easy to end up in wise investments. The same principles that work for increasing the level of savings also apply here. For example, it does individuals no real service to provide for automatic enrollment to increase their savings if the funds go into an employer-sponsored retirement plan that invests poorly—for example, exclusively in the employer's stock. The default investment allocation could be something bland but not harmful, such as a conservative lifestyle fund or a broad index fund. Policy also could work to actively call attention to points on which individuals appear to err. For example, disclosure requirements or other policies could raise the salience of features like mutual fund fees.

Finally, to address that part of low saving that results from the difficulty that individuals can have in exerting self-control, policy might seek to make it easier for individuals to commit to saving and harder for them to procrastinate or give in to short-term temptations. There are two distinct points at which assisting with self-control is crucial for building retirement wealth. The first is when individuals form the intention to save. Policy can assist individuals with following through on their intentions and help overcome inertia in funding retirement accounts through automatic enrollment and automatic escalation, which have been shown to be effective tools.[40] The second is when individuals are tempted to use their retirement funds before they retire. Policy can reduce the temptation through the penalties and fees that are features of most existing tax-favored retirement savings plans.[41] Moreover, it may take illiquid saving vehicles to attract individuals who are self-aware regarding their bounded self-control. On the other hand, features such as the ability to borrow from such plans cut the other way, and they might entail extra costs for individuals who lack perfect self-control.

A closely related form of policy response to the difficulties that individuals face in saving and investing for retirement is to seek to improve and expand their capacity to make good choices through education and efforts to promote financial literacy. In fact, policies that take this approach are distinct from a behavioral approach in a subtle but important way, which we elaborate on in box 4-1.

Assisting with Consumption Planning in Retirement

A related policy goal is to assist individuals with planning their consumption once retired. Because the evidence suggests that that, too, is a problem born of complexity, one approach is to make it easier for individuals to transform their lump sum of retirement wealth into a stream of income. One policy proposal that would accomplish that is to default retirement savings into annuities, at least for a trial period immediately following retirement, during which individuals could opt out.[42] In addition to harnessing the power of defaults for directing behavior, that would both convey information about annuities indicating that they are a standard, implicitly endorsed product and allow individuals the opportunity to learn about the benefits of annuities through experience. A challenge for such a policy is determining appropriate defaults, as heterogeneity in preferences for annuitization and risk characteristics might make different levels and forms of annuities optimal for different individuals. Policy must balance the costs of a mismatch against opportunities to personalize defaults, such as by assigning different individuals to different defaults based on some available criteria.

Another approach could be to work to change the frames in which consumers understand annuities. Evidence suggests that demand for annuities is higher when they are presented in terms of consumption rather than investment.[43] Aside from specifically encouraging annuitization of retirement wealth, policy might generally ensure that rules for drawing down assets from retirement accounts, such as minimum distribution requirements, are well designed and easy to understand.

Social Security

The old-age portion of Social Security represents an entirely different approach to ensuring consumption in retirement. Rather than encourage or complement private life-cycle saving, Social Security acts as a substitute for it. From a behavioral perspective, that has a number of desirable consequences. Most notably, it relieves individuals of some of the complexity and need for self-control that

Box 4-1. *Financial Literacy and Debiasing*

One policy option to address individuals' tendency to save insufficient funds for retirement or to make poor investment choices is education to improve financial literacy. The goal of such a policy would be to improve saving and investing choices by improving the set of tools that individuals use to make those choices. That can encompass improving basic knowledge, such as understanding of concepts like interest rates and diversification; it also can focus on practical knowledge—for example, by educating individuals on the basics of what their saving and investing options are and the relative costs and benefits of those options.

To be sure, there is evidence that individuals who possess higher levels of financial literacy accumulate greater retirement wealth.[a] And there is scattered evidence suggesting that targeted forms of financial education can improve retirement savings—for example, financial education offered through the workplace may be effective at promoting participation in and saving through retirement plans.[b] There is even evidence that a behavioral perspective can inform the design of successful financial literacy programs—for example, teaching simple rules of thumb might be more effective than detailed mathematical concepts.[c]

But while a policy prescription for increasing financial literacy and thus retirement savings in this way seems to follow from the behavioral challenges highlighted in the text—emphasizing, for example, difficulties with knowing how much to save and how and where to invest—there is an important sense in which that is not the case. While lack of financial knowledge can have effects similar to those of behavioral tendencies, there is an important distinction between the two: behavioral tendencies are not, essentially, related to lack of knowledge; they are generally related to limitations and biases in decisionmaking.

While an education and a literacy approach to policy is important in its own right and can complement a behavioral approach in important ways, they also are fundamentally separate. A good way to illustrate that point is to consider the distinction between failing to save adequately for retirement because of lack of understanding of how compound interest works and failing to save adequately for

undermines both private saving and consumption in retirement. To accumulate credits in Social Security while working and then draw steady benefits once retired requires almost no conscious effort on the part of individuals.

The choices that are present in Social Security are sensitive to behavioral concerns. The two main choices in Social Security as it currently is structured are prominent: the choice of when to claim benefits and the choice of whether to work in retirement. While the normal retirement age is sixty-six for individuals retiring in 2010, eligible individuals can elect to take benefits earlier, as young as retirement because of flawed risk assessment, procrastination, or overconfidence. Improving education and literacy can ameliorate the first source of undersaving, but in general it does not address the second.

More broadly, this distinction holds across different domains. For example, while improved health literacy might be an important goal for health care policy, it does not follow from or address the behavioral dimensions of health outcomes.

Finally, note that there is a behavioral analog to literacy and education in what is referred to as debiasing, the process of engaging individuals in some exercise that might lead them to make unbiased choices. There are some techniques for addressing particular biases, but general lessons are elusive.[d] Simply supplying information or understanding, as would be indicated to raise literacy, is generally not sufficient to debias. For example, making people aware that they exhibit a bias is not enough to counteract it.[e]

a. Annamaria Lusardi and Olivia Mitchell, "Baby Boomer Retirement Security: The Role of Planning, Financial Literacy, and Housing Wealth," *Journal of Monetary Economics,* vol. 54, no. 1 (2007), pp. 205–24.

b. B. Douglas Bernheim and Daniel M. Garrett, "The Effects of Financial Education in the Workplace: Evidence from a Survey of Households," *Journal of Public Economics,* vol. 87, no. 7–8 (2003), pp. 1487–1519; Patrick J. Bayer, B. Douglas Bernheim, and John Karl Scholz, "The Effects of Financial Education in the Workplace: Evidence from a Survey of Employers," *Economic Inquiry,* vol. 47, no. 4 (2009), pp. 605–24.

c. Greg Fischer, Alejandro Drexler, and Antoinette Schoar, "Keeping It Simple: Financial Literacy and Rules of Thumb," CEPR Discussion Paper 7994 (London: Centre for Economic Policy Research, 2010).

d. Norbert Schwarz and others, "Metacognitive Experiences and the Intricacies of Setting People Straight: Implications for Debiasing and Public Information Campaigns," in *Advances in Experimental Psychology,* vol. 39, edited by Mark P. Zanna (Amsterdam: Academic Press, 2007), pp. 127–61.

e. Linda Babcock, George Loewenstein, and Samuel Issacharoff, "Creating Convergence: Debiasing Biased Litigants," *Law and Social Inquiry,* vol. 22, no. 4 (1997), pp. 913–25.

sixty-two, or to defer benefits until they are older. Benefit levels are actuarially reduced if claimed prior to normal retirement age and supplemented if claimed later. When it is best to claim benefits for any given individual is a complex determination that depends on personal preferences, life expectancy, and status of the spouse, if there is one. Most workers now claim benefits early—roughly half of retirees claim benefits at 62 and nearly three-quarters do so before their normal retirement age.[44] That may be a mistake for many workers, who would draw a larger expected lifetime stream of benefits if they were to claim at an older age.[45]

A number of behavioral forces might push individuals toward claiming benefits early. In particular, individuals with bounded self-control may find the temptation of early benefits difficult to resist even if they know that they would be better off waiting.[46] There also may be too little assistance for individuals in making this choice, especially for those facing the daunting joint problem of optimally timing their own claim and that of their spouse. The option of claiming benefits at earlier ages conveys information—possibly the sense of an implicit endorsement of retirement at those ages. What is worse, the current popularity of retiring early may be self-reinforcing if it creates a social norm for retiring early. A policy change to steer people toward later retirement ages may therefore be warranted. For example, the benefit claiming process could be changed to create a stronger default at the normal retirement age, or the choice could be framed in ways that seek to promote later retirement.[47]

Individuals claiming Social Security also face the choice of whether or not to continue working and earning income in retirement. Earned income does not affect the benefits of workers claiming benefits at or beyond the normal retirement age, but the benefits of individuals who claim benefits early—between the age of 62 and their normal retirement age—are reduced by $0.50 for each dollar earned above a set threshold ($14,160 in 2010). When they reach normal retirement age, however, their benefits are adjusted upward to compensate for the withheld benefits, and that adjustment is approximately actuarially fair. Unsurprisingly from a behavioral perspective, there is some evidence that people tend to misunderstand this provision, thinking of it purely as a reduction in benefits and not a shift in benefits across time.[48] That is likely to result in distortion of the working and retirement decisions of those in this age range. Presenting the terms of this provision in simpler or more salient terms might assist individuals with decisionmaking with respect to working in retirement.

A behavioral perspective can also inform broader issues in Social Security design. For example, allowing for behavioral tendencies may highlight the importance of assisting individuals with understanding the implications of Social Security for their own saving and investing behavior. While Social Security does insulate individuals from some of the burdens of life-cycle saving, it also adds another dimension to the problem. That is, the life-cycle planning problem becomes how best to accumulate assets and draw assets down given what one expects to draw from Social Security. Optimal levels of saving, investment strategies, and annuity purchases all are affected by the existence of Social Security. The primary approach of policy to this problem to date is for the Social Security Administration to keep covered workers informed of the terms of Social Security. The main conduit for that information is an annual personalized statement informing individuals of their standing in the program and what benefit amounts they can expect. Some evidence suggests that this statement has helped individuals with understanding the terms of their Social Security benefits, but the presentation of information in this statement does not necessarily attend to the behavioral difficulties associated with life-cycle saving.[49]

Finally, behavioral economics also could inform efforts at Social Security reform. For example, the conditions under which privatization of Social Security could improve welfare are likely to be extremely sensitive to behavioral concerns. If the underlying problems that Social Security solves are in fact partly behavioral—suboptimal saving rates and a disinclination to purchase annuity products—rather than the result of market failure, then that reopens the question of whether a series of cross-generational transfers is a better targeted policy solution than forced saving in private accounts. It seems that as long as a private account system was well-designed to counteract those behavioral tendencies—accounts are compulsory; investment choices are simple and few and include a strong, appropriately chosen default; and account balances automatically roll over into annuities on retirement—then the main behavioral challenges could be met.[50] But the primary concern with private accounts from this perspective is that if they are not well designed—if they lay too much complexity or the need for iron-clad willpower at the feet of participants—then they recreate the very problems that they need to solve and they are likely to fail.

Health Insurance

In 2010, after an extended and sometimes heated debate, Congress passed and President Obama signed into law the Patient Protection and Affordability Act, the latest iteration of health care reform. The signature feature of this new law is its intended effect on health insurance coverage. In 2009, the latest year for which there are official estimates, more than 50 million people in the United States—about 19 percent of the nonelderly population—lacked health insurance.[51] The new law is projected to reduce that figure to approximately 8 percent by the time it is fully implemented in 2019.[52] The improvements in coverage are to come about through a mix of subsidies to the purchase of private health insurance and expansions in public programs like Medicaid.

While the policies embodied in the new law target a variety of other goals, such as improving the quality of health care delivered in the United States and slowing the growth of health care costs, its focus on coverage is consistent with the standard public finance analysis of asymmetric information and health insurance policy. Traditional public finance stresses the susceptibility of health insurance markets to adverse selection and the effect of the resulting market failure on the ability of individuals to obtain health insurance. Moreover, it goes on to indicate what some of the important trade-offs involved in expanding coverage are, focusing on the possibility of moral hazard resulting from coverage. And it suggests the design of policies to expand coverage in efficient ways, including implementation of public programs and the subsidization and regulation of private health insurance.

A behavioral approach to the public finance analysis of health insurance informs each of these aspects of policy. In particular, it highlights the variety of ways in which the features of health insurance interact with the behavioral tendencies that individuals exhibit in decisionmaking. That interaction has implications not just for the optimal design of health insurance policy but for the operation of fundamental features of the health insurance market, including adverse selection and moral hazard.

Behavioral Economics and the Market for Health Insurance

In well-functioning markets in which consumers behave according to standard assumptions, lack of health insurance coverage would reflect either decisions by individuals to forgo coverage or simple inability to pay. In those cases, there is little role for the government outside of straightforward redistribution. But where barriers exist to the ability of individuals to obtain coverage due to market failure, more extensive government intervention may be justified.

In considering the role of the state in health insurance markets, public finance traditionally has focused on market failures arising from information problems. Because individuals tend to have an information advantage when it comes to their own health, they can act on their private information in ways that undermine the ability of markets to operate efficiently, or at all. The most serious threat to the health insurance market comes from adverse selection.[53] Health insurance is naturally most valuable to relatively sick or at-risk individuals. But if health insurance attracts the relatively sick, insurers cannot effectively pool risk. The result can be a failure of market supply, as insurers find that they cannot profitably offer health coverage. That leads to a welfare loss, because health insurance is valuable to individuals because it provides for consumption smoothing across health states. As a result, government action to ensure the availability of health insurance can improve market outcomes.

A behavioral approach to the economic analysis of health insurance considers whether and how behavioral tendencies on the part of decisionmakers changes the case for government intervention to ensure health insurance availability. Two possibilities arise. First, behavioral tendencies may interact with asymmetries of information to generate novel selection effects because the impact of adverse selection on the market is mediated by those tendencies. In the standard model, the presumed information advantage of health insurance consumers derives from the assumption that they accurately and reliably translate private information into health insurance purchase decisions. When individuals exhibit behavioral tendencies, their information advantage may play out differently. Adverse selection may be exacerbated or mitigated—it may not operate at all, or it may even be wholly overturned, leading instead to advantageous selection. Second, behavioral tendencies operate alongside selection effects, creating the possibility of demand failure—and welfare losses—that are due to behavioral tendencies alone.

Either possibility follows from intrinsic features of the health insurance purchase decision that make it difficult for individuals to decide in a perfectly optimal manner. First is the sheer complexity of health insurance as a product. Determining whether any given level of health insurance is worth its cost is hard and requires individuals to match the full schedule of plan benefits against their expected health care needs. Moreover, that decision involves risk and uncertainty—in particular an assessment of the likelihood of low-probability events such as illness or disease, features that frequently lead individuals to err.[54] Health insurance decisions also may be especially sensitive to the propensity of individuals to overstate their own chances of positive outcomes and to avoid consideration of unpleasant ones, since considering the need for health insurance is tantamount to considering the likelihood of bad health outcomes. Another important source of error, unrelated to the complexity of insurance products, is the well-documented difficulty that individuals have with projecting their preferences over health states. For example, people systematically overestimate the impact of changes in health status on happiness.[55] If it is hard for people to know what health status or medical care is worth to them, it may be difficult for them to form an accurate assessment of what health insurance coverage is worth to them.

A different class of behavioral obstacles to choosing optimal health insurance arises from the fact that health insurance decisions have an important time dimension. The effects of bounded self-control can be conflicting and even offsetting. The fact that purchasing insurance in the present buys coverage that is likely to pay off only in the future, if at all, creates the possibility that failures of self-control will lead individuals to delay the acquisition of coverage. Conversely, present-biased preferences might make certain forms of heath insurance more attractive. For example, policies with first-dollar or front-loaded benefits will be more attractive than alternatives—first-dollar coverage provides immediate gratification.

Finally, reference-dependent preferences might interact with decisions about insurance coverage. Status quo bias, for example, was first identified in the tendency of individuals to stick with health plans once enrolled.[56] Health insurance itself is a choice between alternative patterns of gains and losses. So, for example, the choice of whether to insure is like a choice between a sure loss, in the form of a premium, and a gamble with some probability of a loss, in the event of requiring health care. Results from behavioral economics suggest that, possibly due to loss aversion, individuals may place a low value on forms of insurance that cover large losses that have a low probability of occurring.[57]

Behavioral Tendencies and Adverse Selection

Behavioral tendencies are a complicating factor in considering the efficient operation of health insurance markets. Because errors can affect how individuals act on any private information about health status, they in turn affect the degree of adverse selection in health insurance markets. There are two different ways in which behavioral tendencies might interact with selection. First, the implicit assumption of the standard model of adverse selection is that individuals correctly recognize their type and act accordingly. But if individuals make errors about their type—about whether they are, say, sick or healthy—that could mitigate adverse selection by reducing the correlation between type and propensity to participate in the market. For example, motivated biases, such as overconfidence, could alter insurance market outcomes.[58] Even if individuals form accurate beliefs regarding their type, they may have difficulty acting on that knowledge. For example, limits to self-control or the curse of knowledge—in this context, the inability of an individual with an information advantage to conceive of others as being without the information—can mean that in the health market agents with private information can have difficulty capitalizing on it.[59] Again, that can limit the potential for adverse selection.

The second way in which behavioral tendencies can affect adverse selection in health insurance is when they lead to behaviors that both affect the propensity to purchase health insurance and correlate with health status. That could exacerbate or mitigate adverse selection, depending on the nature of the correlation. Take the so-called young invincibles, young people who are both disproportionately healthy and disproportionately likely not to buy health insurance. In part, that is a consequence of the fact that the young are, on average, healthier than the rest of the population and therefore find health insurance less attractive. It is likely made worse, however, by the fact that the benefits of coverage might be realized farther away in time for young people or the risks might be smaller, so that the probabilities look indistinguishable from zero. That would exacerbate adverse selection.

The net impact of behavioral tendencies on the market for health insurance therefore is theoretically unclear. The extent to which those tendencies change any conclusions about the market, whether they increase or decrease the extent of adverse selection, is an empirical matter. The results may qualify the effects of adverse selection in ways that modify the scope of productive government intervention or argue for or against particular policy solutions. One study that examined choices across health care plans in an employer setting found evidence that the tendency of employees to stick with default plans led to diminished adverse selection relative to a choice environment in which a default was not available and individuals were forced to make an active choice.[60] Other accumulating evidence that adverse selection is not as prevalent as the standard model leads us to expect is consistent with a possible role of behavioral tendencies in mitigating adverse selection[61]—for example, research findings that risk preferences can overwhelm selection effects in long-term care insurance[62] or findings of advantageous selection in some health insurance markets that appear to be related to cognitive ability.[63]

PRIVATELY SUBOPTIMAL INSURANCE COVERAGE

Separately, behavioral tendencies suggest that individuals may fail to purchase insurance when in fact they would be better off with coverage. Perhaps the most compelling piece of evidence in this regard is that many people fail to take up essentially free insurance for which they are eligible, as in the case of Medicaid and the State Children's Health Insurance Program (SCHIP). Many children lacking health insurance are eligible for Medicaid or SCHIP.[64] While that is surely due in part to costs associated with take-up as well as lack of knowledge of eligibility, a contributing factor is likely to be some form of error in assessing the value of the insurance. Another form of supporting evidence for the proposition that individuals lack health insurance due to decisionmaking errors comes from research investigating the affordability of private health insurance to the uninsured. Many uninsured adults have insurance available either through their own employer or that of a family member.[65] This literature finds that many of the uninsured could afford some type of coverage.[66] Still, while that separates the issues of affordability and choice, it cannot distinguish preference from error.

Behavioral tendencies also may lead individuals to choose policies that are not suitable given their circumstances. The number of dimensions along which health insurance policies can vary—from pricing structures, to coverage and exclusions, to provider networks, and so on—is vast, and many of those attributes are difficult to understand even in isolation. Individuals with limited attention and computational capacity left alone to navigate the market are likely to choose plans with some degree of error. Evidence of this type of behavior comes from the Medicare Part D prescription drug benefit, which allows eligible seniors to choose among private prescription drug plans. One study found that the typical participant in Part D is paying about $500 a year more for prescription drugs in her current plan than she would in the lowest-cost plan that meets her coverage needs.[67] Another found various forms of choice inconsistency: beneficiaries place much more weight on plan premiums than they do on expected out-of-pocket costs of equivalent dollar value; they place almost no value on variance-reducing aspects of plans; and they value plan financial features such as increased cost-sharing even when those features did not reduce their own projected costs.[68] Experimental evidence with even simplified terms shows a similar tendency toward error.[69] Evidence from other settings is broadly consistent with those results.[70]

Decisionmaking errors and inconsistencies therefore are a potential source of welfare loss in themselves, selection effects aside. The possibility of errors along the extensive margin raises the possibility that some fraction of those individuals or families that lack health insurance lack it not because they cannot afford it or simply prefer not to have it but because they make errors in reasoning. Errors along the intensive margin also create the possibility of welfare loss as individuals choose policies that do not maximize their experienced utility. These possible sources of welfare loss at least raise the question of whether government policies might assist individuals with health insurance decisions in ways that raise welfare.

Finally, note that there are important implications of behavioral economics for health policy along other dimensions, such as the overall quality and costs of health care, that are not traditionally part of public finance. We present a brief discussion of these issues in box 4-2.

Setting Objectives for Health Insurance Policy

The general policy goal with respect to health insurance is to ensure accessibility to suitable coverage in the face of both market and decisionmaking failures that can lead to outcomes that fail to maximize social welfare. But policy prescriptions for improving welfare do not follow directly merely from the identification of such failures. Expanding coverage is not costless, and the social benefits of any particular course of action must be weighed against its costs. Moreover, policy actions taken to assist with or guarantee coverage will generate behavioral responses that may partly offset any benefits, and the benefits and costs of policies will not be shared or borne equally by everyone that they affect. Consequently, determining which policies are worthwhile—including both what ends to pursue and the extent to which to pursue them—requires judgment calls about when, on net, policies improve social welfare. While economics cannot make those judgments, it can speak to the nature and terms of the trade-offs that they must resolve.

From a traditional perspective, the main issue to consider, as with social insurance in general, is how to trade off the benefits of expanded insurance coverage against the social costs of the moral hazard that they tend to generate.[71] While the consumption-smoothing benefits of insurance are real for those who gain coverage, that coverage can lead to excess spending on health care as individuals no longer face the true marginal costs of care or the full marginal benefits of engaging in protective activities. Such behavioral responses to coverage make policies that seek to expand public coverage or subsidize private coverage more costly, both in terms of the direct cost to the government as well as overall social costs. And while cost-sharing elements of insurance design, such as deductibles and coinsurance, can mitigate moral hazard, from the perspective of setting policy objectives they serve only to push back to another level of detail the question of

Box 4-2. *Health Care and Public Policy*

Ensuring the proper functioning of health insurance markets is only one of a larger set of public policy concerns related to health and health care. Through insurance programs like Medicaid and Medicare and medical care operations such as the Veterans Health Administration, the government accounts for nearly one of every two health care dollars spent in the United States each year.[a] Consequently, the government has a vested interest in finding answers to a variety of questions related to health care, including how to keep the growth of costs in check as well as how to realize quality health outcomes. Along with the expansion of coverage, those issues were in fact among the major goals of the recently passed health reform law.

A behavioral approach to broader health care questions can be as productive as a behavioral approach to questions of health insurance. A traditional approach to the problem of understanding and improving health care outcomes focuses on incentives for providers and incentives for—as well as the information available to—consumers of health care. A behavioral approach emphasizes the fact that both consumers and providers of health care are imperfect decisionmaking agents and that the impact of traditional policy levers such as financial incentives and information is mediated by behavioral tendencies.[b]

For example, a wide variety of patient behaviors seem more consistent with a behavioral model than the standard model. Individuals may be more or less likely to take recommended protective actions, such as cancer screening, depending on whether the associated risks are framed in terms of losses or gains.[c] They are influenced by anecdotal evidence in making decisions about treatment while ignoring available statistical information.[d] They exhibit evidence of status quo bias toward treatment options.[e] In particular, many patient behaviors are consistent with individuals possessing only bounded self-control. For example, evidence on patient non-adherence indicates that individuals often fail to follow indicated courses of treatment, such as taking medicine as prescribed by their doctor.[f] They also fail to seek necessary care. For example, one study found that only about one-quarter of individuals with diabetes receive the recommended number of blood tests each year.[g] All of that is apart from the effects of behavioral tendencies on broader lifestyle factors, such as smoking, diet, and exercise, which contribute to health outcomes in important ways.

These behavioral tendencies lead to both challenges and opportunities for health care policy design. They indicate, among other things, how policies related to communicating information can be powerful; for example, making information about provider quality and treatment outcomes more transparent and accessible might help individuals choose better.[h] More generally, it indicates how the principles of choice architecture can be applied here.[i] It also indicates that there may be scope for achieving improved health outcomes by assisting individuals adopt health

(continued)

Box 4-2 (*continued*)

behaviors to which they otherwise may have difficultly committing. For example, patients may be well served by incentive schemes that motivate compliance with drug protocols in ways that appeal to behavioral tendencies or by simplified regimens that are easier to follow.[j]

The personal service nature of health care also opens up the possibility of behavioral complications from the supply side, because providers as well as consumers of medical care are imperfect decisionmakers. There is evidence that physicians exhibit behavioral tendencies in medical decisionmaking—for example, in studies that demonstrate status quo bias in choosing among treatment alternatives or the sensitivity of doctors' choice of therapies to whether alternatives are framed in positive or negative terms.[k] Geographic variation in standards of care is consistent with local norms and imperfect learning.[l] Important research findings can go largely ignored in that doctors fail to adhere to evidence-based guidelines.[m] Recommended treatments can vary with specialty.[n] Physicians sometimes even fail to follow simple hygienic guidelines, such as the recommendation to wash their hands adequately.[o]

The implication is that just as policy goals to improve quality or control cost must consider the behavioral tendencies of patients, so too must they consider the behavioral tendencies of physicians and other care providers. For example, findings suggest that government intervention to merely identify and disseminate best practices, such as by supporting comparative effectiveness research, is unlikely to be sufficient in itself to lead to changes in physician behavior. Interventions such as simple checklists, which have been shown to reduce surgery-related deaths by more than 40 percent, suggest the possibilities here.[p] Similarly, part of the promise of health information technology may be in the role that it might play to help overcome such tendencies— for example, through intelligently designed decision support programs.[q]

The reason that we largely set these important and interesting issues aside is that, as important as they are for public *policy*, they are not, in the usual conception, the province of public *finance*, and therefore are largely beyond the scope of this book. More generally, while public finance is an expansive and useful framework for considering the implications of behavioral economics for many aspects of policy, it also is restrictive. While insights from psychological research have applications to a wider range of topics in public policy—from health care to criminal justice to consumer finance—that we do not cover here, it is not for lack of importance but rather a consequence of the focus of our approach.

a. National Center for Health Statistics, *Health, United States, 2009: With Special Feature on Medical Technology* (Hyattsville, Md.: 2010).

b. Richard G. Frank, "Behavioral Economics and Health Economics," in *Behavioral Economics and Its Applications,* edited by Peter Diamond and Hannu Vartianen (Princeton University Press, 2007), pp. 195–222.

c. Daniel J. O'Keefe and Jakob D. Jensen, "The Relative Persuasiveness of Gain-Framed and Loss-Framed Messages for Encouraging Disease Prevention Behaviors," *Journal Communication,* vol. 59 (2009), pp. 296–316; Alexander J. Rothman and Peter Salovey, "Shaping Perceptions to

Motivate Healthy Behavior: The Role of Message Framing," *Psychological Bulletin,* vol. 121, no. 1 (1997), pp. 3–19.

d. Peter A. Ubel, Christopher Jepson, and Jonathan Baron, "The Inclusion of Patient Testimonials in Decision Aids: Effects on Treatment Choices," *Medical Decision Making,* vol. 21, no. 1 (2001), pp. 60–68; Eric C. Schneider and Arnold M. Epstein, "Use of Public Performance Reports," *JAMA,* vol. 279, no. 20 (May 27, 1998), pp. 1638–42.

e. Haiden A. Huskamp and others, "The Impact of a Three-Tier Formulary on Demand Response for Prescription Drugs," *Journal of Economics and Management Strategy,* vol. 14, no. 3 (2005), pp. 729–53.

f. M. Robin DiMatteo, "Variations in Patients' Adherence to Medical Recommendations: A Quantitative Review of 50 Years of Research," *Medical Care,* vol. 42, no. 3 (March 2004), pp. 200–09.

g. Elizabeth A. McGlynn and others, "The Quality of Health Care Delivered to Adults in the United States," *New England Journal of Medicine,* vol. 348, no. 26 (June 26, 2003), pp. 2635–45.

h. Brian J. Zikmund-Fisher, Angela Fagerlin, and Peter A. Ubel, "Improving Understanding of Adjuvant Therapy Options by Using Simpler Risk Graphics," *Cancer,* vol. 113, no. 12 (December 15, 2008), pp. 3382–90.

i. George Loewenstein, Troyen Brennan, and Kevin G. Volpp, "Asymmetric Paternalism to Improve Health Behaviors," *JAMA,* vol. 298, no. 20 (2007), pp. 2415–17.

j. Kevin G. Volpp and others, "A Test of Financial Incentives to Improve Warfarin Adherence," *BMC Health Services Research,* vol. 8, no. 272 (2008); Sandra van Dulmen and others, "Patient Adherence to Medical Treatment: A Review of Reviews," *BMC Health Services Research,* vol. 7, no. 55 (2007).

k. Donald A. Redelmeier and Eldar Shafir, "Medical Decision Making in Situations with Multiple Alternatives," *JAMA,* vol. 274, no. 4 (1995), pp. 302–05; Barbara J. McNeil and others, "On the Elicitation of Preferences for Alternative Therapies," *New England Journal of Medicine,* vol. 306, no. 21 (1982), pp. 1259–62.

l. Elliott S. Fisher and others, "The Implications of Regional Variation in Medicare Spending Part 1: The Content, Quality and Accessibility of Care," *Annals of Internal Medicine,* vol. 138, no. 4 (2003), pp. 273–87; Elliott S. Fisher and others, "The Implications of Regional Variation in Medicare Spending Part 2: Health Outcomes and Satisfaction with Care," *Annals of Internal Medicine,* vol. 138, no. 4 (2003), pp. 288–98.

m. T. S. Carey and J. Garrett, "Patterns of Ordering Diagnostic Tests for Patients with Acute Low Back Pain: The North Carolina Back Pain Project," *Annals of Internal Medicine,* vol. 125, no. 10 (1996), pp. 807–14; D. Di Iorio, E. Henley, and A. Doughty, "A Survey of Primary Care Physician Practice Patterns and Adherence to Acute Low Back Problem Guidelines," *Archives of Family Medicine,* vol. 9, no. 10 (2000), pp. 1015–21.

n. Daniel C. Cherkin and others, "Physician Variation in Diagnostic Testing for Lower Back Pain. Who You See Is What You Get," *Arthritis and Rheumatism,* vol. 37, no. 1 (1994), pp. 15–22; Floyd J. Fowler Jr. and others, "Comparisons of Recommendations by Urologists and Radiation Oncologists for Treatment of Clinically Localized Prostate Cancer," *JAMA,* vol. 283, no. 24 (June 28, 2000), pp. 3217–22.

o. Didier Pittet and others, "Hand Hygiene among Physicians: Performance, Beliefs, and Perceptions," *Annals of Internal Medicine,* vol. 141, no. 1 (2004), pp. 1–8.

p. Alex B. Haynes and others, "A Surgical Safety Checklist to Reduce Morbidity and Mortality in a Global Population," *New England Journal of Medicine,* vol. 360, no. 5 (January 29, 2009), pp. 491–99.

q. James B. Rebitzer, Mari Rege, and Christopher Shepard, "Influence, Information Overload, and Information Technology in Health Care," in *Beyond Health Insurance: Public Policy to Improve Health,* vol. 19, Advances in Health Economics and Health Services Research, edited by Michael Grossman and others (Bingley, U.K.: Emerald Group Publishing, 2008), pp. 43–69.

how best to trade off the benefits of insurance to individuals against its cost to the government and society.

Allowing for behavioral tendencies both changes the terms of the standing trade-offs and reveals new ones. The most substantial revision is to our understanding of behavior under coverage and moral hazard. In general, the extent of moral hazard will be greater or lesser to the extent that behavioral tendencies such as choice errors or failures of self-control change the way in which individuals respond to coverage. So, for example, while moral hazard suggests that people with insurance will overconsume drugs or doctor visits, self-control problems might deter individuals from doing so or even lead them to underconsume those services. A substantial body of evidence indicates that individuals do not make decisions about how to consume health care in perfectly optimal or consistent ways (some examples are discussed in more detail in box 4-2), and such behavior may mitigate the moral hazard associated with health insurance. Moreover, measures to combat moral hazard, such as cost sharing, may in fact reduce demand for care below the efficient level or distort care decisions inefficiently. Alternatively, moral hazard could be exacerbated by, for example, choice errors resulting from coverage making the costs of services harder to perceive.

The overall result may operate along two distinct dimensions of moral hazard: the use of health services under coverage and health behaviors under coverage. First, behavioral tendencies and moral hazard may become confounded. For example, we might mistake behavior such as poor diet or failure to exercise by insured individuals as due in part to moral hazard—they do not face the full cost of the health expenses that they may incur as a result of such behaviors—when those behaviors may in fact be primarily the result of imperfect self-control. Second, the way that moral hazard operates with respect to decisions regarding the use of health care may be modified by behavioral tendencies. For example, while insurance can in principle create incentives to consume excess care, in the case of unpleasant procedures or those with only long-term benefits, such as colonoscopies, that effect may be offset by behavioral tendencies that lead individuals to consume less care. Or if moral hazard pushes individuals to consume excess care, for example, in the form of prescription drugs, that effect may be modified by behaviors such as those that lead to imperfect drug adherence. The key implication for policy is that in drawing conclusions about the social welfare implications of alternative policies for expanding health insurance, the costs associated with moral hazard must be considered in context rather than assumed to follow from behavior consistent with standard assumptions.

The possibility that behavioral tendencies mediate moral hazard in such ways is consistent with some evidence on the health consequences of cost sharing in insurance plans. Pertinent evidence includes results from the RAND health insurance experiment, which randomly varied levels of cost sharing. On one hand, the RAND experiment did find that increased cost sharing led to reductions in use, consistent with standard theory.[72] However, the standard model also predicts that the response will be efficient, in that what individuals cut back on is the excess care that they consumed due to moral hazard. While most RAND participants in general did not see adverse health outcomes, the reduction in use due to increased cost sharing had some adverse health consequences along some dimensions for some groups.[73] Moreover, recent research has found a number of instances in which increasing cost sharing had effects consistent with those predicted by the behavioral model. One study finds that increased cost sharing for office visits and drugs among a group of retirees led to lower use of those services but increased use of costly hospital services.[74] Other research finds qualitatively similar results, such as the finding that limits to prescription drug benefits can decrease use in ways that lead to adverse health outcomes and that higher costs of cancer screenings appeared to depress use in inefficient ways.[75] Research that finds that individuals respond in more efficient ways when the structure of cost sharing conveys more information about the value of treatment also is consistent with this view.[76]

A behavioral approach also illuminates challenges that policymakers must resolve that the standard model fails to consider at all. How should policymakers take results that suggest that individuals under-demand health insurance in ways that lead to welfare losses? The biggest issue presented by a behavioral approach to expansion of coverage is addressing the welfare consequences of individual decisionmaking that fails to maximize utility. There are several forms of challenges here. When it appears that individuals commit choice errors by opting for the wrong level or kind of health insurance, policy must take a stance on whether those choices are truly due to error or are merely the expression of unusual preferences. When it appears that because of a failure of self-control individuals fail to make decisions about health insurance coverage that are in their own long-run or considered best interest, policy must decide whether to favor the short-run, impulsive self or the long-run, restrained self. Finally, policy decisions may have to account for the possibility of reference-dependence in preferences for health insurance. Policy can affect the reference points with respect to which individuals judge the relative desirability of alternatives, and it can influence individuals' perceptions of health insurance—whether they see it as a loss or a gain. Both actions affect choices as well as welfare.

Health Insurance Policy Design

The key insight from behavioral economics for the design of policies to increase access to coverage is that coverage rates are a function not only of market failure due to information asymmetries but also behavioral tendencies on the part of individuals. Increasing health insurance coverage is therefore not simply an issue of making insurance affordable; it also involves helping individuals make optimal decisions about both the level and nature of coverage. In addition, the policy response to adverse selection and moral hazard must consider the ways in which behavioral tendencies affect how those forces operate.

Public policy in this area reflects two basic approaches, both of which can be informed by a behavioral perspective. One is to promote the function of private health insurance markets through a combination of subsidies that make health insurance more affordable and regulations that encourage pooling and discourage selection, both in group and nongroup health insurance markets. The other is to provide health insurance coverage directly through public programs, which can target vulnerable populations by setting eligibility parameters and can be explicitly designed to pool risks and avoid adverse selection. The psychology of targeted individuals plays an important but distinct role in the operation of each type of policy environment.

Promoting Access to Health Insurance in Group Markets

A central way that the government encourages private health insurance coverage is through the tax subsidy to employer-provided insurance. Premiums on group coverage sponsored by an employer are treated as untaxed compensation, creating a subsidy relative to insurance purchased with after-tax income. That encourages coverage through a variety of channels. By subsidizing premiums it increases the affordability of coverage for workers; by operating through employers, it creates natural risk pools that serve to mitigate adverse selection; and by making health insurance a relatively valuable component of compensation, it encourages employers to offer health insurance as a benefit.

However, this system of subsidizing health insurance has its drawbacks. For example, it has the practical effect of linking health insurance coverage with employment. One result is that individuals who separate from employment suffer the dual shock of loss of income and loss of health insurance coverage. That in turn has the effect of impairing labor mobility and thereby decreasing the efficiency of labor markets because workers are more reluctant to leave jobs when doing so means losing their health coverage. It also has questionable distributional features, as the value of the tax benefit of the exclusion increases with income. And it leaves a lot of people out—if an individual is unemployed or if his or her employer does not offer coverage, the benefits of the subsidy are unavailable.

For those reasons among others, recent reforms have shifted the focus away from a system built around employer-based coverage. A behavioral perspective on the health insurance problem rehabilitates the argument for employer-based coverage somewhat, though it adds its own set of qualifications. Most important, what the employer-based system does that can be difficult to recreate in other contexts is to provide individuals a source of assistance and guidance with insurance choices that they may otherwise find difficult.[77] Rather than leaving individuals completely on their own to choose among available levels and types of health insurance, employers who sponsor coverage necessarily take steps to assist with the insurance purchase decision. By lessening opportunities for committing choice errors, that approach may improve outcomes relative to a system that simply subsidizes individual purchases of health insurance. Qualified human resource officials pick the set of plans to be offered, and they can provide guidance with making choices from that restricted set. Moreover, individuals might find it easier to make smart choices from the few policies offered by the typical employer than from the dozens of policies that they might confront in the open market.

Employer-sponsored health insurance also can help individuals to overcome delays in purchasing coverage due to bounded self-control, as employer agents can assist with meeting deadlines and help with forms or other barriers that might lead individuals to procrastinate. Finally, because employer-sponsored plans are paid for through paycheck withholding, individuals may be more willing to take coverage that way—for example, because of reference-dependence—than when they have to pay premiums directly.

There also are countervailing behavioral considerations to employer-provided coverage. First among them is that the costs of employer-sponsored insurance can be obscure to workers. That is due in part to the complicating nature of the income tax exclusion in calculating the true costs of premiums; it also is due to the fact that employers typically deduct only a part of premiums from paychecks, an amount that is usually reported to employees, and cover part of the premium directly, an amount that often is hidden from employees. The result is that individuals can have a hard time knowing what the true cost is of the health insurance offered to them through their employer, and that can promote choice errors on the part of individuals in deciding whether to take coverage and in choosing among plans. For example, individuals may overconsume health insurance if they misperceive their premium contribution to be the total cost of coverage. Recent health care reform legislation requires firms to disclose the total cost of health insurance premiums on pay statements, which will make the cost of coverage at least somewhat more salient.

Reforms to employer-sponsored coverage that are informed by behavioral insights also are possible. For example, many employees have insurance available through their job but fail to take it up; the new reform law will encourage take-up through employers by mandating health insurance coverage at the individual level starting in 2014. Evidence suggests, however, that financial incentives alone, such as those that would result from failing to take up insurance in the face of the mandate, may be an imperfect instrument for encouraging take-up at work.[78] Other, more behavioral, levers to encourage take-up are possible. Policy could, for example, follow the lead of employer-sponsored retirement plans in allowing and encouraging firms to enroll employees in health insurance plans by default. The health care reform law takes some steps in this direction—it will eventually require large firms that offer health insurance to automatically enroll new hires.[79]

PROMOTING ACCESS TO HEALTH INSURANCE IN NONGROUP MARKETS

The other approach employed to encourage health insurance coverage in private markets is to subsidize the direct purchase of coverage by individuals in the non-group market. The nongroup market has been the focus of much policymaking attention in recent years, in large part because a substantial portion of the unin-sured are in this market because they lack access to employer-sponsored cover-age. Notably, the recent health care reform legislation seeks to improve overall coverage largely by increasing participation in the nongroup market. It does so by offering new subsidies for health insurance purchased in this market and by creat-ing new health insurance exchanges in which a nongroup policy can be purchased.

As promising as the nongroup market is as a platform for reform, it has a number of disadvantages from a behavioral perspective. The main behavioral challenge is whether the nongroup market is too complex to expect individuals to navigate it successfully. The number of health insurance plans—and the num-ber of dimensions along which they vary—can be daunting. Dozens of available plans differ in coverage, pricing, and cost-sharing provisions. Combine that with a process of sifting through options that can be somewhat arduous in the best of circumstances, from obtaining quotes to getting underwriting to acquiring cover-age, and the possibilities for failures of self-control, in addition to simple choice errors, begin to multiply. The experience of Medicare Part D, which indicates that individuals have difficulty with choosing well for prescription drug coverage alone, provides a cautionary case.

The recently enacted national health reform legislation and the recently implemented plan in Massachusetts are examples of reforms that use nongroup markets as the lynchpin of efforts to expand coverage. To encourage individuals to take up health insurance in these markets, the policies combine subsidies with an income-related fine that is collected through the tax return. The experience in Massachusetts, in which the uninsurance rate is now only 2.7 percent, suggests that that combination of incentives can be effective in overcoming whatever behavioral barriers to take-up the complexity of such a market presents.[80] That result and the promise of the new national law also are consistent with the opera-tion of some behavioral tendencies. Mandates to purchase health insurance may, for example, create a social norm with respect to insurance coverage that rein-forces take-up. Behavioral economics also offers other possible levers for further encouraging take-up in this model by manipulating the presentation or struc-ture of the penalty for noncompliance. For example, the fine could be presented either as a gain or a loss—such as, say, a loss of a personal exemption on one hand or a tax credit for being insured that is taken away on the other.

In the future, policy also might automatically enroll individuals through exchanges, and it could make enrollment sticky by making it a hassle to opt out. Those mechanisms might be deployed through employers, even when employers do not themselves sponsor the insurance, in much the same way that auto-IRA proposals work for retirement savings. Automatic features of the tax system also could be an integral part of making enrollment as easy as possible. Automatic enrollment outside the context of a public program naturally raises the question of what plans individuals would be automatically enrolled into. Such a policy could force a choice, but it might need to include provisions for structuring or assisting individuals with that choice. Or policies might designate a default plan—potentially by random assignment to private plans meeting certain criteria or by assignment based on risk factors like age.

A behavioral perspective also suggests that the design of the insurance exchange will be of central importance in any such reform efforts. While the Massachusetts experience suggests that take-up levels can be high under such a plan, the difficulties that individuals can have with choosing well among alternative plans remains, so policies must be concerned with the choice environment that they create. Policy can structure the choice of plan, for example, by limiting variation in plan attributes and structuring the presentation of alternatives—such as with the color-coded categories of plans in the Massachusetts model. Policy features such as decision aids might assist with choice. In the experience with Medicare Part D, personalized information about plan costs was found to lead to lower costs without observable declines in plan quality.[81] The evidence on the effectiveness of information provision that is not personalized is more mixed.[82] The development of markets for third-party advice or assistance also might improve choice. Publicly funded third parties could be employed to create competition for advice or assistance services by, say, randomly assigning enrollees to those parties, who would be rewarded for things like ensuring customer satisfaction, keeping people in plans, keeping costs down, improving average health outcomes of customers, and so on. Those third parties would gain or lose market share based on their performance along those dimensions.

EXPANDING ACCESS IN PUBLIC PROGRAMS

Finally, some uninsured individuals are eligible for public insurance programs such as Medicaid or SCHIP, which present opportunities for policy reform that take a behavioral approach to improving take-up rates.[83] Take-up in those programs is imperfect, despite being very low cost to participants.[84] Behavioral tendencies such as being discouraged by channel factors are suspected of playing a role in take-up in many public programs.[85] There is evidence, for example, that a difficult take-up process hinders take-up of Medicaid and that lack of awareness of the program can be an issue with SCHIP.[86]

In general, design principles that encourage enrollment in private plans—simplification, assistance, and so on—can be used with public programs as well. In addition, for public programs such as Medicaid or SCHIP, some form of automatic enrollment may be more feasible.[87] For example, many of the children eligible for Medicaid or SCHIP live in families that file a federal income tax return. Given the fact that the tax return already contains much of the information necessary to determine Medicaid eligibility, some have proposed methods to align the Medicaid enrollment process with the tax filing process to promote enrollment in these programs.[88]

Recent experimentation with using information from tax returns to assist with application for college financial aid provides a model for how such an approach could be made to work as well as evidence that it may be effective.[89] Reform also might work to encourage enrollment by setting up a system to allow and create incentives for third parties to assist with enrollment.[90] Another model is to build enrollment assistance into the health care system, so that, for example, hospitals, which already have an incentive to enroll eligible patients, do so systematically.[91]

Unemployment Insurance

The recent recession has been characterized most notably by exceedingly harsh labor market conditions, bringing the unemployment rate into double digits for the first time in a generation. But even in the best of times, the United States labor market is extremely dynamic—before the recession the average month saw around 5 million job separations and 5 million new hires.[92] Regardless of whether job loss is due to cyclical or frictional forces, it comes at a direct cost to individuals. Job loss has an immediate impact on a family's ability to pay for basic needs such as food and shelter. Finding a new job is difficult, especially in a worsening job market. The government provides assistance to individuals after job loss, primarily through unemployment insurance, as a way to help cushion the difficulties.[93]

From the perspective of standard public finance, the government does so for a number of reasons, but in large part because of the inability of the private market to effectively provide mechanisms by which individuals can smooth income and consumption across unemployment spells. The standard analysis of the problem emphasizes the role of asymmetries of information in leading the market to underprovide those mechanisms, and it goes on to consider the ways in which public provision of unemployment benefits trades off against the moral hazard that those benefits create, in particular the way that they can blunt incentives to return to work. And it also suggests designs for policies that deliver those benefits while minimizing the resulting inefficiencies.

A behavioral approach recognizes the information problems that plague this market and goes on to consider the ways in which behavioral tendencies contribute to the difficulties that individuals face both in smoothing consumption and in returning to work. It stresses in particular the role that bounded self-control and other decisionmaking biases can play, along with traditional moral hazard, in causing unemployment insurance to increase the length of spells of unemployment. It also suggests how policy might respond to those challenges.

The Psychology of Job Loss

Given the consumption-smoothing benefits of unemployment insurance, we might expect the private market to respond to individuals' need for assistance after job loss by providing insurance that would pool risk across individuals. Absent such insurance products, each individual could still spread his or her own risk over time through precautionary saving, although that is likely to work well only for small losses. In principle, individuals also could borrow to smooth consumption during unemployment, although it can be difficult to do so except at very high interest rates without assets to use as collateral, such as one's home for a home equity loan.

In practice, the key piece of this market, unemployment insurance, is unlikely to exist without government intervention. In the standard public finance analysis, the key problem is that private insurance against unemployment is not available due to asymmetries of information. Individuals who know that they are the most likely to lose their jobs would be the most likely to buy insurance, leading the pool of those seeking insurance to be adversely selected. As the insurer increases the price to cope with high payouts, the pool willing to purchase insurance concentrates even more among those with the greatest risk of job loss and a private market for insurance is not sustainable.

While the information problems in this market are severe—compare the all-but-complete absence of private unemployment insurance to the weakened but still existent markets for private annuities or health insurance—there are behavioral dimensions to the problem of unemployment as well. Two dimensions of behavior stemming from the psychology of job loss might have consequences for welfare that could be addressed by unemployment policy. First, individuals may not optimally self-insure; second, they may return to work at suboptimal speeds and engage in suboptimal search.

PRECAUTIONARY SAVINGS AND SELF-INSURANCE

A behavioral approach to this problem considers the complicating element of behavioral tendencies that tend to undermine the already limited ability of individuals to self-insure against job loss. In principle, individuals could save while working to provide a buffer of income to pay for household expenditures while searching for work, but behavioral tendencies might mean that individuals do not accumulate optimal levels of precautionary savings. For example, all of the difficulties detailed above that individuals have with life-cycle saving may apply to precautionary saving as well. The complexity of determining the desired level of savings is itself a deterrent to saving. Figuring out how much to optimally save is a complex problem involving estimation of the risk of job loss, the duration of unemployment, flexibility of consumption expenditures, ability to borrow, earnings at a future job—all of which could vary over time. Moreover, savings related to job loss would interact with savings for health care, disability, education, and retirement—and with the tax treatment of different forms of saving.

Even if a credible third-party expert could help with the computation of the level of savings, issues of procrastination and misperception would remain. In addition to bounded self-control leading individuals to consume out of earnings rather than save, individuals also may be deterred from saving by a desire to avoid contemplating unpleasant outcomes such as unemployment, fueled in part by the likelihood that individuals will be overconfident or overly optimistic with respect to their own employment. Perception of one's job performance and likelihood of being retained may be systematically too high, in that most people believe their own performance to be above average.

Some evidence is consistent with individuals failing to save optimally as a precaution against unemployment. Many households have too little savings to replace any substantial portion of their income lost through unemployment.[94] Another piece of evidence of complexity is the prevalence of crude rules of thumb for precautionary savings—for example, to save the equivalent of six months of wages.

Returning to Work

Another potential source of welfare loss in unemployment is due to behavioral tendencies that may lead individuals to remain out of work for inefficiently long periods of time. That is, even in the absence of unemployment insurance and the disincentive to return to work that it creates, individuals might remain unemployed beyond what would be optimal due to behavioral forces. Two are likely to be of special importance: bias and error in expectations about wages and the search process, and time-inconsistent preferences with respect to work and leisure.

If behavioral tendencies lead individuals to form biased, mistaken, or reference-dependent expectations about the search process, individuals may search for inefficient lengths of time. For example, imperfectly optimizing individuals may set their wage expectations using shortcuts—for example, by focusing not only on the current market valuation of their skills but also how current wage offers compare with their previous wages. That could be due simply to a limited capacity to accurately gauge the labor market or to a tendency to judge the fairness of wage offers relative to wages observed in the past. There is some evidence that past wages inform reservation wages.[95]

Depending on the sign of the error, setting wage expectations that are inaccurate may lead individuals to search for too long or not long enough. When the error is such that individuals set wage expectations that are higher than justified, the problems may be compounded by reference-dependence. If losses loom larger than gains, as they do in many domains, then taking a lower wage on a new job may be an especially large hurdle to overcome and may deter returning to work. There is some evidence from other contexts that workers may have reference-dependent preferences in earnings.[96] Finally, individuals also may form biased expectations about the search process that may lead them to remain unemployed for longer than is optimal. For example, if individuals are overly optimistic or overconfident about the prospects of finding a new job, they may put too little effort into searching, which may prolong spells of unemployment. There is some evidence that individuals may be overly optimistic about reemployment prospects in this way.[97]

The other channel through which behavioral tendencies could lead to an inefficient length of unemployment is present-biased preferences with respect to work and leisure. By definition, those counted as unemployed state a preference for wanting to find a job. Yet, time-use studies also indicate that on an average day, an unemployed person does not spend much of his or her time searching.[98] It is possible that the best search strategy involves making many inquiries and then waiting for replies. But as with other difficult and unpleasant activities, individuals may procrastinate and put off searching until another time. That is, while their long-run preferences are to search more now in order to improve their chances to regain employment, their short-run preferences are to not search because searching creates disutility. Thus, when individuals are impatient or afflicted by bounded self-control, unemployment spells may be inefficiently lengthy.[99]

Defining Goals for Unemployment Policy

Given the set of policy problems that unemployment insurance policy has to contend with, policy responses must reflect judgments about how to manage competing objectives and the various costs and benefits of alternative policies. In order to think through the comparative equity and efficiency of policies that provide assistance after job loss, policymakers need to define their goals. There are no right answers; defining goals involves instead making normative judgments that will set the scope for analysis.

In the standard model, the major trade-off that unemployment policy must weigh is the moral hazard that unemployment insurance can create.[100] By softening the blow of job loss, unemployment insurance diminishes incentives to search for and return to work, and more generous unemployment benefits are associated with longer spells of unemployment.[101] Policy therefore must weigh those effects against the welfare benefits generated by the income smoothing that unemployment insurance makes possible. The design of unemployment insurance and proposals for reform frequently focus on making this trade-off more favorable by reducing the force of moral hazard.

Behavioral tendencies complicate the moral hazard problem because they change how we understand the behavior of individuals seeking work. Behavioral economics introduces the possibility that disincentives to return to work created by unemployment insurance interact with standing behavioral barriers to returning to work, such as biased wage expectations and procrastination. In addition, allowing for behavioral tendencies identifies entirely new judgments that policy must reflect, such as whether to favor long- or short-run preferences or different conceptions of preferences in, say, encouraging individuals to return to work.

The interaction of behavioral tendencies with moral hazard can change our understanding of the terms of that trade-off substantially because it requires us to reinterpret the behavior of individuals seeking reemployment. In particular, it allows that the failure to search for or reluctance to accept employment may not reflect diminished incentives so much as behavioral tendencies. Individuals might intend to seek and take employment but fail to follow through on their intentions because of procrastination or some general failure of self-control. Or individuals may turn down offers not because of the incentives created by unemployment insurance but because they hold reference-dependent preferences with respect to wages based on their pre-separation wage. Notice that in some cases, rather than creating a trade-off for policy in which the consumption-smoothing benefits for recipients compete against the efficiency costs to society, this creates a situation in which the trade-offs are ameliorated or even eliminated outright. As a result, the interests of society at large and the targets of policy are in alignment rather than in competition—both the individual and society are made better off if spell length is reduced.

Some evidence of behavior by the unemployed is consistent with this behavioral interpretation. For example, one set of findings indicates that while benefits lead individuals to take longer to return to work, the delay is not associated with improved quality of the match between worker and job.[102] That is consistent with unemployment benefits increasing length of unemployment by, for instance, indulging procrastination. Evidence that exhausting benefits does not lead to substantial increases in the rate of reemployment also is consistent with a model in which individuals fail to return to work for reasons besides moral hazard.[103] Some evidence from job search assistance that indicates that merely requiring individuals to register with a program is sometimes sufficient to spur them to return to work also is consistent with behavioral explanations about the motivations of the unemployed.[104] So too are the generally disappointing results of some past experiments testing the effect of lump-sum rewards as an incentive for reemployment—distant future rewards would not be expected to be effective incentives for procrastinators.[105]

Behavioral tendencies also identify wholly new judgments that policy must reflect—for example, the importance of closing the gap between stated intentions to save for unexpected events like job loss and lack of action to actually save, of closing the gap between stated intentions to search intensively during unemployment and lack of intensity in actually searching, and of adjusting expectations of future income to correspond less to previous wages and more to labor market conditions. To the extent that the social goal involves making the individual better off, the policymaker needs to take a stand on whether that individual's welfare is measured in a long-run sense or as the sum of a sequence of short-term considerations. Individuals also may be making errors, by, for example, underestimating the risks of job loss and saving too little as a result. Finally, when the way that an individual considers a choice like a new job depends in part on some reference point, like the wage earned at a previous job, then a policymaker who is in part attempting to make the individual better off needs to take a stand on the extent to which that reference point should be taken as given or considered part of the set of things that the policy could influence in order to make that individual better off.

Policy Responses to Unemployment

Given the objectives and trade-offs that unemployment insurance embodies, traditionally policy responses to unemployment have addressed the failure of the private market to provide insurance that provides benefits after job loss by mandating participation in an insurance pool and then structuring benefits so as to minimize moral hazard. In the United States, for example, mandatory payroll taxes finance a state-provided unemployment insurance benefit that typically lasts for up to six months. There also is a smaller element of policy that focuses on helping individuals directly with searching for a job and returning to work.

Behavioral insights have design implications for these policies along a number of possible dimensions. First, a behavioral approach suggests that policy can operate directly to improve the ability of individuals to smooth consumption out of private savings. Second, it informs the design of unemployment compensation so as to create effective incentives to return to work in the face of behavioral tendencies such as biased wage expectations and bounded self-control. And third, it lends new weight and focus to policies such as job search assistance that can directly address some of the biases and difficulties that individuals have with responding accurately to the opportunities available in the labor market.

Precautionary Savings and Self-Insurance

One possible goal of policy is to assist individuals to self-insure against job loss by creating mechanisms that allow them to accumulate precautionary savings in advance of unemployment spells or to borrow against future earnings. For example, findings from behavioral economics indicate that there is a potential role for policy to help realign intentions and actions in activities like saving and searching for a job, where there is a potential disconnect between intention and action. Even with a government benefit, savings can provide a cushion after job loss that goes beyond government-backed assistance. Successful policies might, for example, import some of the innovations used with such great effect in retirement saving, such as automatic enrollment, and apply them to saving vehicles more appropriate for precautionary saving.[106]

Another approach would be to create an entirely new choice environment in which to save and borrow, such as through the imposition of private unemployment insurance accounts. Many alternatives have been proposed to address other traditional concerns.[107] Limitations of self-insurance for unemployment spells can be offset by benefit designs that focus more directly on larger, longer-term losses. The cost of borrowing during unemployment spells can be lowered by using mandatory paycheck withholding for repayment following reemployment, potentially combined with income-contingent repayment amounts or limited recourse against other assets for those who do not have enough labor earnings to repay. Note also that individuals might treat unemployment accounts differently from unemployment benefits. They might, for example, exhibit different labor supply or saving responses to contributions than to taxes. And they might treat drawing down balances differently from collecting benefits while unemployed for the purpose of determining consumption or length of unemployment spell: for example, people might feel more or less entitled to available funds. Finally, note that a drawback to these policies is that they might still be relatively complex; policies need to be careful not to recreate elements of the behavioral problem that discourages precautionary saving in the first place. Publicly provided unemployment insurance has the advantage of protecting behavioral participants from the complexities of preparing for a spell of unemployment on their own. In addition, such policies would have to attend to the possibility that individuals with bounded self-control may be tempted to overborrow while unemployed.

Unemployment Compensation and Incentives to Return to Work

Supporting the unemployed while encouraging their speedy return to work is a primary goal of unemployment compensation. The main design challenge for policy traditionally is taken to be balancing the provision of efficient mechanisms for making cash available when there is no employment income against the tendency of benefits to slow down job search and reemployment. Behavioral economics identifies the additional psychological barriers to job search and reemployment noted above. First, separated individuals may form biased wage expectations that can slow their return to work. Second, individuals may procrastinate in searching for a job or accepting reemployment even when such delay is against their own long-run self-interest.

Policies such as unemployment insurance seek to preserve in beneficiaries optimal incentives to search for and return to work. Procrastination and other expressions of bounded self-control complicate the problem of maintaining the motivation to search for and accept work. It suggests that the effects of benefits on search intensity are not a product of financial payments from continued unemployment but a more subtle interaction among benefits, incentives, and willpower. Especially problematic for policy, those tendencies may serve to blunt the force of design features intended to align incentives. Far-off time limits or reemployment bonuses that benefit individuals in the long run may provide little incentive to individuals who choose their level of search effort day to day.[108]

In response to those challenges, policy might create innovative incentive schemes that recognize the role of self-control in returning to work. The main incentive built into unemployment insurance as it exists is its time limit. Unemployment insurance might experiment with smaller, more immediate, and more frequent reminders and incentives to search in order to motivate workers with bounded self-control. So, for example, instead of tying rewards and penalties to reemployment, unemployment insurance might offer rewards or impose penalties tied to objectives such as making a specific number of active employer contacts in a week. Another possible direction for policy is to attempt to overcome imperfect self-control by creating a principal-agent relationship in which placement agents rather than unemployed individuals themselves receive reemployment bonuses. A final possible set of reforms would consider the issue of identity framing and whether search effort depends on whether individuals identify as workers. The hypothesis is that when unemployment benefits stop, identification as a member of the labor force can weaken and with it the motivation to search for a job. One possible proposal would be to experiment with or study extensions of benefits to test for the importance of that effect.

A policy response to biased wage expectations and reference-dependence might be wage-loss insurance, proposals for which exist in many forms.[109] Wage-loss insurance, whereby individuals are paid a portion of the difference between the wages of their old and their new job, could reduce the perception of how much is lost by taking a new job. By manipulating the realized value of wages and making job offers more attractive, wage-loss insurance averts to some degree the impact of biased wage expectations and mitigates the effects of loss aversion. In the longer run, it can smooth the painful but sometimes necessary process of psychological adjustment to lower-wage employment. There is some evidence of improved employment outcomes from a wage-loss insurance demonstration.[110] Consideration of proposals for wage-loss insurance might weigh the possible behavioral advantages, and any demonstration projects or evaluations of wage-loss insurance might take care to test for the possible importance of behavioral tendencies. Note that to the extent that reference-dependence in wages is an important factor in accepting job offers, it does call into question somewhat the likely efficacy of partial wage insurance at getting people back to work—it might work better as full insurance initially, though this conflicts with targeting limited funds efficiently.

Employment Services and Job Search Assistance

Finally, a related but distinct issue raised by a behavioral model of job loss is that irrespective of coverage by unemployment insurance, individuals may remain out of the workforce for an inefficiently long period simply because they find the job search daunting due to its complexity, because of individual biases toward wage offers and the process of searching itself, and because of bounded self-control. As a result, individuals and society in general may benefit from services that assist individuals with finding jobs. They may improve the speed with which individuals return to work and improve the quality of employee-job matches. Employment services and job search assistance might address this issue.

Job search assistance policies as they exist are usually found to be fairly cost effective, which may reflect in part the fact that they serve a behavioral need.[111] Programs include information services as well as active job search assistance and labor exchange activities. On one hand, the surprising effectiveness of low-intensity job search assistance in speeding reemployment may be due in part to the role that it plays in assisting workers with the adjustment to new wage expectations and in managing the complexity of job search. On the other hand, a behavioral view of unemployment suggests possible innovations. These services also could work to directly address behavioral tendencies. The programs might, for instance, seek to engage in active attempts to debias wage expectations.

5

Externalities and Public Goods

It has been famously labeled an inconvenient truth: the burning of fossil fuels, along with a number of other activities that modern economies have become accustomed to or depend upon, is contributing to global climate change.[1] If current patterns of use continue unabated, the environmental, social, and economic consequences of global warming may be severe.[2] As a result, the matter of how to address this issue has been a staple of policy debates both in the United States and around the world for at least the last two decades. Proposals to stem carbon emissions and thereby slow the rate of global warming range from cap-and-trade schemes to carbon taxes to stricter command-and-control regulations. But all seek to respond to the same underlying issue, which is that markets on their own do not appear to create incentives that lead people to consume and behave in ways that result in socially optimal levels of carbon emissions.

Why do markets fail to produce efficient outcomes in this case? The underlying problem is that the long-term costs associated with climate change are largely not reflected in the private costs and benefits associated with the goods and activities that lead to carbon emissions. As a result, individuals consume those goods and engage in those activities at inefficiently high levels. Because gasoline is too cheap, people drive too much, and so on. No single individual or entity has the private motivation to cut back on energy use in anything but a trivial way. The result is aggregate levels of emissions that are inefficiently high and looming global warming with all its consequences.

In general, such causes of market failure are labeled externalities in public finance, and climate change due to excess carbon emissions is only one—albeit perhaps the most striking—example of such a market failure in action.

Externalities are the classic cause of market failure, and they represent the classic case for government intervention in markets. They represent the failure of the price system at the most basic level. In the presence of externalities, markets set incorrect prices, in that private prices do not reflect true social costs and benefits. As a result, the private equilibrium is not socially optimal, and market outcomes are no longer presumptively efficient. A similar logic holds for public goods, a special case of externalities.

The welfare costs of externalities and public goods can be understood to arise due to the fact that external conditions lead to inefficient levels of production and consumption. Where there are negative externalities, the market allows too much activity. Where there are positive externalities or public goods, the market provides too little activity. As a result, government intervention—in the form of taxes, subsidies, regulation, tradable permit schemes, and so on—may improve economic efficiency by moving the level of activity back toward an efficient level.

But when the conditions that lead to externalities and public goods arise— along with how those conditions translate into efficiency costs—depends in large part on the preferences and behavior of individuals. In the example above, excess carbon emissions result from individuals responding to the fact that those costs are not reflected in prices. In general, deviations from the usual assumptions about how individuals behave change the conclusions about when we can expect externalities and public goods to arise and how they will affect the equilibrium outcome in the economy when they do. If, for instance, individuals do not respond to the unpriced costs of carbon emissions in accordance with standard assumptions, the effects can change—other-regarding individuals might voluntarily internalize those costs, mitigating the consequences of the externality; short-sighted or error-prone individuals might ignore or fail to perceive even the costs of carbon that they do face, exacerbating the consequences.

Correspondingly, the nature and form of policy interventions to guarantee efficient outcomes may change when we allow for their interaction with behavioral tendencies. Financial levers such as taxes and subsidies may no longer be necessary or sufficient. When behavioral tendencies lead individuals toward socially optimal outcomes, policy may be able to work with those tendencies. When behavioral tendencies operate to push outcomes further away from the social optimum, policy may have to correct not just the externality but also the decisionmaking error or inconsistency.

The key insight of behavioral economics for understanding the causes and consequences of externalities is that when externalities are present, private choices have public consequences—for good or ill. In this chapter, we discuss the potential implications of behavioral economics, first for externalities in general, then for the special case of public goods, and finally for some particular questions related to education policy.

—*Externalities*: Market failures due to externalities are one of the more conceptually straightforward issues in public finance from the standard perspective. Behavioral tendencies change both how we understand the effects of externalities and the challenges of correcting for them. In general, the effect of externalities on levels of economic activity will be mediated by behavioral tendencies; those tendencies could even cause externalities to arise where they otherwise would not. Correcting externalities efficiently becomes complicated by the nonstandard response of individuals to prices and incentives.

—*Public goods*: The special case of externalities that are consumed in the aggregate can lead to the existence of public goods, which the market will tend to underproduce, thereby requiring governments to either provide them directly or create conditions under which private markets will provide them. A behavioral approach identifies ways in which the standard market misstates the private equilibrium and clarifies the terms of the trade-off between the private and public provision equilibria. It further suggests new ways to guarantee the adequate provision of public goods.

—*Education*: An important set of economic policies has to do with the development of human capital through education, an activity supported extensively by the government in part because of the positive externalities that derive from education and in part because the production of education has some properties of a public good. Behavioral economics can inform some of the policy challenges particular to education.

In working through the behavioral dimensions to each of these areas, we again follow our framework of considering in turn the ways in which behavioral economics changes our diagnosis of the problem, the judgments that the problem requires, and the policy prescriptions that follow.

Externalities

Externalities arise when actions by individuals affect others in ways that are not mediated by the price system. Consumption as well as production can generate externalities, which can be positive as well as negative. The standard model predicts that in the presence of externalities, levels of economic activity will be below or above efficient levels as individuals choose and behave in a way that makes their private costs equal to their private benefits on the margin. From that understanding of how externalities translate into welfare loss, the standard model derives a menu of policy options for correcting externalities. For example, policy can set taxes and subsidies or otherwise change the costs and benefits that people face in making decisions in order to create incentives that more accurately reflect social costs and benefits. It can set regulations in order to enforce outcomes closer to the social optimum. And it can attempt to operate directly on the underlying market failure—for example, by assigning previously unspecified property rights.

Behavioral economics opens up some new ways that externalities can operate as well as new policy problems and solutions. Behavioral tendencies change the way in which externalities translate into efficiency results and can sometimes generate externalities directly. The psychology of motivation also identifies a new set of trade-offs that face policymakers in addressing externalities in important ways. And a behavioral approach changes the nature of the design challenges that policy must meet, while presenting a new set of levers for policy to operate on and with.

Because the way that behavioral tendencies alter the standard conclusions about both the consequences and correction of externalities necessarily depends heavily on the decisionmaking context, it is useful to give concrete examples of behavioral implications in specific cases. Below, we make extended reference primarily to externalities that arise in two domains: first, environmental externalities, especially negative externalities related to energy consumption, such as described in the example of carbon emissions and global warming; second, public health externalities, such as the positive externalities that arise when there are social benefits above and beyond the private benefits to activities like vaccination.

Behavioral Causes and Consequences

The standard economic analysis of externalities starts from an understanding of what externalities are and how they cause markets to fail. There are two parts to this analysis. The first part defines what externalities are and how they arise. The case of negative environmental externalities, as in the case of carbon emissions, is illustrative. The condition that defines the externality is that environmental conditions that affect the welfare of some individuals are partly a function of activities by firms and individuals that do not consider the impact of their activities on others when making production or consumption decisions. That is, when firms and individuals engage in activities that harm the environment, they do so without full regard for the external costs that those activities impose. For the most part, that is tantamount to the observation that the private prices that firms and individuals face when they make consumption and production decisions do not reflect the full marginal social costs of their activities.

The second part to the analysis is deriving what that means for social welfare—why and how market outcomes fail to be efficient in the presence of externalities. In the case of negative externalities, the consequence for social welfare in the standard analysis is that when individuals and firms make consumption or production decisions based on a set of private costs that are below the social costs, they engage in inefficiently high levels of economic activity. Again, take the case of negative environmental externalities. Firms that do not face the full costs of polluting will pollute more than is efficient, consumers who do not face the full costs of energy use will use more energy than is efficient, and so on.

The socially optimal amount of, for example, gasoline consumption and driving occurs when the social marginal costs of driving, including the costs to the environment, are equal to the marginal benefits of driving. But individuals will drive until the private marginal costs equal the marginal benefits. And because the private cost of driving does not include all of the associated social costs—for example, the costs in terms of the contribution to climate change—the private cost is lower than the social costs. Individuals therefore tend to drive more than is socially optimal. The collective result is an economy that is not operating efficiently in the face of negative environmental externalities. Overall welfare is diminished, resources are misallocated, and incentives to innovate are muted.

Behavioral economics changes not only how the conditions that define an externality lead to welfare outcomes but also when those conditions are likely to be present. On one hand, behavioral tendencies mediate the translation of externalities into welfare outcomes. Where the standard model suggests a straightforward logic—individuals who do not face the full costs of their actions engage in inefficiently high levels of economic activity—a behavioral approach emphasizes that behavioral tendencies mediate how the failure to face those costs translates into behavior and thus into welfare. On the other hand, behavioral tendencies might themselves create the conditions that define an externality or lead to outcomes that mimic those of an externality, even when the standard analysis would suggest that externality conditions are not present. A behavioral approach suggests that even when individuals face the correct prices or incentives, they may still engage in inefficient levels of economic activity, due, for example, to a failure of self-control. It also identifies new ways in which the behavior of individuals can affect the welfare of others.

Environmental externalities provide a useful illustration of the case in which behavioral tendencies change how individuals respond to externalities. The psychology of individuals affects both the way in which environmental externalities arise and translate into social costs as well as the effectiveness of the standard types of policy responses. For example, the presence of other-regarding preferences means that social norms serve as an important mediating factor in the decision to engage in environmentally harmful activities, even when prices do not reflect that environmental impact. That green alternatives—in architecture, in cars, in consumer choices more generally—have recently become fashionable in some circles has had much less to do with any changes in relative prices than with social preferences. A lot of people want to be seen in a Toyota Prius hybrid, gas prices aside. And those forces create both challenges and opportunities for environmental policy that the standard analysis largely neglects.

Public health provides useful examples of instances in which behavioral tendencies create the conditions of externalities—or conditions that are tantamount to externalities—directly. When individuals make choice errors or exhibit failures of self-control, those deviations can impose external costs on others. Conversely, bounded self-control and limited attention can make individuals sensitive to the actions of others in ways that they would ordinarily not be. These types of behavioral externalities have broadly similar social welfare characteristics and policy implications as ordinary externalities, but they are due primarily to decision-making failures rather than failures of the price system. So, for example, when individuals have bounded self-control, negative externalities are generated when other individuals engage in tempting activities—such as smoking or eating—in their presence. Below, we explore each of these cases in greater detail.

Psychology and the Efficiency Costs of Externalities

Behavioral tendencies may change the efficiency costs of even textbook examples of externalities, such as environmental externalities. The reason is that consumer behavior in the face of externalities is a joint product of the incentives that individuals face, especially in terms of prices, and the decisionmaking process by which they interpret and respond to those prices. Imperfect optimization, bounded self-control, and nonstandard preferences all mean that understanding the relationship of prices to social cost is no longer sufficient for understanding how individuals behave in the face of prices that deviate from marginal social costs. The way that social costs are reflected or not reflected in prices is only one component of what determines outcomes. The essential feature of a behavioral approach is to emphasize that how individuals respond to externalities is a more complex function of prices and other factors.

The case of energy use and associated environmental externalities illustrates some of the specific ways that behavioral factors and price incentives can interact.[3] For example, individuals face gas prices that are too low, in that they do not reflect the social costs of the associated carbon emissions; as a result, individuals tend to consume inefficiently high levels of gasoline. Note that in addition to consumption decisions on the margin, the amount of gasoline that individuals consume depends in part on the choice of car that they purchase—whether they select a hybrid or an SUV, for example. While under standard assumptions individuals fully build in the difference in operating costs due to differing fuel efficiencies when making a purchase decision, it may be difficult for behavioral individuals to do so. The fact that fuel costs are in the future may lead time-inconsistent individuals to discount them heavily. Similarly, the cost difference may not be salient for or easily calculated by an imperfectly optimizing person. As a consequence, individuals may purchase cars that lead them to consume gasoline in excess of even their private optimum—and further still from the socially optimal level.

Because the welfare effects of externalities depend on the extent to which economic activity in the presence of an externality deviates from the social optimum, in general the possibility that behavioral tendencies modify the level of economic activity can either mitigate or exacerbate the social costs of the externality. In some cases, such as the choice of car and its implications for gasoline consumption, behavioral tendencies may work to reinforce the effect of the externality and aggravate social costs. In other cases, behavioral tendencies could work to offset the effect of the externality. The particular implications of behavioral tendencies for the effects of externalities depend on the specific interaction of the externality and the relevant features of individual decisionmaking and the choice context.

One set of factors that affect how individuals behave in response to externalities derives from the fact that individuals are imperfect optimizers. To a large extent, the welfare consequences of externalities arise because individuals face the wrong price, a private price that does not reflect social costs. As a result of limited attention and computational capacity, individuals respond to prices not necessarily as they are, but as they are construed. The construed price that individuals respond to may be the private price, the social cost, or something else entirely. Limits to attention mean that individuals may respond differently to prices depending on their salience. Limits to computational capacity suggest that individuals may respond to misconstrued prices or imprecise rules of thumb about how prices operate.

Evidence of the importance of limited attention in influencing how individuals respond to environmental externalities is widespread. One area in which the effects of attention appear to be significant, for example, is residential energy use. While energy use in the home is more or less continuous, its cost is salient for most individuals only once a month, when the energy bill arrives. As a result, individuals can seem insensitive to energy prices when instead they may be inattentive to them.[4] A number of recent interventions have tested whether increasing the salience of energy prices by providing individuals with more real-time information about costs can affect behavior. Some evidence suggests that providing households with an energy meter that displays the real-time cost of consumption can reduce their energy use relative to that in households with standard meters.[5] There is preliminary evidence that even qualitative indicators of real-time energy prices provided to households can encourage conservation.[6] One review of this literature concludes that such improved price and usage feedback measures tend to reduce residential energy consumption by between 5 and 15 percent.[7] Following from results like those, there also is speculation that part of the improvement that individuals see in fuel economy when using hybrid cars is due to the real-time feedback that those cars give on fuel use.[8]

There also is some evidence for effects of limited computational capacity on such decisions. The price schedules for many activities with environmental consequences are complicated, and the relationship between costs and behavior can be opaque. As a result, individuals may simply have difficulty correctly understanding the cost structure of environmentally significant choices. For example, one recent study finds that individuals tend to make a computational mistake in interpreting the relationship between fuel economy when it is expressed as miles per gallon and the relative fuel costs of cars.[9] And there is qualitative evidence that individuals understand residential energy price schedules imprecisely.[10] In general, individual consumers appear to have only an imperfect understanding of the energy consumption or savings consequences of their behavior.[11] When consumers make choices based on a misconstrued understanding of price and cost, the outcomes of externalities become less clear.

Another set of factors that influence how externalities impact behavior derives from the fact that individuals have only bounded self-control. As a result, even when individuals perceive the correct private prices, they may form consumption plans with respect to those prices that they have difficulty executing. In particular, decisions to engage in many activities that have consequences for the environment have a nontrivial time dimension. Myopic individuals or individuals who are vulnerable to temptation or procrastination might be deterred from or enticed into taking actions that help or harm the environment in ways that interact with the effects of prices. For example, evidence from the way that consumers trade off the upfront costs of appliances with the energy costs of using them is consistent with impatience.[12] Another key element of environmentally sensitive decisions is the complicating role of channel factors. Individuals tend to make those choices that are relatively easy for them to make, which again may either attenuate or aggravate the effects of private prices distorted by the externality. The marginal costs of separating trash from recyclable materials are somewhat trivial, but all of us probably have thrown something recyclable in the trash at some point just because it was easier.

Finally, reference-dependence may also play a role in how individuals make decisions about energy and the environment. For example, there is evidence of status quo bias in the choice of energy suppliers when individuals are able to select among alternatives.[13] The result may be to blunt the price incentives that the ability to make such a selection confers.

The effects of imperfect optimization, bounded self-control, and reference-dependence are broadly consistent with emerging findings that individuals frequently fail to take environmentally protective actions even when they appear to be in their private interest.[14] For example, while compact fluorescent light (CFL) bulbs are generally cost saving relative to standard bulbs, few people buy them. Similarly, although many individuals would save money over time by selecting a more fuel-efficient car, they do not. And while such choices may simply reflect preferences for incandescent bulbs or fuel-inefficient cars, they are consistent with imperfect optimization and bounded self-control. These behavioral tendencies also are consistent with one recent study finding that large investments in energy efficiency in the United States could be achieved at a negative net cost—that they would result in private cost savings before even considering the environmental benefits.[15]

However, there is at least one potentially important set of countervailing factors that derives from features of other-regarding preferences and how they interact with environmentally significant choices. When individuals care about the welfare of others and their welfare is determined in part by how they are perceived by others, that can complicate the relationship between energy prices and behavior. While the fact that the prices of environmentally harmful behaviors are too low tends to encourage those behaviors, the net effect of the discrepancy is modified because of the way in which preferences are interdependent among individuals. Individuals may wish to make pro-environmental decisions out of a general tendency to act in pro-social ways. They may norm their behavior relative to that of others. And they may be sensitive to how others view their actions.

Mounting evidence shows the role of other-regarding preferences in shaping behaviors that affect the environment. One set of evidence comes from a series of studies of residential energy consumption that find that providing information to individuals about how their energy consumption compares with that of their neighbors can reduce consumption.[16] Another study found that simple appeals to social norms alone had a similar effect.[17] Framing behaviors in terms of social norms or expectations may promote environmentally conscious behavior even when there are no direct benefits to individuals. For example, one study finds that individuals can be encouraged to reuse towels in hotel rooms by indicating that that is what most other people do.[18] Consistent with the importance of other-regarding preferences, the effects of interventions to promote efficiency are sometimes found to be stronger for individuals possessing characteristics indicating pro-environmental preferences.[19] Finally, there also are some reasons to believe that individuals take into consideration how others view their choices in making decisions with environmental consequences. For example, one often hypothesized reason why the Prius sells relatively well compared with other, more conventionally styled hybrid cars is that its distinctive styling allows consumers to signal their pro-environmental behavior to others.[20] Consistent evidence from the field finds that individuals are more likely to respond to appeals to conserve energy when their response is made public.[21]

In sum, what we see in the case of environmental externalities is that how the conditions of the externality (some social costs associated with energy consumption are not reflected in the prices of energy that consumers face) translate into economic outcomes that determine the social welfare effect of the externality (overconsumption relative to the social optimum) depends on how those conditions interact with features of individual decisionmaking. While the forms of the interactions noted above were specific to the case of environmental externalities, the principle tends to be a general feature of externalities in the presence of behavioral decisionmakers. The effects of externalities on levels of economic activity—and thus on social welfare—depend on their interaction with behavioral tendencies.

Behavioral Economics and Externality Conditions

In addition to complicating the analysis of existing externalities like pollution and greenhouse gas emissions, behavioral tendencies also can create externality conditions or externality outcomes in situations where the standard analysis would consider no externality to exist. Because even when people face prices or other incentives that reflect social costs or benefits, or those costs appear to be internalized for other reasons, or there is no apparent effect on others, behavioral tendencies serve as a reason to revisit the standard conclusions. There are, broadly, two mechanisms by which behavioral tendencies might lead to externalities or externality-like outcomes. First, even when prices or incentives are such that consumers face private costs and benefits that should lead them to socially optimal levels of activity, they may engage in levels of activity above or below optimal levels because, for example, of errors of choice or failures of self-control. Where that affects the well-being of others, the social welfare results are tantamount to an externality. Second, new externalities can arise because behavioral tendencies admit new channels by which the actions of individuals might impact others. When individuals have, for example, bounded self-control or limited attention, actions of others that serve to erode their willpower or distract their attention impose external costs.

For understanding how behavioral tendencies can lead directly to externalities or to what amounts to an externality, we draw on examples from public health. Public health issues serve as good examples because they can highlight both mechanisms described above. On one hand, when individuals make errors with respect to decisions about their own health or display bounded self-control in adopting healthy behaviors, there can be external consequences for the health of other individuals. On the other hand, limits to computational capacity and self-control, along with other-regarding preferences, mean that the health of individuals depends on actions taken by others in ways that the standard model typically would not consider.

When prices and incentives are right, individuals should not engage in suboptimal levels of activities that affect other people, because the costs or benefits that those activities impose are built into the incentives that they face. But behavioral actors might make suboptimal choices anyway, due to either choice errors or failures of self-control. The result looks analytically similar to an externality—production or consumption levels are off their optimum, and others are affected. This is the other side of the same coin described in the case of environmental externalities, where behavioral tendencies mediate the response to the incorrect incentives created by an externality: those tendencies also mediate the response to correct incentives in the absence of an externality. So even when markets otherwise exist and are functioning properly, the economic outcomes may be the same as if an externality existed. The difference is that the breakdown is not operating through failure of the price system, but through failures of individual decisionmaking that happen to have social consequences.

For example, consider the potential for errors on the part even of individuals facing the proper incentives to affect the health of others. As described in more detail in box 4-2 in chapter 4, individuals often make imperfect decisions about health care. One typical finding is that individuals often fail to adhere to drug regimens.[22] In all but unusual cases, the private benefits for any individual to adhere to a medication regimen vastly outweigh the private costs and should lead the individual to consume in the socially optimal way. By essentially any calculation of private costs and benefits, it is worthwhile for individuals to take the full course of pills prescribed. There is no real market failure here; the cost of the marginal pill is zero. But individuals do fail to follow drug regimens, perhaps because they miscalculate or misperceive private costs and benefits or simply forget to take their pills even though they mean to do so. Their failures, however, have negative external consequences. Individuals may remain contagious carriers of disease, failure to take a full course of antibiotics might promote resistant strains of bacteria, and so on. Another example of such behavior is when individuals fail to seek necessary care. For example, behavioral tendencies might lead individuals to be less likely to be tested for certain conditions, which might contribute to the spread of disease.[23] In cases such as these, the government faces an externality problem that is not just complicated by behavioral tendencies but is entirely due to them.

An important, though admittedly special, case of this type of externality is an intergenerational externality that arises due to the behavioral tendencies of parents or caregivers.[24] Ordinarily we think of the welfare of their children as being internal to the welfare function of parents, so that parents will tend to provide optimal levels of care to their children. However, imperfectly optimizing caregivers will provide imperfect care, even when incentives are in fact aligned. Parents, in the long run, might want to have made particular investments in their children, but in the short run they might find themselves making inconsistent or imperfect choices. For example, parents may want to raise healthy kids, but find that today it is easier to go to McDonalds to eat than to cook. Because childhood outcomes are tied to parental choices, those outcomes also are linked to parental shortcomings. The self-control problems of parents with respect to, for example, food choices have external consequences for children. In that way, parents' behavioral tendencies might contribute to public health problems such as childhood obesity.[25]

Behavioral tendencies also can lead to new forms of externalities because they create new ways for people to be affected by the actions of others. Most obviously, other-regarding preferences can lead to new externalities. By definition, other-regarding preferences create a situation in which some aspect of an individual's welfare is in the choice set of other individuals, who may or may not consider that fact when making choices. Many of the interesting examples of these types of externalities are related to redistribution (see, for instance, the discussion of positional externalities in chapter 6, "Poverty and Inequality"). No less important in general, however, and more important for understanding topics related to traditional externalities, are externalities that arise due to the limitations highlighted by behavioral economics. When individuals have only limited attention or computational capacity, actions by others that distract their attention or complicate their choices impose external costs. Similarly, when individuals have only bounded self-control, actions by others that make it more difficult to exercise willpower impose external costs.

Consider, for example, the role of self-control and willpower in making healthy or unhealthy lifestyle choices. Healthy choices, such as going to the gym, quitting smoking, or abstaining from unhealthy foods, often require some measure of self-control, which behavioral economics often indicates individuals possess to only a limited degree.[26] The externality here arises because the behaviors of others can make it harder for individuals to exert self-control. When an individual's self-control is limited, actions by others that increase temptation impose an external burden on that individual: the person must exercise willpower to avoid doing something that he or she intended to abstain from or succumb to the temptation. For example, exposure to products like junk food, cigarettes, and alcohol impose a cost on individuals trying to avoid or limit their intake of such goods. Such costs are not priced to firms or individuals who expose others to those goods. For example, a variety of research finds that individuals consume more food when consumption is promoted by social cues, an effect consistent with the behavior of others having an eroding effect on willpower.[27] To the extent that such factors contribute to findings such as those that show network effects in obesity, such types of willpower externalities may be significant for social outcomes.[28]

Just as individuals have bounded self-control, they also have only limited attention and limited computational capacity to devote to choices related to decisions about health. As a result, actions by individuals that lead to the proliferation of choices or increase the complexity of choices impose an external cost on other individuals, while actions that make decisionmaking easier have external benefits. Complexity or attentional externalities like these are not important in the standard model, but they can be significant in a behavioral approach. For example, firms that seek consumer attention may impose costs on consumers by making them focus their attention on product features that may prevent them from making optimal choices.[29] For example, while food products might be required to carry labels that display nutritionally relevant information in some standardized way, firms and advertisers might be able to redirect the consumer's attention to other product features that are not relevant to their nutritional value.[30]

These examples from public health show how behavioral tendencies can lead directly to externality conditions or functionally equivalent conditions. Note that while we have used public health examples in this case (of behavioral tendencies creating externalities) and environmental externalities in the former case (of behavioral tendencies interacting with more conventional externalities), this distinction is for illustrative purposes only. The particular implications of behavioral economics for externalities in any given domain are unlikely to fit cleanly or exclusively into one category or the other. For example, the positive public health externalities that arise in the case of vaccinations are cause for the government to support and encourage vaccinations due to entirely traditional logic. But note how this problem is potentially complicated by features of individual decisionmaking, such as limited computational capacity or forms of reference-dependence, that may tend to further distort private decisions about vaccinations.[31] Conversely, there can be cases of behavioral externalities in environmental decisionmaking.

Finally, note that the externality framework developed by public finance may provide a useful way of thinking about inconsistent decisionmaking even when the consequences are primarily internal to the decisionmaker. Discussion of such cases—internalities—is given in box 5-1.

The Role of Government

Addressing externalities requires policymakers to resolve trade-offs about the relative social value of alternative courses of action. In particular, policy choices must reflect judgments about social welfare outcomes in alternative states of the world—for example, about the benefits of reducing carbon emissions through a corrective tax compared with the benefits of inaction or the costs of implementing a carbon reduction policy. Policy choices also express judgments on how to treat individuals.

In the standard analysis of externalities, very little judgment of this sort is required of policymakers. The social welfare implications of choosing alternative states of the world follow nearly directly from the identification of the problem. There is some private equilibrium, with one set of outcomes, and it is compared to achievable equilibria under policy alternatives. Absent government intervention,

Box 5-1. *Internalities*

The analysis of how externalities lead to social welfare costs and their implications for policy can be extended to provide a useful way of thinking about how decision-making errors or failures of self-control affect individual well-being and how policy might respond to them. This approach treats such errors or failures as leading to within-person externalities or internalities. The concept of an internality is defined with reference to a model of decisionmaking in which individuals have multiple, possibly conflicting preferences—such as short-run, myopic preferences and long-run, patient preferences. The actions of one of these selves—say, the failure of the short-run self to decide to save sufficiently for retirement—can have consequences for the long-run self. The effect is like an externality that is internal to the individual—an internality.[a]

The best-studied example of a decision that may involve an internality is smoking. Smoking can generate welfare costs not only because of the externalities associated with tobacco smoke but also because of an internality that may be associated with smoking: a myopic, misinformed, or addicted self might be imposing costs on the long-run self, the self that wants to quit smoking but that for one reason or another finds it difficult. The source of the inconsistency can be a result of time-inconsistent preferences, as with hyperbolic discounting, or a result of the physical and psychological properties of addiction.[b] Given a judgment about which self, if any, policy ought to favor, this approach identifies some scope for policy to improve welfare. Commonly, in the case of smoking, the judgment favors the long-run self, the self that wishes not to make a habit of smoking or wishes to quit.[c]

Given that diagnosis of an internality and a judgment regarding which self policymakers wish to favor, policy prescriptions for mitigating smoking can be designed and implemented. Here the usefulness of the analogy to externalities becomes clear: policy can draw on the menu of responses already formulated to address externalities to improve outcomes in the case of the internality. Much as a negative externality such as pollution can in principle be abated by the imposition of, for example, corrective taxes, so too can a negative internality such as smoking. In the case of internalities, such corrective taxes are frequently (and somewhat unfortunately) labeled sin taxes, and they can in principle improve welfare.[d] Available evidence suggests, for example, that taxes on cigarettes may in fact improve the welfare of some individuals by discouraging them from smoking.[e] Alternatively, this logic suggests a role for regulatory policy with respect to cigarettes and other tobacco products similar to regulation applied to externalities such as environmental externalities. Regulations that limit the availability of cigarettes to consumers or the ability of firms to advertise tobacco products may help individuals to exercise self-control and realize their long-run preferences.[f]

Smoking is just one example of an activity that can be thought of as generating an internality. Any decision whereby an individual seems to be choosing against the well-being of some conception of self due to difficulty in forming or expressing consistent preferences can be thought of in that way. For example, weight and obesity problems can involve self-control with respect to decisions about eating and exercising.[g] Such decisions need not necessarily involve addiction or even self-control problems—consumers make purchases that they may later regret due to, for example, the influence of other-regarding preferences or limited attention. Again, policy can respond to such internalities in ways that are analogous to its response to an externality. Subsidies to exercise or to relatively healthy foods—or taxes on unhealthy foods—might effectively address internalities associated with exercise and diet.[h] Consumer protection regulations such as the Federal Trade Commission's cooling-off rule, which provides individuals with the right to return some kinds of merchandise, might be a response to internalities with respect to consumer purchases.[i]

The concept of an internality offers a convenient framework for understanding the welfare costs of self-control failures and choice errors, the trade-offs to be weighed in considering interventions to address outcomes, and the design challenges in establishing and implementing policy responses. But that convenience should not obscure two limitations to this analysis. The first is that while labeling these outcomes internalities or within-person externalities highlights useful structural similarities to the case of externalities, the two cases are categorically different problems for policy. Externalities are a clear case of failure of the price system. Internalities do not by themselves represent a market failure. Internalities might be more properly likened to the problem of redistribution, in which the outcome of the market is, according to some criteria, suboptimal but not necessarily inefficient. That highlights the second limitation of internalities as a concept, which is that teasing out the policy implications of the conditions that they describe is inextricably tied up in an understanding of welfare economics from a behavioral perspective. What the concept of internalities captures might more descriptively be labeled simply as choice errors and failures of self-control. Policies intended to address these issues are in this sense an uneasy fit with public finance.

As a result, the appropriate place of internalities in the domain of public finance is not at all clear. Our approach, here and throughout the book, is to not take failures of self-control or errors of choice—internalities—by themselves as a separate topic of inquiry but to consider these features of decisionmaking as they interact with topics in public finance. We argue that choice errors and self-control failures

(continued)

Box 5-1 *(continued)*

such as those that arise in conjunction with cigarette smoking, while an important dimension of public policy broadly and public health policy specifically, are not necessarily brought into the field of public finance by virtue of labeling or modeling them as an internality. The concept of the internality is useful, but it is probably best applied not as a way of importing such policy problems into public finance, but as a way of exporting some of the insights from public finance to the analysis of those policy problems.

a. R. J. Herrnstein and others, "Utility Maximization and Melioration: Internalities in Individual Choice," *Journal of Behavioral Decision Making,* vol. 6, no. 3 (1993), pp. 149–85.

b. Jonathan Gruber and Botond Koszegi, "Is Addiction 'Rational'? Theory and Evidence," *Quarterly Journal of Economics,* vol. 116, no. 4 (2001), pp. 1261–1303; B. Douglas Bernheim and Antonio Rangel, "Addiction and Cue-Triggered Decision Processes," *American Economic Review,* vol. 94, no. 5 (December 2004), pp. 1558–90.

c. B. Douglas Bernheim and Antonio Rangel, "Behavioral Public Economics: Welfare and Policy Analysis with Fallible Decision-Makers," in *Behavioral Economics and Its Applications,* edited by Peter Diamond and Hannu Vartiainen (Princeton University Press, 2007), pp. 7–77.

d. Ted O'Donoghue and Matthew Rabin, "Studying Optimal Paternalism, Illustrated by a Model of Sin Taxes,*" American Economic Review,* vol. 93, no. 2 (May 2003), pp. 186–91; Jonathan Gruber and Botond Koszegi, "Tax Incidence When Individuals Are Time-Inconsistent: The Case of Cigarette Excise Taxes," *Journal of Public Economics,* vol. 88, no. 9–10 (2004), pp. 1959–87; Ted O'Donoghue and Matthew Rabin, "Optimal Sin Taxes," *Journal of Public Economics,* vol. 90, no. 10–11 (2006), pp. 1825–49.

e. Jonathan H. Gruber and Sendhil Mullainathan, "Do Cigarette Taxes Make Smokers Happier?" *Advances in Economic Analysis and Policy,* vol. 5, no. 1 (2005).

f. John Beshears and others, "Early Decisions: A Regulatory Framework," *Swedish Economic Policy Review,* vol. 12, no. 2 (2005), pp. 41–60; B. Douglas Bernheim and Antonio Rangel, "From Neuroscience to Public Policy: A New Economic View of Addiction," *Swedish Economic Policy Review,* vol. 12, no. 2 (2005), pp. 99–144; Joni Hersch, "Smoking Restrictions as a Self-Control Mechanism," *Journal of Risk and Uncertainty,* vol. 31, no. 1 (July 2005), pp. 5–21.

g. Christopher J. Ruhm, "Understanding Overeating and Obesity," Working Paper 16149 (Cambridge, Mass.: National Bureau of Economic Research, July 2010).

h. Gary Charness and Uri Gneezy, "Incentives to Exercise," *Econometrica,* vol. 77, no. 3 (2009), pp. 909–31; Leonard H. Epstein and others, "The Influence of Taxes and Subsidies on Energy Purchased in an Experimental Purchasing Study," *Psychological Science,* vol. 21, no. 3 (2010), pp. 406–14; Jason P. Block and others, "Point-of-Purchase Price and Education Intervention to Reduce Consumption of Sugary Soft Drinks," *American Journal of Public Health,* vol. 100, no. 8 (2010), pp. 1427–33.

i. Colin Camerer and others, "Regulation for Conservatives: Behavioral Economics and the Case for 'Asymmetric Paternalism,'" *University of Pennsylvania Law Review,* vol. 151, no. 3 (2003), pp. 1211–54.

for example, in the case of carbon emissions, individuals respond purely to private costs. Applying some intervention, such as a carbon tax, leads individuals to respond to a new set of incentives. In addressing negative externalities through price mechanisms, even the particular mechanisms creating those incentives are assumed to be relatively unimportant. A carbon tax and a cap-and-trade scheme for carbon emissions are roughly equivalent in terms of social welfare results under some standard assumptions. When there are important judgments to be made, they often have to do with the distributional implications of policies. For example, in the case of climate change, there is an important judgment regarding how to trade off the costs of carbon abatement to current generations against its benefits to future generations.

Viewing these issues through a behavioral lens complicates them substantially. It changes both how we understand the trade-offs to weigh in choosing among policy alternatives, and it adds new trade-offs to the mix by requiring in some cases judgments on how to weigh the interests of possibly conflicting selves. With respect to resolving trade-offs across policy alternatives, the presence of behavioral tendencies makes the judgments less than straightforward. As discussed above, the equilibrium assumed by the standard model to obtain in the absence of government intervention may be altered by individuals acting in error or in pro-social ways. And the form of policy may matter for social welfare in new ways, especially with respect to distributional consequences. Moreover, the possibility of behavioral tendencies means that policy must sometimes take a position on the presence and treatment of those tendencies directly. The determination of whether and how to tackle an issue like willpower externalities in the consumption of unhealthy foods must reflect some judgment about when behaviors reflect preferences and when they are, in fact, failures of self-control—and if they are failures of self-control, how to weigh the welfare of the short-run self against that of the long-run self.

Trade-Offs across Policy Alternatives

Evaluating the relative social welfare implications of policies responding to externalities is complicated by behavioral tendencies. What appears relatively mechanical in the standard analysis now involves trade-offs. Judgments have to be made about how to treat the social welfare implications of the ways in which behavioral tendencies interact with both an externality itself and any intervention.

In general, policy responses change the way that behavioral tendencies interact with the incentives created by an externality, making the effect of implementing the policy on social welfare less straightforward. Take the case of environmental externalities. If individuals are, say, ignoring the energy costs of automobiles in making purchase decisions in the absence of a carbon tax, the implementation of such a tax could change not just the incentives that individuals face but also their propensity to make the error. A simple projection of what the impacts of such a tax would be on fuel consumption and social welfare based on the responsiveness of individuals to the price of gas alone thus leads policymakers to misstate that counterfactual.

The most important way that behavioral tendencies interact with externalities is probably that extrinsic incentives—in the form of taxes and fees—can sometimes crowd out or weaken intrinsic incentives, such as the incentive to adhere to norms.[32] As a result, the extent to which individuals voluntarily internalize an externality might be weakened by policy intervention, creating a trade-off for policy. Pro-social behavior of that sort appears to be susceptible to crowding out.[33] There is some evidence, for example, that individuals might be less willing to donate blood when offered a monetary incentive to do so.[34] Putting a price on a behavior can even under some circumstances appear to license it.[35] In the context of environmental externalities, a social norm that leads individuals to engage in pro-environmental behaviors might be weakened—or even overturned for some—by the imposition of taxes. Absent a carbon tax, individuals might feel social pressure to buy a car with a hybrid engine, but once a carbon tax is in place, some individuals might feel free to buy a gas-guzzler again, because by paying the tax, they feel that they have met their social obligation. Naïve comparisons of policy alternatives that do not allow for this type of crowding out are likely to draw inaccurate conclusions about social welfare.

Trade-Offs within and across Individuals

Policy responses to externalities also have to reflect judgments about how to make trade-offs both across individuals and across possibly conflicting preferences within individuals. Behavioral tendencies affect some of the terms of the former, by changing some of the distributional implications of alternative policies. And it creates the latter set of trade-offs entirely.

Even in the standard analysis, policy responses to externalities have to consider their possible distributional consequences. For example, a carbon tax would affect different segments of the population in different ways, and policy has to reflect judgments about how to weigh the interests of the different groups. A behavioral approach does not in general change this feature of policy responses to externalities, but it does add one important modification. An important class of policy responses to externalities, discussed in greater detail below, is the assignment of property rights. While such policies have distributional effects in any event, those effects are likely to be substantially different in the face of reference-dependent preferences, which suggests that valuation of such rights is not independent of assignment.[36] Policies that involve the creation or assignment of rights thus have to reflect a judgment about how to treat those effects.

Behavioral tendencies create an entirely new set of judgments that externality policy must reflect to the extent that those tendencies allow for the possibility that individuals exhibit inconsistent preferences that interact in some ways with externalities. Those judgments have to do with assessing the potential role of choice errors and self-control failures in creating externalities or leading to externality conditions. In particular, policy reflects judgments about whether choices reflect errors or preferences or whether to favor the short-run self or the long-run self. For example, a policy response to an intergenerational externality necessarily reflects some judgment about whether that externality indicates an error or failure on the part of the parent or indicates the parent's true preferences. This is true even in the case of traditional externalities. Corrective policies with respect to energy consumption, for example, embed some judgment about whether, for example, individuals are making errors in trading off operating costs in making automobile purchase decisions.

Correcting Externalities

The standard policy responses to externalities draw on available policy levers to generate an outcome closer to the social optimum than is achieved in the unregulated market. Those responses can be collected into three broad categories: manipulations of the costs and benefits associated with an activity generating an externality—for example, corrective taxes and subsidies—that direct agents toward consuming and producing socially optimal quantities; regulations and mandates directing consumption and production toward optimal levels; and correction of the underlying market failures, such as by assigning property rights or finding legal or technological ways to get agents to internalize the externalities.

Behavioral economics changes the nature and qualifies the operation of policies in each category. Encouraging or discouraging behavior may not be a simple matter of changing prices; incentives also have to be changed in a way that is salient to agents with limited attention, clear to agents with limited computational capacity, and so on. The same limitations create new opportunities to use regulation to ameliorate externalities in relatively efficient ways. And nonstandard preferences may provide new ways to correct the underlying market failure that externalities represent.

PRICES AND INCENTIVES

Perhaps the most straightforward policy response to the presence of an externality is to impose corrective taxes, or some variant of corrective taxes, in order to move outcomes toward the social optimum. This approach treats the policy problem as essentially one of solving pricing errors. In the case of environmental externalities, for example, polluting or emitting carbon is viewed as being too cheap, in that the private cost does not reflect the social cost. Policy interventions that make private costs more reflective of social costs solve that problem. They can do so by means of price corrections, taxing goods that create negative externalities and subsidizing goods that create positive externalities so that consumption and production arrive at socially optimal levels.[37] While there are various specific mechanisms for establishing those prices—taxes, effluent fees, tradable permits, and so on—in this framework they operate in broadly similar ways.

A behavioral approach suggests that the ability of policy to correct externalities through price adjustments is less straightforward. As described above, standard assumptions about how individuals perceive and respond to price signals are unlikely to hold. Individuals make choice errors, fail to exhibit self-control, and hold nonstandard preferences, all of which serve to mediate the impact of price signals on behavior. That creates both a challenge and an opportunity for price- and incentive-based policy responses to externalities. On one hand, standard price adjustments are no longer likely to be sufficient to generate the desired behavioral response. On the other hand, price levers are no longer the only tools available to policymakers—they can employ nonprice levers that appeal directly to the psychology of individuals.

The limits of prices in correcting externalities follow directly from the same behavioral tendencies that interact with the externality in the first place. In general, when agents are imperfect optimizers, prices cannot be assumed to be effective. Policy must be designed specifically to account for how individuals construe and respond to prices. Such a design must have at least two dimensions. First, price incentives interact with how individuals perceive and understand them. A corrective tax on gasoline that individuals do not perceive or understand will not be effective in reducing carbon emissions. Second, in order to be effective, price incentives may have to be of a magnitude or structure capable of correcting both the market failure and the decisionmaking failure. For example, in order to be effective, a tax on cigarettes may have to be set in a way that both corrects for any externalities that their consumption produces and overcomes the effects of myopia and temptation.

One design principle that follows from these observations is that price correction mechanisms that are easily perceived and understood by individuals are more likely to generate the desired behavioral response. That principle can be put into practice in part by making taxes more salient to consumers. For example, studies find that people do not always perceive sales taxes when posted prices do not reflect those taxes.[38] So for consumption taxes to serve as effective corrective taxes, they may have to be made visible to the consumer in the price. That may argue in favor of regulations that require prices to be posted inclusive of taxes (as is typically the case with gasoline).

Corrective taxes also are more likely to generate the desired response when the underlying price schedule is transparent to consumers. For example, a carbon tax might be highly effective at reducing consumption of gasoline because gas prices are highly salient—consumers are all but forced to stand at the pump, watching the price ring up.[39] On the other hand, even an otherwise salient carbon tax may be a blunt instrument for encouraging conservation in residential energy, where price schedules are more complex, less transparent, and not as obviously connected to consumer behavior. Innovations in the way that residential energy use and pricing is conveyed to individuals may be required for prices to be an effective lever to promote conservation. For example, subsidizing the adoption of new smart meter technologies, which convey information about energy cost and use more directly to consumers, is a logical extension of these ideas.

Another design implication that follows from the limitations of prices as levers is that levers may be more effective when designed to operate on firms rather than consumers. For energy policy, that raises the question of whether policies should target, say, extraction and generation firms or consumers of their products.[40] While there are practical considerations in any event, standard theory generally suggests that policies within this class lead individuals and firms to respond in ways that make such policies broadly equivalent—it suggests, for example, that all other things being equal, a cap-and-trade policy that directly affects firms will have largely the same effects as a tax faced directly by consumers. Behavioral tendencies on the part of consumers, however, provide an opportunity for policies directed toward consumers to fail—consumers may fail to even notice such a tax. Conversely, policies that operate on firms tend to lead to cost increases that are harder to ignore.

Limitations on their effectiveness aside, there is a separate design implication of a behavioral approach to the use of price corrections to address externalities, which is that prices may have to simultaneously correct both the market failure and the decisionmaking failure in order to achieve the social optimum. If part of the problem with, for example, people consuming too much gasoline is that individuals are making an error about the future marginal costs of gas relative to the upfront costs of fuel efficiency in cars, then a tax that merely sets private costs of a gallon of gasoline equal to the social costs might not be sufficient to achieve the desired level of reduction in consumption. Note that even when the tax is salient in the price of gasoline, this problem remains.

So in some cases corrective taxes may need to double up on the end user, holding everything else constant. It might in this example be efficient to have a final tax rate that pushes prices well above social costs in order to generate socially optimal outcomes. The potential need for policies that operate on both margins is perhaps most evident in the case of behavioral externalities arising due to errors on the part of individuals that lead them to consume inefficiently low levels of health care that have implications for public health. Here, policies such as free care or even negative copayments that might be worthwhile for society are motivated by the behavioral error alone.

If behavioral tendencies make getting prices right more difficult, they also create other levers for affecting incentives and behavior. The behavioral tendencies that individuals exhibit may mean that policy can structure choices in order to encourage conservation even without changing financial incentives. For example, as discussed above, interventions to clarify the relationship of residential energy use and costs to consumers can lead to conservation even without changes in prices.[41] Policy also can set choice architecture to affect desired outcomes—for example, to favor energy conservation. For example, in areas where households can choose among alternative energy providers, defaults could be set in favor of green energy suppliers. Behavioral levers can even be activated by prices. For example, the striking effectiveness of a nominal per bag tax in the District of Columbia at discouraging the use of plastic shopping bags is at least consistent with the possibility that the tax itself was instrumental in changing social norms.[42]

An especially effective behavioral lever appears to be social influence, operating through other-regarding preferences.[43] For example, studies find that simply providing households with information on how their residential energy use compares with that of their neighbors can lead to significant decreases in consumption.[44] In this way, policy can be set to activate social norms for conservation. Note that we might prefer nonprice levers even when price manipulations are available and effective because nonprice levers in general are cheaper. Optimal policy is likely to be some mix of price and nonprice levers.

Note that an important limitation on the use of behavioral levers is the potential ability of firms to undo them. For example, while effective in pilot studies, a policy to reduce residential energy use by providing information about what neighbors use is effective only to the extent that firms distributing energy do not have incentives to take countervailing actions. If they do, the firms will have the last word in influencing consumers, and they might set their marketing or sales techniques to offset the effects of such messaging. What might work better, again, is to focus policy not on consumers but on the firms. For example, if policy worked to set the pricing structure for such firms so that they had incentives to reinforce behavioral levers—or even develop their own—such as by decoupling profits from quantities sold, they might instead harness their marketing capabilities to steer consumers toward energy efficiency rather than fight it.[45]

REGULATION

Another approach to correcting externalities such as environmental externalities is through regulation. Regulation usually is disfavored in standard economic models relative to market-based solutions, for a variety of reasons. Regulation imposes high information requirements on policymakers, and it can have high administrative and compliance costs for producers. Most important, regulation can be an inefficient way to reduce environmental harm because it does not take advantage of price mechanisms to ensure that reductions in actions creating externalities are undertaken where those reductions are least costly.

One consequence of the presence of behavioral tendencies is that, under certain circumstances, the case for regulation is rehabilitated somewhat. That is due in part to the results discussed above: price mechanism solutions do not look so straightforward from a behavioral perspective. Simply regulating certain outcomes can avoid the need to rely on individuals to respond to price corrections in desired ways. When externalities are due to or exacerbated by behavioral tendencies, regulations can have substantial impacts without having severe consequences for economic efficiency.

Consider again the case of environmental externalities and energy conservation. As noted above, some behavioral tendencies seem to have the effect of pushing individuals toward harmful environmental outcomes even when conservation is in their private interest. So, for example, use of CFL bulbs often is in the private interest of individuals, but they fail to buy them, and fuel-efficient cars that pass cost-benefit tests still may be passed over. Getting corrective prices to work in such cases can be difficult. The alternative is simply to regulate desired outcomes. Regulations mandating efficiency standards for light bulbs that incandescent bulbs cannot meet, for example, might be more effective in promoting use of CFL bulbs than other means, and they may not even be that harmful to consumers. To take another example, the fact that raising corporate average fuel economy (CAFE) standards is calculated to be net cost saving due to their impact on private expenditures on fuel alone, even before considering their social benefits, is at least consistent with this view.[46]

For other regulations, such as disclosure, a behavioral approach indicates both challenges and opportunities. On one hand, programs such as Energy Star use labels to reduce some of the computational complexities of choosing energy-efficient appliances, and to that extent, they may be effective in reducing energy use. On the other hand, such policies have to contend with and address behavioral tendencies on their own terms. For example, requiring the posting of fuel efficiency of cars in terms of miles per gallon may be rendered ineffective by the difficulties that individuals have in translating such information into fuel costs. Moreover, it might be that getting people to focus on one set of things can lead them to ignore other things.[47] So, for example, focusing attention on the relative efficiency costs of appliances might cause individuals to pay less attention to, say, the source of the energy used to power such appliances. In general, the lesson from behavioral economics is that disclosure does not necessarily lead to understanding when the recipients of the disclosure are imperfect optimizers.

Addressing Underlying Failures

One approach to correcting externalities is to correct the conditions that led to the externality. For example, in the case of environmental externalities the underlying market failure often is due to the failure to completely specify property rights. One possible way to address that failure is to assign property rights to the resource in question. Doing so can lead interested parties to internalize the externalities, allow for bargaining, or create markets that lead to efficient levels of pollution.

A behavioral framework creates both challenges and opportunities for addressing externalities in this way. In the case of ordinary externalities, such as environmental externalities, behavioral tendencies may lead individuals to act as though they have internalized the externality even in the absence of any actual change in incentives or property rights. When behavioral failures are the source of the externality, such as willpower externalities, policy can seek to address the decisionmaking failure directly. On the other hand, reference-dependent preferences might cause bargaining solutions to externalities to fail.

In the case of environmental externalities, behavioral tendencies, in particular other-regarding preferences, suggest the possibility of encouraging individuals to internalize externalities to some extent through voluntary appeals. That is, some policy response will occur if people are just asked in a particular way. The evidence suggests that people seem to internalize more than the standard model would predict and that this tendency can be activated through messaging. For example, there is some evidence that public campaigns asking individuals to reduce their energy consumption can be effective.[48] As a result, there may be opportunities for encouraging voluntary solutions as opposed to simply charging, taxing, and fining. Public policy might consider such appeals and coordination efforts as alternative means of internalizing and correcting externalities. Any such efforts are unlikely to be a complete solution to environmental externalities by themselves, but they could be part of an effective portfolio of policy responses. Finally, policy must be cognizant of the fact that extrinsic incentives may crowd out intrinsic incentives; price corrections therefore should be designed to minimize crowding out.

In the case of behavioral externalities, the underlying conditions that lead to the externality are not market failures but failures of decisionmaking. Just as policy can attempt to address the market failures that lead directly to environmental externalities, here policy can attempt to correct decisionmaking conditions directly. For example, policy efforts to simplify decisionmaking problems for parents may reduce intergenerational externalities. Similarly, policies that provide commitment devices directly to individuals might serve to reduce the incidence of willpower externalities.

Finally, the tendency of individuals to hold reference-dependent preferences complicates some forms of policy interventions. One traditional set of policy responses to the problem of externalities is to assign property rights to one of the involved parties, thereby creating a market for the resource in question and resolving the externality. The Coase theorem specifies that, setting aside transactions costs, the efficiency of this type of solution does not depend on which party the property rights are assigned to.[49] However, reference-dependent preferences can lead individuals to have higher willingness-to-accept valuations than willingness-to-pay valuations of resources.[50] As a result, Coasian solutions to externalities have welfare consequences that may depend on assignment or may fail outright.

Public Goods

Public goods are a special case of externalities in which an individual's utility is determined in part by the aggregated actions of others. The classic example of a public good is public safety, such as that provided at the federal level by national defense: what any individual experiences in terms of increased safety (or whatever else) from national defense activities is a function of the aggregate total of defense provided. It is an externality because that total is determined by the sum total of everyone's contributions to national defense, of which any individual can choose only his or her own contribution. Another example of a public good is the knowledge generated by research and development—absent legal barriers like patents and copyrights, new discoveries in general benefit society at large. Public goods frequently are defined in terms of the qualities that ensure that they enter utility functions in this way: they are nonrival (they can be consumed by multiple individuals simultaneously) and nonexcludable (one cannot prevent people who have not paid for the good from accessing it).

Psychology and the Public Goods Problem

The standard analysis of public goods starts from the observation that in the absence of government intervention, private equilibria will underprovide public goods. That follows in part from the assumption that individuals are purely self-interested. While society would be better off with a greater aggregate level of provision, each individual also has an incentive to free ride. The result is a private equilibrium in which the public good is provided in quantities below the social optimum. The government can in principle improve the unregulated outcome by acting to move the level of the public good provided closer to the optimal level.

Because, as with externalities in general, the way in which public goods arise and translate into welfare losses depends on how individuals form preferences and make choices, deviations from narrow self-interest can change the nature or the magnitude of the problem posed by public goods for the economy. On one hand, behavioral tendencies might operate to create or undermine the conditions that lead to a public goods problem. For example, if preferences are nonstandard, individuals' utility may contain new arguments that have the properties of a public good. On the other hand, behavioral tendencies mediate the way in which the conditions that define a public good lead to welfare losses. For example, if individuals hold other-regarding preferences, they may voluntarily contribute to the provision of public goods to a greater extent than the standard model predicts.

Behavioral externalities could in principle affect the conditions that make externalities public goods—that is, the extent to which goods are rival or excludable. In practice, however, those conditions usually are determined by technological features of goods that are unlikely to have a strong behavioral component. Consumption by others—rivalry—is unlikely to be affected by behavioral factors. Excludability can be affected by behavioral factors, but that also is unlikely in general. Still, in special cases, behavioral features of decisionmaking and preferences could allow for new types of public goods, in much the same way that they can lead to externalities. The most prominent example of such an outcome is when other-regarding preferences take the form of individuals caring about the overall distribution of income. In that case, other-regarding preferences lead the income distribution to be a public good.[51] We discuss that case more fully in chapter 6, "Poverty and Inequality."

More commonly, behavioral tendencies interact with existing conditions that lead to a public goods problem to change the implications for welfare outcomes. Of particular importance for public goods is the way that other-regarding preferences might affect the private provision of public goods. In the standard model, individuals privately provide public goods to some extent, but at suboptimal levels.[52] With other-regarding preferences, individuals might voluntarily contribute to public goods at greater levels.[53] Revisiting the examples of public goods above, individuals might voluntarily contribute toward public goods such as public safety measures because of either their direct concern for the well-being of others or their susceptibility to social pressures not to free ride. Or they might engage in research and development activities without expecting to capture the full economic returns to doing so to the extent that they value other benefits, such as how the activity contributes to their identity or to how they are viewed by others. To the extent that such forces lead individuals to voluntarily contribute to public goods at greater levels than would be predicted by the standard model, the problem of public goods, in terms of social welfare, will be mitigated and the scope for government intervention may be reduced accordingly.

Evidence that individuals seem more willing to contribute to public goods voluntarily than the standard model would predict comes from both the lab and the field. Much of the direct evidence comes from laboratory experiments. Decades of laboratory experiments consistently find that when individuals play public goods games, the levels of contributions to public goods are relatively high.[54] The evidence is consistent with individuals having other-regarding preferences of some form that lead them to place a higher value on contributions than assumptions of narrow self-interest would suggest, although questions regarding the particular form of their preferences or the mechanism by which their preferences lead to public goods contributions are less settled. There is evidence that contributions are driven both by preferences directly for making the contribution as well as by preferences over the outcomes of others.[55] There also is some evidence that preferences for fairness and cooperation play a role in stimulating contributions.[56]

Evidence from the field is generally consistent with the hypothesis that individuals tend to contribute more to public goods than standard models would generally predict. For example, private contributions to public goods such as public radio stations and public schools are not explained well by the standard analysis.[57] To the extent that charities provide public goods, the extent of charitable contributions is at least circumstantial evidence that a model of pure self-interest does not match real-world behavior.[58] Similarly, observed relatively high levels of tax compliance are consistent with nonstandard preferences promoting voluntary contributions to the public goods financed by taxes.[59]

Trade-Offs Facing Policymakers

Solving the public goods problem requires policymakers to make judgments about the relative social value of alternative levels of government involvement to secure the provision of public goods. The provision of public goods faces important trade-offs along at least two dimensions. First, the public provision of public goods may tend to crowd out the private provision of public goods. Second, the provision of public goods reflects judgments about the value of public goods to individuals, which determines the optimal level of provision.

A behavioral approach changes the terms and nature of those trade-offs. It changes how we understand the trade-off between public and private provision because it allows for preferences that change the way in which private provision responds to public provision. It also has the potential to inform judgments about valuation of public goods.

The primary trade-off that society and policymakers must weigh in setting public goods policy is how the public provision of public goods can crowd out the private provision of public goods. Because how individuals respond to public policy in making private contributions to public goods is a matter of choice and preference, behavioral tendencies can modify the terms of the trade-off. In the standard model, with self-interested individuals, the crowding out can be substantial and under some conditions complete.[60] The other-regarding preferences that lead individuals to contribute voluntarily to public goods might counterbalance it, depending on the particular form they take.[61] Evidence from experiments typically finds incomplete crowding out, consistent with participants holding nonstandard preferences.[62] Empirical evidence on crowding out, which typically finds that public policies crowd out private donations only incompletely, also is consistent with a behavioral approach.[63]

In addition to mediating the usual mechanisms by which public provision can crowd out the private provision of public goods, behavioral economics adds a new channel in the form of motivational crowding out. Findings from psychological studies suggest that extrinsic motivations can crowd out intrinsic motivations rather than add to them. There is some evidence that policies that encourage private contributions to public goods by providing financial incentives to make such contributions might have the effect of weakening any intrinsic motivation that may have served to encourage contributions. One experiment, for example, found evidence that monetary incentives crowded out intrinsic incentives to contribute to charities by reducing the benefit that contributing offered in terms of how individuals are viewed by others.[64] In another study, individuals reported that they were less willing to make sacrifices to accommodate the location of a public good when offered monetary compensation.[65]

Finally, public policy with respect to public goods must reflect judgment calls about the level of public provision that is optimal, because in general it is difficult to create a practical mechanism for revealing preferences related to public goods. Those judgments are likely to be complicated in some ways by a behavioral approach. Allowing that individuals hold nonstandard preferences could alter what optimal levels might be or how costs might be distributed.

Providing Public Goods

The standard policy response to the public goods problem is for the government either to provide the good directly or to create conditions under which others will supply them; in principle, public policy can thereby secure optimal levels of public goods.[66] There are a variety of possible approaches. The government might provide for public safety by providing for it directly, such as through national defense or law enforcement expenditures. Note that even so, government provision is not necessarily government production: for example, in the case of national defense, the government both operates programs directly, such as by fielding an army, and contracts with private providers, such as for the manufacture of weapons systems. The government also might work to create the conditions necessary for others to provide public goods; for example, governments may give groups or entities the right to enforce exclusivity, such as with patent and copyright protection for individuals who engage in research and development. Finally, the government can provide incentives to individuals or groups to increase the purely voluntary provision of public goods. The deductibility of charitable contributions from income taxes can be viewed, in part, as such a policy.

Behavioral economics does not do much to change the nature of government provision, which does not depend substantially on individual decisionmaking. But it does speak to the set of conditions under which the government might elicit the provision of public goods by others. On one hand, it suggests that policy can foster conditions under which individuals will provide public goods on a voluntary basis; on the other, it can inform the financial and nonfinancial incentives established to encourage individuals to contribute to public goods.

That individuals appear willing to make voluntary contributions to public goods in excess of what the standard model predicts is well established in the literature. Going beyond the mere sign effect, in principle such research could inform the shape of policy to ensure that voluntary contributions are not discouraged—for example, by suggesting conditions under which voluntary contributions are more or less likely, conditions that policy might seek to promote. One way policy might do that is to take note of when and how public provision is more or less likely to interact with other-regarding preferences to lead to crowding out of private contributions. For example, there is some evidence from experimental results that crowding out is more severe when the link between taxation and the public provision of public goods is more salient.[67] Such evidence might militate against funding public goods with dedicated taxes or levies and favor funding those goods out of general revenue. Overall, governments might seek to provide public goods in ways that somehow complement private efforts rather than substitute for them.

Behavioral economics also may inform government policy that establishes financial and nonfinancial incentives to encourage private contributions to public goods. For example, the tax deduction for charitable contributions in part serves to draw in private contributions, and charitable contributions are sensitive to the generosity of that subsidy.[68] Behavioral economics suggests that how individuals respond to such subsidies depends on how the subsidies are perceived in addition to the level of subsidy. For example, matches have been found to be more effective than rebates at encouraging contributions, possibly due to the increased salience of a match or to the lower computational requirements; that finding might have implications for the way that tax preferences for charitable contributions are structured.[69] Even with matches, responses can be unexpected—for example, they may be highly nonlinear.[70] Finally, behavioral tendencies point to other levers that might be used to encourage private contributions to public goods. For example, behavioral tendencies may help to explain the effectiveness of lotteries in encouraging contributions.[71] Similarly, they may explain findings showing that the social context of giving can affect contribution levels.[72]

Finally, note that in seeking to promote the private provision of public goods, the government is presented not only with new opportunities due to behavioral tendencies but also with new challenges. In particular, behavioral tendencies might lead to problems with the market for private provision. For example, the market for soliciting private contributions might easily become congested as private and public organizations compete for the limited attention of contributors. Similarly, if individuals make contributions based on preferences for contributing, rather than preferences over outcomes, as some of the evidence described above suggests, that will diminish any tendency that this market might have toward identifying effective providers. Finally, if people have preferences over the mix of public goods provided by society, the mix itself will have public good qualities and the government might be uniquely well suited to take on a coordinating role. These factors point to some advantages to public provision even when private contributions are possible.

Education

A policy topic that combines elements of both externalities and public goods, with special importance for both the economy and society at large, is education. In the United States, the government at various levels both provides for and produces free primary and secondary education. Tertiary education, while not free, is heavily subsidized both through loan and grant programs as well as through public universities and community colleges. Government involvement is justified in part because education generates positive externalities.[73] Education also has some of the properties of an impure public good. Due in part to those factors, private provision of education would likely be below the socially optimal level.

That said, the policy problem surrounding education is multidimensional and complex, and not all of its aspects have important behavioral dimensions or are topics of study for public finance. However, many elements of education policy do intersect with both the psychology of decisionmaking and the analysis of how relevant markets may fail to operate efficiently or desirably. In particular, students and parents face a number of decisions regarding how to navigate an educational career, and those decisions interact not only with the policy problems but also with the policy design challenges inherent in education. Here we highlight two decisions about education for which the effect of behavioral tendencies is likely to be of particular significance: those about the amount of education to obtain and those about the institution at which to obtain it.

Incentives and Attainment

A primary problem that education policy must solve from the perspective of traditional public finance is that in the private equilibrium, levels of educational attainment will be too low relative to social tastes due to the positive external benefits that derive from education. The standard approach is to focus on the cost side of the ledger, providing either free or heavily subsidized educational opportunities in order to encourage attainment. From the standard perspective, giving students and their families incentives to attain an education is not foremost, and for good reason: the private returns to education are generally found to be substantial.[74] If policy can provide adequate educational opportunities at little or no direct cost, individuals should have strong private incentives to take advantage of those opportunities. Yet despite access to education and strong private incentives, approximately one-quarter of American students fail to complete high school,[75] and college completion rates also have been falling in recent years.[76] The results are something of a puzzle from the standard perspective.

Those results are consistent, however, with students and parents exhibiting behavioral tendencies, such as imperfect optimization or bounded self-control. Those tendencies may interact with the externality itself to further depress private educational choices below socially optimal levels. For example, parents and students alike may find it difficult to understand the costs and benefits associated with the choices that they face. Moreover, students in particular may have time-inconsistent preferences. The costs of staying in school are immediate and salient, while the benefits accrue only long into the future. For individuals with bounded self-control, the temptation to leave school may be difficult to resist. Evidence that policies such as compulsory schooling laws both increase educational attainment and in doing so generally lead individuals to be better off is consistent with individuals making behavioral errors.[77] Because of the externalities to educational attainment, the failure of individuals to complete their education has consequences for social welfare.

As in the case of environmental externalities, effective policy design for education might have to address behavioral tendencies directly or address them in addition to the externality. One particularly promising avenue in this regard is to provide students and parents with more immediate incentives for students to achieve academically. Providing short-run, salient incentives might work around the tendency of time-inconsistent or imperfectly optimizing individuals to place too little weight on the long-run benefits of education. There is some evidence from other contexts—other countries and noneducational programs—that providing students or their parents with direct incentives can be effective.[78] Current experiments with conditional cash transfers as incentives for educational attainment in several city school districts in the United States are especially noteworthy. One study finds that incentives to increase high school achievement in New York City led to significant improvements, but only for students who entered high school academically prepared.[79] Another study finds evidence from experiments in several cities suggesting that incentives for specific activities, such as reading books, can be effective in increasing educational achievement, while incentives for educational outcomes, such as test performance, are largely ineffective.[80] Both sets of results are broadly consistent with a behavioral perspective on educational incentives and achievement. Note finally that concerns that the possibility that extrinsic incentives might crowd out intrinsic motivations to learn and achieve are heightened in the context of education.[81] Policies to promote educational attainment through direct incentives must therefore be carefully constructed to test for and avoid such an effect.

Related evidence and an opportunity for policy design come from studies on the college application process, financial aid, and college attendance. Here again, where the standard model suggests that individuals understand and respond optimally to the benefits associated with applying to college and for financial aid, a behavioral approach suggests that individuals may have difficulty engaging in what can be a complex process in an optimal fashion. For example, evidence that marginal changes that make it easier to apply to an additional college can materially affect where students attend college is consistent with the view that individuals optimize in college application and selection in only some approximate sense.[82] One result is that policies to subsidize and encourage college attendance may have to attend to behavioral tendencies in order to be effective. For instance, the complexity of applying for and receiving college financial aid may be a barrier to the effectiveness of such policies when individuals are imperfect optimizers.[83] The Free Application for Federal Student Aid (FAFSA), the gateway form for qualifying for college financial aid, is notoriously complex. One experiment that provided assistance with completing the form found that the assistance led to significant increases both in applying for financial aid and in college attendance.[84] In part because of that research, the Department of Education has recently taken steps to simplify the aid application process.[85]

School Choice

Education policy faces the design challenge of how to effectively and efficiently deliver education to students. Most elementary and secondary education in the

United States is not just funded but also provided directly by the government through public schools. From the perspective of traditional public finance, this form of delivery can be justified in part by the public good features of education, but the case for public provision of education is in general not as strong as the case for public support of education. In part for that reason, innovations such as charter schools, open enrollment policies, and school voucher programs are increasingly common.

Economic principles suggest that one way to improve the productivity of schools is to harness market forces to promote competition and innovation. However, the evidence on direct effects of choice on student outcomes is mixed,[86] and evidence that choice leads to competition that produces improved equilibrium outcomes is modest.[87] That seems to be due in part to the way that parents and students choose among schools. Emerging evidence suggests that individuals and families do not necessarily focus on academic performance when choosing schools in the way that the logic of school choice typically, if often implicitly, assumes.[88] As a result, the effects of choice on student outcomes may be muted. Moreover, when parents do not select schools based on academic performance, the hoped for competitive pressures may not arise.

The mixed results may also be due in part to behavioral impediments to building well-functioning markets for schooling. The problem of choosing among schools is intrinsically complex. In New York City, where students have a choice of high schools, the directory of high schools runs to hundreds of pages.[89] Behavioral economics stresses that individuals with limited attention and limited computational capacity will find it difficult to make such choices optimally. One direct test of the role of information in school choice found evidence that simplifying information presentation with respect to school quality led to improved school choices along that dimension, which in turn led to academic gains.[90] Those results suggest that outcomes are sensitive to how choice is presented and structured and that choice architecture is an important element of education choice policy.

6

Poverty and Inequality

Roughly one in seven Americans, more than 43 million people, lived in poverty in 2009.[1] In the United States, poverty is defined as having a low level of market income in absolute terms—that is, as living below the poverty line. For a family of four, for example, that meant a total family income of less than $21,756. Incomes at that low level both reflect and create undesirable conditions, not only for individuals who suffer directly the hardships associated with poverty but also for societies and economies that allow such conditions to persist. As a result, economic policy often seeks to address the issue of poverty. Social and transfer policies work both to alleviate hardship and to provide individuals and families with the tools and opportunities necessary to escape poverty.

The rate and depth of poverty in the United States is all the more striking for the way that it compares with the vast wealth of Americans at the other end of the income scale. In 2009, households at the 90th percentile of the income distribution earned more than 11 times as much as households at the 10th percentile. Moreover, over the last thirty years the gap between rich and poor has widened to levels not seen since before the Great Depression. The fraction of total income accruing to the richest 10 percent has been more than 45 percent in recent years, up from roughly one-third of income thirty years ago.[2] As with poverty, addressing economic inequality often is an object of public policy. Inequality can be a source of lost social welfare on its own terms, and it also can both be a sign and a cause of other undesirable social and economic outcomes.

If anything, static poverty and inequality figures disguise the nature of the challenges these conditions pose for policy. For one, the economic conditions that many individuals face are quite volatile. For most income-poor households, there is frequent cycling above and below the poverty threshold, so that they are persistently living on the margin of being either poor or near-poor.[3] In fact, according to recent analyses chronic poverty in the United States is relatively uncommon. Estimates suggest that while only 2 percent of the population lived in poverty continuously from 2004 through 2007, approximately 31 percent of the population had at least one spell of poverty lasting two or more months during the same four-year period.[4] Because of such chronic financial fragility, a variety of triggering events can easily undo years of hard work to climb out of poverty. Therefore, policy interventions may seek to target the frequency and severity of changes in income experienced by many poor individuals, in addition to targeting levels of income.

Both poverty and inequality are issues for policy in part because of the way and extent to which they interact with mobility. If poverty were primarily a temporary condition through which individuals passed on their way to a better life, or if inequality figures were merely a snapshot of a highly mobile society, there might be less cause for concern. But in many instances that does not seem to be the case. Increasingly, evidence suggests that there is in fact less economic mobility in the United States than in other developed countries.[5] As a result, policy also is concerned with promoting mobility. Many policy responses to poverty and inequality do not simply focus on static transfers of income but seek to promote mobility by, for example, supporting work and savings.

Questions about poverty and inequality and volatility and mobility can be tricky ones for economic analysis, because often the underlying issues are normative. They involve not just efficiency but also equality, and economics alone cannot answer questions about what is just and equitable. That said, public finance provides an intellectual framework for tackling those questions, even when it cannot ultimately provide the answers. It provides a way to think about the problems, to measure the conditions, to work through the implications of various assumptions, to delineate the trade-offs that policy must negotiate, and to gauge the relationship of policy design to policy objectives.

The issues of social welfare, poverty, and inequality thus differ in character from issues related to market failure, such as asymmetries of information or externalities. Whereas with market failures unregulated outcomes were clearly inefficient, poverty and inequality can exist in efficient economies—they may simply be undesirable in some sense. Still, a traditional approach to public finance can incorporate an analysis of issues related to poverty and inequality. It typically begins with identifying a concept of social welfare and the ways in which poverty and inequality might depress social welfare. It goes on to recognize some of the trade-offs that are inherent in addressing poverty and inequality, and it produces some principles for the design of policy responses.

Findings from psychological studies are relevant at every level of this approach. They change how we understand the nature of the policy problem: the causes and consequences of poverty are mediated by behavioral tendencies, as are the implications of income inequality for social welfare. They change the nature and terms of the trade-offs that antipoverty and redistribution measures must consider: the welfare implications of transferring resources across individuals and the frontier of alternative possible policy outcomes also depend on behavior and psychology. And they change the design requirements of effective transfer policy: on the one hand, policy design must consider behavioral tendencies; on the other, policy can look to behavioral insights for new levers and opportunities. This chapter discusses the behavioral dimensions of policy design, including the following:

—*Social welfare.* For the purposes of public finance, the consequences of poverty and inequality typically are captured through some measure of social welfare. The standard economics of poverty and inequality shows how those conditions can lead to lower social welfare than under alternative distributions of income. A behavioral approach modifies our understanding of both the causes and consequences of poverty, with implications for the social welfare costs of poverty. It also identifies new ways in which inequality might translate into welfare loss.

—*Moral hazard.* Policies that reduce poverty may also have unintended side effects. Perhaps the primary trade-off that policy responses to poverty and inequality must weigh is that between the benefit of addressing those conditions and the cost due to the moral hazard that such policies can create. Behavioral tendencies may change the terms of that trade-off or confound it. The welfare consequences of behavioral tendencies that mimic traditional moral hazard can be much different from those in the standard case.

—*Targeting.* The other key policy trade-off in addressing poverty and inequality derives from the general inability of policymakers to distinguish those who require assistance from those who do not. As a result, policy responses often have to trade off two types of errors in targeting, false positives and false negatives. Due to behavioral tendencies, the terms and nature of the trade-off can be slightly modified.

—*Program design.* Public finance derives a set of principles for designing efficient and effective programs to address poverty and inequality. Such programs seek to deliver benefits to targeted individuals with a minimum of error, to provide benefits in such a way that they translate most efficiently into the desired outcomes, and to structure benefits in order to minimize distortions to incentives, especially work incentives. Behavioral tendencies mediate how individuals respond to programs in ways that complicate each of those objectives; principles of program design therefore must be modified accordingly.

Below, we draw out the implications of behavioral tendencies for poverty and inequality policy by considering the behavioral dimensions of the policy problem, the required judgments, and the design of the policy response.

Psychology and Social Welfare

The primary traditional approach to considering the role of government in the context of public finance proceeds from the concept of a social welfare function, which represents overall social welfare as an aggregation of individual utilities.[6] Determining the form of the social welfare function and evaluating it is in general beyond the scope of economics.[7] However, within this approach, public finance can work through the implications of alternative conceptions of individual utilities and their aggregation for social welfare. By doing so, it can be seen that in many common conceptions of the social welfare function, poverty and inequality can leave social welfare below its maximum. For instance, if social welfare is taken to be the sum of individual utilities, and individual utility functions exhibit diminishing marginal utility, redistributing income from the wealthy to the poor can improve social welfare, all other things being equal. While public finance cannot determine the precise magnitude and nature of many of the social welfare costs of poverty and inequality, based as they are on normative evaluations of utility and welfare, it does provide a coherent theoretical framework for considering those costs. Within that framework, we can consider the implications for policy of different assumptions about how individual utilities aggregate into social welfare.

There is also a separate, related rationale for a policy response to some forms of poverty and inequality that is derived from an empirical and positive approach that identifies the social costs of poverty and inequality. This approach usually focuses on poverty and inequality as instrumental—in effect, focusing on the externalities that poverty and inequality may generate—rather than as ends in themselves. That is, the problems that policy must solve in addressing poverty and inequality are due not only to the way that they affect social welfare through preferences but also to the costs that poverty and inequality may impose on society at large. So, for example, recent evidence suggests that on net, investments in early childhood education that target disadvantaged children improve social welfare.[8] There also is some evidence of social costs to inequality. For example, it has been suggested that inequality may lead to adverse health outcomes for society at large.[9] Where poverty and inequality impose such costs, a policy response may improve welfare.

A behavioral approach to understanding the role of government in addressing poverty and inequality modifies our understanding of how poverty and inequality translate into social welfare losses. With respect to inequality, the nonstandard forms of preferences identified by behavioral economics—other-regarding preferences and reference-dependent preferences—change our assumptions about the form of individual utility and thereby social welfare, opening the door for inequality to translate into social welfare loss in new ways. With respect to poverty, allowing for behavioral tendencies changes the way that we understand the causes and consequences of poverty and thereby may change our understanding of the social costs of poverty. Note that although we maintain our concentration on the psychology of judgment and decisionmaking, behavioral economics also may inform social welfare through the incorporation of insights from the psychology of happiness and subjective well-being. Box 6-1 gives a brief introduction to those concepts.

Preferences and Inequality

The social welfare costs associated with inequality derive from a variety of factors, including beliefs about what is just or fair, concern for the welfare of others, and judgments about whether and how the well-being of an individual is or should be interrelated with that of others. Because attitudes toward those questions are largely a matter of normative belief—the domain of philosophical reasoning, religious convictions, and moral sentiments—positive economic analysis is insufficient for determining when redistribution is justified and at what level. As noted above, however, while the role of economics in determining the appropriate extent of redistribution is somewhat limited, economic analysis can inform decisions about redistribution through the study of the empirical bases and logical consequences of alternative claims. One important area of investigation includes assessing the validity of alternative assumptions, both implicit and explicit, about the nature and shape of individual preferences: different levels and forms of redistribution are more or less justifiable depending on the structure of individual preferences.

To the extent that economic analysis can incorporate and analyze the implications of beliefs, concerns, and judgments that justify choices of alternative possible income distributions, it works through social welfare functions that, in turn, rest on the assumed structure of the underlying preferences of relevant agents. Claims about those preferences often take the form of testable—but often untested—assumptions about the nature and structure of underlying beliefs, values, or tastes. Economic analysis is well-suited to assessing the evidentiary basis for such claims. Behavioral findings, especially as they relate to possibly nonstandard forms of preferences, challenge and update assumptions about the form of individual preferences as well as about how they aggregate into social welfare.

Conclusions about the welfare impact of various levels or forms of redistribution may change as a result.

Two findings from behavioral economics about the shape of preferences are of particular importance to understanding the social welfare consequences of inequality. The first is that individuals exhibit behavior consistent with holding preferences over the welfare of others, both in absolute and relative terms. The second is that individuals appear to hold preferences over the process that generates economic outcomes such as the income distribution.

INTERPERSONAL PREFERENCES AND SOCIAL WELFARE

Behavioral economics finds evidence, in various forms of other-regarding preferences, that individuals appear to be only imperfectly self-interested. That is, people seem to care about the absolute well-being of others. There is evidence for behaviors consistent with forms of other-regarding preferences from altruism to envy. For example, the data on charitable giving—in particular the fact that Americans engage in so much of it—and other forms of private or voluntary redistribution are at least weakly consistent with altruism.[10] There also is a variety of evidence from laboratory experiments that individuals often tend to express what appears to be a preference for more equal distribution of resources than pure self-interest would predict.[11]

Other-regarding preferences of this sort have two main implications for the social welfare costs of inequality, which work in opposing directions. One implication is that because of the interdependence of preferences, the impact of inequality on social welfare is greater. In addition to whatever consequences of inequality emerge due to the way in which individual utilities are aggregated into social welfare, there may now be costs of inequality that enter directly through individual utility. For example, if individuals have preferences for positive outcomes of others, inequality can depress social welfare in part through its effects on those individuals' utility. A similar effect can also operate through preferences that individuals may hold over the distribution of income as a whole.[12] As a result, the magnitude of the problem posed by inequality may be greater than under standard assumptions, and the scope for government action to improve on unregulated outcomes by redistributing income or other goods may be expanded. On the other hand, the same preferences might lead individuals to engage in more voluntary redistribution than the standard model would predict. To the extent that such voluntary redistribution addresses the social costs of inequality even in the absence of government intervention, the magnitude of the problem posed by inequality may be less than under standard assumptions, and the scope for government action to improve on unregulated outcomes might be diminished.

Box 6-1. *Happiness and Social Welfare*

A set of findings from psychological studies with possible implications for social welfare that we set aside in our analysis has to do with happiness and subjective well-being. This growing body of research seeks to understand both what people say makes them happy and how they experience happiness. In doing so, it has observed a set of empirical regularities about happiness and well-being. One branch of the literature documents the relationship between characteristics of experiences and their consequences for happiness—for example, that the peak and the end of experiences disproportionately influence whether those experiences are coded as enjoyable or not. It also finds, to take another example, that there are systematic deviations between experienced well-being and recalled well-being.[a] Another branch examines the relationship of various particular experiences and states— income level, age, and so on—to happiness. Some studies find, for example, that across individuals in the United States, happiness increases with income.[b]

The potential uses of this research for questions involving social welfare are straightforward. If economists can take happiness or well-being as measured in this literature as indicative of utility, that provides the corresponding entries for individuals in the social welfare function, and policy evaluations can proceed accordingly. Some have proposed creating national measures of happiness or well-being based on this research and reasoning and using them in policymaking as an indicator of social welfare.[c] Policy evaluations can logically proceed using happiness data in this way. An example of policy analysis that is based on happiness research is the finding that cigarette taxes can make smokers happier, possibly by helping them commit to a course of action that they otherwise could not commit to because of a failure of self-control.[d] A variety of other possible implications for economic analysis and policy are possible.[e]

That said, the tractability of incorporating findings from the happiness and well-being literature into public finance is far from clear. There are at least two barriers. One has to do with some of the limitations inherent in this research and in its application to building social welfare functions for use in public finance analysis. Perhaps the most important is that the question of when happiness or well-being measures can be taken as an indicator of utility, in the sense that it would enter a social welfare function, is not obvious. Even under the assumption that the methods used in this literature are measuring happiness in a meaningful and accurate way, any particular measure of happiness or satisfaction is not necessarily identical

---

In conjunction with other-regarding preferences, reference-dependent preferences also may play a role in mediating how inequality translates into social welfare loss. Individuals may form preferences over their relative position in the income distribution, not just their absolute standing. When individuals hold preferences over their relative place in the distribution of income or other

with utility. As a result, those measures may not get as far toward empirically identifying a social welfare function as they first appear to do.

The other has to do with some practical considerations and the definition and scope of research agendas. From the perspective of public finance, the happiness research gets into deeper questions about the nature of welfare and utility that really precede public finance as well as into open philosophical and political questions about the role of the state that are beyond its scope. In part what the happiness research does is get back to more fundamental questions of welfare economics that, for reasons discussed in chapter 3, we choose to set aside for the narrower purposes of public finance. From the perspective of behavioral economics, the happiness research can similarly be separated out as a line of inquiry in psychology from the research on judgment and decisionmaking on which we have focused. While the two are obviously related on some level—judgments and decisions reflect beliefs about happiness and well-being—a clear functional distinction remains.

For those reasons, we largely set aside the research on happiness and well-being, both in this narrow instance of addressing questions of social welfare and throughout our development of a behavioral approach to public finance. The happiness and well-being literature is an important research agenda and one that is likely to ultimately inform public policy in key ways. But it is not clear that public finance is the best conduit for its insights.

a. Daniel Kahneman, Peter P. Wakker, and Rakesh Sarin, "Back to Bentham? Explorations of Experienced Utility," *Quarterly Journal of Economics,* vol. 112, no. 2 (1997), pp. 375–405.

b. David G. Blanchflower and Andrew J. Oswald, "Well-Being over Time in Britain and the USA," *Journal of Public Economics,* vol. 88, no. 7–8 (2004), pp. 1359–86.

c. Daniel Kahneman and others, "Toward National Well-Being Accounts," *American Economic Review,* vol. 94, no. 2 (2004), pp. 429–34; Daniel Kahneman and Alan B. Krueger, "Developments in the Measurement of Subjective Well-Being," *Journal of Economic Perspectives,* vol. 20, no. 1 (2006), pp. 3–24.

d. Jonathan Gruber and Sendhil Mullainathan, "Do Cigarette Taxes Make Smokers Happier?" *Advances in Economic Analysis and Policy,* vol. 5, no. 1 (2005).

e. Bruno S. Frey and Alois Stutzer, "What Can Economists Learn from Happiness Research?" *Journal of Economic Literature,* vol. 40, no. 2 (2002), pp. 402–35; Rafael Di Tella and Robert MacCulloch, "Some Uses of Happiness Data in Economics," *Journal of Economic Perspectives,* vol. 20, no. 1 (2006), pp. 25–46.

outcomes, it creates a new way in which the welfare of individuals is interconnected and thereby a new way in which inequality might translate into welfare loss. That might suggest that higher levels of redistribution can be optimal than in the standard case.[13] Such preferences also can have seemingly perverse implications for the social ordering of alternative distributions of income. For example, because individuals care about their relative place in the distribution, improvements in the welfare of some can have negative effects on the welfare of others.[14] There is some evidence that individuals hold such preferences and that they can have such consequences—for example, one study finds that individuals' subjective well-being is diminished by having higher-earning neighbors.[15]

A particular implication of relative and positional concerns for how inequality affects social welfare is that those effects are likely to be stronger in some domains than others.[16] For example, they might be stronger for goods that are more visible or for forms of income and consumption that are more easily observed. Other domains may inspire intrinsically relative preferences, depending either on their status as merit goods or on beliefs about the importance of relative position particular to those goods. For example, it may be the case that preferences for goods like health care and education, perhaps because they are so closely identified with establishing equality of opportunity, will have strong relative components. Whatever the reason that they arise, the relative strength of positional preferences across domains can contribute to the relative social welfare impacts of inequality across domains.

PREFERENCES FOR JUSTICE AND FAIRNESS

An aspect of other-regarding preferences with special implications for the social welfare consequences of inequality has to do with fairness. In addition to displaying evidence of preferences over economic outcomes, both for themselves and others, in both relative and absolute terms, individuals also exhibit preferences over the process that generates the distribution of income. In particular, individuals exhibit preferences for fairness.[17] Like preferences for redistribution in general, much evidence for preferences for fairness comes from laboratory experiments.[18] As a result, redistributive policies may be justified to foster fairness or to counter perceived unfairness in market outcomes.

Like direct preferences for equitable outcomes, preferences for fairness could have contradictory effects for the social welfare consequences of inequality. Evidence that the strength of individual preferences for redistribution is explained in part by beliefs about the relative roles of luck and effort is consistent with the idea that preferences for fairness can magnify the social welfare consequences of inequality and call for a greater role of the state in addressing inequality.[19] However, to the extent that voluntary redistribution, such as giving to charities, is driven by preferences for fairness, the extent of the welfare loss and the scope for government action to improve private outcomes is diminished.

Finally, like preferences over outcomes, preferences over processes extend to domains other than income and may have greater effects on the social welfare implications of inequality in some domains than in others. It might lead to stronger social welfare losses from inequality, where issues of fairness and opportunity are especially acute. For example, preferences for fairness might lead to especially strong social welfare impacts where inequality has consequences for children, because of the perception that the advantages or disadvantages of children are unearned. For that reason, the social welfare consequences of inequality in areas like education—and the corresponding role for government—might be intensified by fairness concerns.

Behavioral Tendencies and Poverty

Poverty presents special problems for economic policy, in part because of the way that poverty may affect social welfare directly. Even under approaches to social welfare where inequality is of little consequence, poverty can still matter for social welfare. That is in part because the particular hardships associated with poverty are of special concern and lead to distinctive consequences for social welfare, so transfer policies designed to reduce poverty may have a relatively high payoff in terms of social welfare. Even without other-regarding preferences, for instance, if marginal utility of income is sharply diminishing, poverty might have especially strong social welfare effects.

Poverty also has consequences that operate not through preferences and the social welfare function but directly on economic and social outcomes. Poverty therefore might lead directly to outcomes with undesirable economic and social consequences. For example, poverty might lead to poor health and public health outcomes. Poverty also can interact with market failures to magnify their consequences. For instance, when individuals are credit constrained, poverty might lead individuals to invest in suboptimal levels of education.

Behavioral economics shows how the conditions of poverty can interact with elements of decisionmaking to change our understanding of both the causes and consequences of poverty and thereby the consequences of poverty for social welfare or other economic outcomes. The fact that individuals are imperfect decisionmakers means that they can make errors or suffer from failures of self-control that can contribute to impoverishment directly or mediate the way that poverty leads to undesirable outcomes. That may affect how the conditions of poverty translate into social costs or detract from social welfare directly. The result is to change how we view the nature of the problem that poverty poses for economic policy. On one hand, behavioral tendencies can be a cause of some forms or some aspects of poverty, which has potential implications for social welfare. On the other hand, behavioral tendencies can generate or explain some of the consequences of poverty for social welfare and economic outcomes.

BEHAVIORAL TENDENCIES AS CONTRIBUTING FACTORS TO POVERTY

How and whether poverty creates a drag on social welfare can depend in part on what we understand the causes of poverty to be. There are a number of possible reasons poverty might impose social welfare costs, but a central mechanism is a function of the type of preferences over process described above. If individuals care about fairness and process, then the social welfare costs of poverty may be larger to the extent that poverty is due to bad luck or circumstance or smaller to the extent poverty is due to bad behavior or decisions. The underlying concern is about unearned poverty. As a result, understanding the causes of poverty has significance for understanding the social welfare impact of poverty. While in principle standard economic analysis has all of the tools necessary to answer that question, in practice it may be the case that without carefully allowing for behavioral tendencies the analysis will tend to draw incomplete or inaccurate conclusions. Behavioral economics speaks to several important dimensions of the distinction between earned and unearned poverty, whether it is well defined, and where the preponderance of the evidence on the causes of poverty comes down.

One key insight from behavioral economics is that what through the lens of standard economics might appear to be deviant behavior is, in reality, just behavior.[20] For example, while standard economic analysis might look at a poor individual's failing to exhibit self-control—in, say, failing to save adequately—and label that a failure on the part of the poor, behavioral economics recognizes it as a common human failing. Choice errors or failures of self-control are universal features of human decisionmaking. In some circumstances, they contribute to or deepen poverty, but that is not necessarily an indication that the poor are behaving worse than the non-poor. The poor may just be employing the same judgment heuristics and falling prey to the same biases as everyone else. Their failings may not be the result of individual shortcomings, but rather systematic mistakes that everyone is vulnerable to making. Ignoring that possibility may lead to an inappropriate discounting of the social welfare costs of poverty.

Moreover, the same behavioral tendencies might matter more for the poor than for the non-poor. For example, for those with little savings, small errors in planning could lead to outsized consequences for well-being. Similarly, the impacts of failures of self-control might be disproportionately consequential for the poor.[21] As a result, both the visibility and consequences of imperfect decisionmaking on the part of the poor may be higher than for other groups that have more generous margins for error.[22] In addition, elements of other-regarding preferences, to the extent that they allow for individuals to be influenced by social norms and the construction of identity, might work to reinforce aspects of poverty.[23]

Behavioral Tendencies and the Impact of Poverty

The social costs of poverty also are a function of the effects of poverty on other outcomes, and much of the rationale for antipoverty policy is derived from an understanding of those effects. As a result, antipoverty policy proceeds from an understanding of how the conditions of poverty translate into economic or social outcomes. That depends in part on the decisionmaking process of those in poverty. Traditional models emphasize the way that the conditions associated with poverty can affect the terms of cost-benefit decisions to engage in productive or pro-social behaviors.

Behavioral economics brings a new dimension to that aspect of the poverty problem by allowing that the conditions associated with poverty can affect the decisionmaking process directly. For example, the stresses and difficulties associated with living in poverty might require an individual's limited attention or limited computational capacity to be diverted to urgent decisionmaking tasks at the expense of others that might have consequences for social and economic outcomes. Individuals who are constantly worrying about how to pay the rent every month may find it difficult, for example, to devote attention and computational resources to decisions about education or health care. The result might be that the conditions of poverty can sometimes lead directly to undesirable outcomes.

A mechanism that is likely to be of particular importance in generating such effects is the interaction of the conditions of poverty and bounded self-control. The constraints and stresses that are an inevitable byproduct of poverty may lead individuals to demonstrate more short-sighted or time-inconsistent behavior than they would in the absence of such conditions. If willpower is costly to exercise, external conditions may erode willpower.[24] Evidence suggests that the type of environmental factors that co-vary with poverty and that create stress can affect how individuals make decisions, especially with respect to time and risk. For example, there is some suggestive evidence that when individuals face increased levels of stress or a higher cognitive load, they may discount the future more heavily.[25] The stresses associated with, say, living in higher-crime neighborhoods, having generally poorer-quality social services, or having more strained social networks—stresses that might be experienced by the economically disadvantaged—may adversely affect decisionmaking and thereby economic and social outcomes.

Finally, economic instability may present especially difficult challenges for the income poor. In addition to generally experiencing more earnings volatility, the poor have a higher likelihood of experiencing unexpected adverse financial events and material hardship (missed bill payments and the like). Economic instability not only means financial uncertainty for poor individuals, it also takes an extra toll on the ability to focus, to plan, and to weigh future consequences.[26] In the context of economic instability, individuals may respond effectively some of the time, but they often respond in ways that are counterproductive, consuming already scarce resources without improving long-term prospects.

Trade-Offs in Transfer Policy

Setting the level and form of transfer policy to correct a given assessment of the problems posed by poverty and inequality requires judgments about policy trade-offs. Transfer and redistribution policies, perhaps more than any other policies in public finance, are ultimately dependent on judgment calls by society and policymakers. Making those calls involves consideration of trade-offs across alternative policy states—for example, how much to trade off the protections of redistribution against the disincentives to work that they create. It also involves welfare trade-offs across individuals—judging whether on net social welfare is improved by transferring income from one group or individual to another.

The traditional model incorporates those trade-offs, and while it cannot resolve them, it comes to a standard set of conclusions regarding their terms. The main trade-off across policies in this model is broadly captured as being between equity and efficiency.[27] While policies that improve equity can in principle improve outcomes, in practice they may come at some cost to economic efficiency as individuals change their behavior in response. The specific manifestation that is of primary concern for the narrow purposes of transfer policy is the efficiency cost due to the moral hazard that such programs can create and its effects on labor supply in particular. A related set of trade-offs is due to the fact that policymakers typically cannot observe the characteristics by which they would like to identify recipients of benefits. Finally, redistribution motivated by improvements in social welfare due to moving income or resources across people necessarily reflects judgments about relative utilities.

Behavioral economics changes the terms and nature of the trade-offs involved with income support and redistribution. For example, the equity-efficiency trade-off is largely a result of the distortion to incentives that transfers necessarily create. But the way in which individuals respond to those distortions is affected by behavioral tendencies. In addition, when and how transfers from one individual to another might improve welfare depends on assumptions about the nature of preferences. Behavioral economics, in allowing for nonstandard preferences such at other-regarding preferences, may change those assumptions. Moreover, choice errors and self-control failures create the possibility of welfare-improving intrapersonal transfers. Of course, such transfers then necessitate a new set of judgments about when they are worthwhile.

Redistribution and Information

The general trade-off between equity and efficiency that transfer policy must navigate has many specific components. The costs, in terms of efficiency, arise from the distortions that the policy introduces into the economy. On one hand, important and considerable distortions are created by raising revenue from individuals in order to fund transfer policies; however, we defer discussion of that component of welfare until chapter 7, "Taxation and Revenue." On the other hand, distortions are created directly by providing benefits or guarantees to individuals as part of transfer policies. The goal of policymakers in executing these transfers is to minimize the welfare costs to the extent possible; because the costs usually cannot be eliminated outright, the goal of society is to judge what levels and forms of redistribution are worth what costs. However, because welfare costs depend on the behavioral response to distortions, the psychology of preference and choice matters for outcomes.

The key trade-offs from the perspective of providing benefits to eligible individuals follow from information asymmetries between the government and program beneficiaries. The first trade-off is due to the difficulty of observing work effort, which can lead income support policies to create a moral hazard, and it is broadly similar to the type of moral hazard problem posed by social insurance. The second is related to the ability of policy to target benefits, which becomes an issue when policymakers cannot observe perfectly whether individuals belong to the class for which transfer policies are intended.

Moral Hazard and Behavioral Tendencies

Perhaps the key dimension to the efficiency costs associated with transfer policies is the moral hazard that they may create in recipients. By insulating recipients from the full consequences of adverse economic events or unproductive activities, the incentives that those recipients have to protect themselves against those events or to engage in economically productive activities are diminished. Of particular interest for income support policies is the moral hazard created with respect to work incentives. By cushioning the blow of low labor income, such programs can reduce incentives to seek and take employment. That comes at a cost to economic efficiency.

A behavioral approach to the problem of moral hazard created by redistribution emphasizes the coincident forces of behavioral tendencies for covered individuals, in particular, how bounded self-control can reinforce—or supplant—moral hazard. Individuals who fail to seek work when they receive benefits may intend to do so but fail to follow through; in that case, what appears to be a diminished incentive to work may in fact be the result of procrastination. Furthermore, benefits may exacerbate the tendency to procrastinate; there is some evidence that welfare programs might have such an effect.[28] Limits to attention and computational capacity also can play a role in moral hazard. For example, individuals may misperceive the terms of income support policies, leading them to over- or underestimate their benefits, with subsequent effects for the moral hazard that they generate. Such effects may change the terms of the trade-offs for policy dramatically: rather than having competing interests, recipients and society in this case have aligned interests; that is, there may cease to be a trade-off altogether. So, for instance, when transfer policies lead to failure of self-control in seeking work, it may be in the interest of both society and the beneficiary to have benefits structured in a way that encourages work.[29] Note finally that behavioral tendencies may interact with the moral hazard due to transfer policies in the same way that they interact with the moral hazard due to unemployment insurance; see chapter 4, "Asymmetric Information," for an extensive discussion of that topic.

Targeting Behavioral Recipients

One way in which policy seeks to minimize the efficiency costs of redistribution is by targeting specific populations to receive transfers. That is difficult even in standard models, because there is a presumed information asymmetry between policymakers and individuals with respect to knowledge about who is truly needy.[30] As a result, policymakers employ specific targeting methods, such as tagging based on observable characteristics, or ordeal targeting.[31] Because of the imprecision of such methods, they can lead to errors of either commission or omission—that is, they can lead to benefits being claimed by individuals for whom they are not intended, and they can lead to intended individuals failing to receive benefits. Either comes at a cost to program efficiency.

The goals of targeting can thus create a set of trade-offs that policy has to resolve. While more generous benefits can come at a cost to efficiency, attempts to target precisely may leave qualified individuals without benefits. Efficient screening depends crucially on having an accurate model of how individuals will behave in response to such measures, but that is complicated by behavioral tendencies. To the extent that individuals respond to targeting measures in imperfect ways, the features of the trade-off may differ from those under standard assumptions. Of particular concern is the possibility that behavioral tendencies interact with screening mechanisms in ways that undermine their efficiency. For example, when individuals put off filling out benefit applications because they tend to procrastinate or because doing so is a hassle, screening may be ineffective. Worse, the screen may actually work in the wrong direction. The hassle costs associated with complex program rules or application procedures may be a relatively more serious barrier for the sort of low-income populations that are the ostensible targets of the policy.

Welfare Comparisons

Income support and transfer policy also must reflect trade-offs across individuals. While redistributive policies must reflect judgments about how to trade off welfare across individuals, positive economics has long since abandoned formal models in which it is possible to make interpersonal utility comparisons. As a result, public finance can contribute to understanding this trade-off in only the most basic, abstract terms. Nevertheless, considering—even at the level of a textbook exercise—the implications of alternative forms of the social welfare function and alternative assumptions about individual utility for, for example, the optimal form and level of redistribution, may help policymakers to understand the implications of policy alternatives.

The main implication of behavioral economics for such an exercise has to do with incorporating other-regarding preferences into the analytical framework. As discussed in more detail above, individuals hold interpersonal preferences in a variety of forms. Allowing for interdependencies between individual utilities changes the welfare dynamics of redistribution. The relative desirability of different levels or forms of redistribution therefore changes, according to social welfare criteria, when allowing for such preferences.

A related implication of behavioral economics involves intrapersonal transfers. The idea of intrapersonal transfers comes from the conception of choice errors or self-control failures as representing multiple (possibly conflicting) preferences that individuals hold. To the extent that policy takes into consideration, for example, the possibility that poverty imposes costs through its interaction with bounded self-control, as described above, it will have to reflect some weighting of the short-run versus the long-run interests of the individuals concerned. Many of the same issues that arise in setting optimal policy for interpersonal transfers arise in setting policy for intrapersonal transfers.

Behavioral Economics and Program Design

Given some social focus on addressing the consequences of poverty, redistributing resources in the face of inequality, or promoting income mobility, policymaking faces the problem of designing programs that achieve those goals effectively and efficiently. In the United States, policies that tackle them go by a variety of names—income support policies, transfer policies, welfare policies—and include a wide variety of specific measures, including traditional cash transfers, tax credits, food and housing assistance, and subsidized health insurance. But while the policies are varied, they share a common goal—to provide assistance efficiently—and therefore they have a common set of design challenges. Among the central challenges are how to reach those in need, how to effect desired outcomes among beneficiaries, and how to provide benefits without distorting the incentives and behavior of recipients.

Because the effectiveness of programs in meeting such challenges depends in part on how individuals respond to the availability of services or to the receipt of benefits, behavioral tendencies on the part of individuals will mediate program outcomes. In general, the findings of behavioral economics may complicate the relationship between policy objectives, policy design, and behavioral response. Individuals can no longer be assumed to respond to some objective conception of the incentives that a program creates; instead, they respond to their possibly imperfect construal of those incentives or only to the extent that their bounded self-control allows, and so on. A behavioral approach integrates psychological insights into the analysis of program design in order to better understand what works and what does not and to suggest possible innovations.

In that way, behavioral insights can improve our understanding of each of the three central challenges for program design noted above. A behavioral perspective on how individuals perceive benefits and respond to rules for eligibility and participation can inform our understanding of how take-up and targeting operate in social programs. A behavioral view of how individuals respond to benefits and make decisions about their use can improve our understanding of how programs affect desired outcomes. And a behavioral approach to understanding how individuals make decisions to work when they receive or are eligible to receive benefits can suggest how best to deliver benefits without distorting incentives.

Take-Up and Targeting

With few exceptions, income support programs in the United States target specific populations defined by particular characteristics, circumstances, or means. Programs target an array of groups, often defined by age, disability or health status, family composition, or economic means. In order to restrict the benefits of any given program to qualifying individuals, it is necessary to screen prospective recipients to determine whether they meet the eligibility criteria. In practice, that determination often is made by requiring that individuals actively apply for benefits and demonstrate their eligibility. As a result, the effectiveness of income support programs in delivering benefits to targeted individuals is a joint function of who is targeted by the policy, which is defined by eligibility rules, and who takes them up, which is determined by individual behavior.

Given the elective nature of participation in such programs, not all eligible individuals apply for or take up benefits. And as an empirical matter, the take-up rate—the fraction of eligible individuals who actually receive benefits—of most income support programs is far from perfect. That the take-up rate is a result of choices made by potential beneficiaries is clearest in the case of programs that pay benefits to all individuals who apply for assistance and who meet eligibility criteria. The Supplemental Nutrition Assistance Program (SNAP, formerly known as the food stamp program), for example, is an entitlement program, meaning that by law all qualified applicants receive benefits. Still, estimates suggest that only about two-thirds of eligible individuals received food stamps in 2007.[32] A similar example is the earned income tax credit (EITC), which pays benefits to every qualified tax filer who claims the credit on his or her tax return. Even with this simple administration mechanism, the EITC is estimated to reach only approximately 75 percent of eligible households.[33]

Imperfect take-up rates raise two distinct sets of issues for policy design. The first is that low participation rates mean that the program is not delivering benefits to some eligible individuals. Given that the goal of such programs is to provide assistance to eligible populations, incomplete take-up may be an indicator that those populations are not well served by the program. The second issue with low participation rates is that where there is heterogeneity of needs within the eligible population, there is the possibility that propensity to take up does not reflect those underlying needs. To the extent that it is a goal of policy to target benefits to the relatively needy, with incomplete take-up there is reason to question whether programs meet that goal.

The standard model of the take-up decision treats the choice of whether or not to claim benefits as a straightforward cost-benefit problem. Presumptively eligible individuals weigh the value of the stream of benefits that they could expect to receive as program participants against the costs of applying for and collecting those benefits.[34] The costs of program participation take at least two forms: transactions costs (the direct costs associated with claiming and keeping benefits) and stigma costs (the subjective sources of disutility that are associated with receiving benefits). In this model, policies fail to reach the intended recipients if the costs that they impose are large relative to the benefits that they deliver. Another feature of this model is that those costs can lead self-selection of individuals into the program to work as an automatic targeting mechanism.[35] For example, in means-tested programs that provide more generous benefits to more disadvantaged recipients, the neediest of the eligible population will benefit more from the program and will be more likely to take it up, while the program will be least attractive to those in the least need. In this scenario, imperfect take-up rates can be consistent with—and even an element of—optimal policy design.

An alternative framework for understanding the take-up decision comes from behavioral economics. While a behavioral approach is consistent with the basic cost-benefit structure of the standard model, it relaxes that model's implicit assumption that individuals evaluate and act on costs and benefits in an optimal manner.[36] The significance of this approach is that it permits explanations for the observed imperfect take-up of income support programs that do not categorize it simply as the expression of individual preferences. Instead, under this model, individuals may fail to apply for benefits because they do not know of or understand programs, because they procrastinate, or because they are distracted by the minor costs associated with claiming benefits. The implications of a behavioral model of take-up differ considerably from those of the standard model. In particular, low take-up rates are potentially more troublesome in this framework because they may be evidence of imperfect decisionmaking or failure of self-control on the part of individuals who would, in fact, benefit from participation. Moreover, while in the standard model low take-up can complement efficient screening because individuals to whom benefits are more valuable are more likely to take them up, that is not necessarily the case in a behavioral model. If, for instance, the neediest individuals have less access to information on programs or are more discouraged by the hassle costs of applying for benefits, then imperfect take-up could be consistent with self-selection into programs working in a way that actually undermines efficient targeting.

Determining the relative roles of standard and behavioral factors in low take-up and its consequences is ultimately an empirical issue. Take-up has been the subject of extensive research.[37] The role of behavioral tendencies is suggested in part by the generally unsatisfactory fit of the standard model with evidence on take-up. On one hand, transactions costs exist and constitute at least a partial explanation for why take-up rates of income support programs are so far short of perfect. For example, the take-up rate for food stamps appears to be higher in years when and in states where the time between recertifications is longer and the effective transaction costs therefore lower.[38] Similarly, research on the sensitivity of take-up rates to program benefits often finds that the propensity to claim benefits increases with benefit generosity, which is consistent with the existence of fixed costs of enrollment.[39]

On the other hand, while the transaction costs associated with benefit take-up are real, in most programs they are modest relative to benefits. Traditionally economists have suggested that the stigma costs of income support might explain much of the balance of program nonparticipation. When surveyed, respondents do indicate that stigma is a contributing factor in forgoing benefits.[40] However, solid empirical evidence that stigma is a major cause of program nonparticipation has proven elusive. For example, the replacement of paper food stamps with electronic benefit cards, which may have reduced the stigma associated with food stamps, has been found to have some effect on participation, but the results are not dramatic.[41]

A behavioral approach points to other factors that can inhibit take-up, and it is consistent with some evidence. One way in which behavioral tendencies might depress take-up is through the interaction of limited attention or computational capacity with what are sometimes complex eligibility rules. Consequently, some eligible individuals may fail to take up benefits not as the result of a considered decisionmaking process but out of ignorance or confusion. For some smaller or more obscure programs, eligible individuals may not even know that the benefit is available. For example, one study of child-care subsidies found that some eligible women reported not applying for benefits because they were unaware of the program.[42] With larger, better-known programs, eligible individuals are more likely to be aware of benefits but may mistakenly believe that they would not qualify to receive them, or they may not form accurate expectations about the level of benefits for which they would qualify. In one study of food stamp take-up, a majority of eligible, nonparticipating households reported not claiming food stamps because they did not believe themselves to be eligible.[43] Finally, even when individuals believe that they may be eligible for particular benefits, they may not know how to go about applying for or claiming them.

In a similar fashion, individuals may be put off from participating in programs when the benefit schedule itself is complicated or obscure. Evidence that very minor differences in program presentation can have significant effects on program take-up is consistent with that observation. The clearest available example of that effect is from research on the design of the Saver's Credit, which offered a subsidy to low-income families for contributions to retirement savings accounts. In that study, a program that differed from the Saver's Credit only in how benefits were presented to individuals led to increased take-up.[44] It appears that making the program easier to understand and its incentives for saving more salient increased participation.[45]

A separate behavioral insight for understanding the take-up decision is the way in which individuals respond to the type of minor transaction costs associated with enrolling for means-tested benefit programs. Two factors may contribute to making those costs more serious deterrents to take-up than they may appear in the standard model. First, transaction costs associated with take-up may create channel factors—the small factors that channel behavior toward or away from a particular action—that discourage participation.[46] The result is that the types of small costs associated with take-up—sometimes referred to as hassle costs—might have a bigger impact on participation than the standard accounting would indicate. Second, individuals may tend to procrastinate in applying for and claiming benefits. Taken together, the hurdles to claiming benefits can be numerous and diverse—including filling out forms, visiting offices, participating in interviews, taking finger prints, and collecting and producing documentation—and they can channel individuals away from enrollment and create opportunities for procrastination. Perhaps the best evidence of this type of effect in take-up decisions comes from outside transfer policy in studies of participation in employer retirement benefit plans, which indicate that changes to enrollment procedures that eliminate even very minor application burdens can lead to dramatic increases in participation.[47] Similar behavioral tendencies are likely to operate in social programs in ways that depress take-up.

Finally, in addition to identifying channels through which take-up rates in social programs might become inefficiently low, behavioral economics also raises the possibility that imperfect take-up may lead to inefficient screening. That is, in addition to failing to lead to efficient levels of participation, behavioral tendencies might also lead to an inefficient mix of participants. Of particular concern is the possibility that the most disadvantaged individuals will be most susceptible to processing constraints or limits to self-control and so be less likely to take up and participate in programs. While much research on take-up supports the standard view, suggesting that benefits are going to those most in need, there is scattered evidence to the contrary. For example, one study of public housing take-up found that the lowest-income households were less likely to get benefits.[48] There also is evidence of inefficient screening in the Supplemental Security Income (SSI) and Disability Insurance (DI) programs.[49] One study of enrollment in a subsidized health insurance program found that those who failed to enroll tended to be both more economically disadvantaged and in worse health than those who did enroll.[50] Findings such as those are at least consistent with the possibility that behavioral tendencies contribute to inefficient screening in some instances.

A behavioral view of take-up suggests a number of implications for policy design. One is that making it easier for individuals to qualify for and perceive the terms of benefits may have high returns in terms of increased take-up rates. Simplifying the application process—requiring fewer forms, using automatic or default enrollment, and so on—could have large effects on take-up, as could making benefits easier to understand—for example, by offering matches instead of credits. Note, however, that different approaches may have different implications for targeting. Defaults might bring in a different mix of individuals, in terms of program-relevant characteristics, than, say, simplifying forms, which in turn might have effects that differ from those that result from simplifying benefit schedules.

A slightly deeper implication is that the complex eligibility that criteria programs set in order to target benefits precisely may come at greater costs than traditional economic analysis suggests. That is, many times qualification procedures or benefit schedules are complex not because policymakers have failed to attend to the costs of multiplying complexity but because they want to have a sophisticated targeting technique. Simplification in such programs would then tend to come at some cost to the ability to target benefits.[51] The key behavioral insight is that when individuals are imperfect decisionmakers, marginal reductions in complexity can lead to a marginal deterioration in the ability to screen out ineligible applicants that may generate first-order improvements in take-up rates among those who are eligible.

The standard model can miss that potential asymmetry, and it is likely to lead to policies that overemphasize exacting eligibility criteria that come at great cost to participation but offer little practical gain in targeting efficiency. A good example of that is found in the context of federal programs for college financial aid. Recent research suggests that the complexity of the application for college financial aid may serve as a deterrent both to applying for assistance and to attending college.[52] At the same time, research has argued that a simplified application process could target recipients nearly as well as current methods.[53] Taken together, the implication is that, in part due to behavioral factors, the cost-benefit profile of marginally more precise targeting in financial aid achieved by imposing greater burdens on applicants is less favorable than the standard analysis might suggest.

Finally, a slightly more subtle interpretation of the behavioral lesson for program design is that it is not necessarily program complexity itself that comes at the cost of participation or screening efficiency, but the complexity of the program as experienced by eligible individuals. The complexity of underlying program parameters such as eligibility criteria affects the take-up decision only to the extent that individuals are required to deal with it directly. Policy might, therefore, retain complex eligibility rules but shift the burden of applying those rules from the applicant to the government. In order to determine the eligibility of applicants, administering government agencies could be granted access to existing sources of data on earnings or family status and existing sources of administrative data could be modified to meet the needs of income support programs. Proposals to determine, for example, the eligibility of children for public health insurance programs using data from tax returns follow that approach.[54]

An alternative way of maintaining complex program rules while decreasing the burden on program applicants is to transfer some of the costs of take-up to third parties, such as nonprofits or businesses. That appears to be a promising policy response, especially in areas where there is scope for third parties to have material incentives to assist individuals in taking up benefits. For example, hospitals and other organizations have had some success in enrolling eligible individuals for Medicaid, in part by taking on some of the responsibility for completing the application process on their behalf.[55] Another example is the EITC; tax preparation firms, which can benefit from helping individuals claim the credit, are thought to be partially responsible for the relatively high take-up rate for that program.[56] In general, the tax system may be an attractive platform for delivering benefits, given its relative automaticity, the way that requirements for tax reporting intersect with requirements for benefit applications, and the robust network of third parties that has arisen in tax preparation. The success of a recent experiment that encouraged the take-up of college financial aid by taking information from individuals' tax returns at the time of filing and using it to assist them in completing the application demonstrates the potential of such an approach.[57]

Benefits and Outcomes

Another fundamental design challenge for programs that provide assistance directly to recipients is to structure benefits to promote the types of outcomes intended. While take-up of programs is necessary to achieve program goals, it is not in general sufficient. The ultimate goal of a program like SNAP might be thought of as reducing hunger or food insecurity, and programs like TANF (Temporary Assistance to Needy Families) and the EITC might be judged by whether and to what extent they alleviate any of a variety of hardships associated with material deprivation. However, delivering benefits is not identical to producing outcomes. For transfer policy to be successful, it must look beyond whether it can get benefits to those in need in order to determine whether those benefits achieve program goals. A behavioral approach can help in making that evaluation because many aspects of program effectiveness are determined by how recipients respond to and make use of benefits. For example, the extent to which SNAP benefits lead to reductions in hunger and food insecurity will be a joint product of the form and level of the benefit, on one hand, and the decisionmaking process by which recipients decide how to spend and consume, on the other.

A behavioral approach to evaluating the relationship between benefits and outcomes creates both challenges and opportunities for program design. The main challenge is due to the way that behavioral tendencies tend to mediate how benefits translate into outcomes. The opportunities that behavioral tendencies present are twofold. First, programs may be able to achieve outcomes through designs that are tailored to assist individuals with behavioral tendencies. Second, there may be new, behavioral levers by which program design may influence outcomes.

The primary challenge in designing programs to affect particular outcomes is that when individuals fail to respond to benefits as predicted by the standard model, that failure can have consequences for the way that benefits translate into outcomes. An important example is seen in how benefits are paid out over time. The time path of benefit payments will not necessarily match the time path of the expenses that benefits are intended to assist with. In the standard model, individuals are able to realize their preferences for how to structure their consumption over time subject only to whatever external constraints they face on saving and borrowing. In general they are assumed to be capable of transforming income from benefits into optimal consumption and outcomes. A behavioral approach relaxes and amends those assumptions. It allows for limitations in optimization and self-control that can lead individuals to have difficulty managing income in order to achieve optimal consumption patterns, in ways that can have implications for program outcomes.

Possible evidence of such an effect comes from the Supplemental Nutrition Assistance Program. Like many transfer programs, SNAP typically delivers benefits monthly. The distinctive feature of SNAP is that benefits can be used only for goods in a particular category of expenditure, food. Food is directly linked to an observable aspect of well-being, namely, nutrition and caloric intake. The result is that the timing of benefit delivery can be linked explicitly with the specific outcomes that the program is intended to foster. In the case of food, presumed preferences for consumption smoothing are reinforced by biological constraints that compel individuals to have an approximately smooth demand for calories over time. Studies that track the caloric intake of SNAP beneficiaries, however, find violations of consumption smoothing. In particular, evidence suggests that caloric intake by food stamp recipients ebbs over the course of the month following receipt of food stamps. One study found that among food stamp recipients, daily caloric intake declines on average by approximately 0.4 percent per day following benefit receipt, or about 8 food calories per day over that period.[58]

That result is consistent with a number of possible behavioral factors. One set of explanations focuses on the fact that the mismatch between the monthly delivery of benefits and the higher frequency at which consumption and purchasing decisions are made leaves individuals with a planning problem. Individuals may devote insufficient attention to planning how to consume out of their food stamp income and make errors. One piece of evidence that is consistent with planning errors is that, in some studies, calorie cycles are found to be more pronounced among those who shop less frequently.[59] Or the planning process might be complex for individuals with only limited computational capacity. If individuals incorrectly valued food stamps relative to cash, that could lead to overconsumption of food early in the month. Evidence from food stamp cash-out experiments that indicates that food expenditures are cyclical for participants paid in food stamps but not for participants paid in cash is consistent with that type of error.[60] So too is evidence that households sometimes treat food stamps as being worth less than their face value in cash.[61]

A largely separate behavioral explanation for the declining caloric intake over the course of the month comes from the difficulty that individuals may have committing to a time-consistent consumption path. Survey responses to time-preference questions that indicate that relatively impatient households are more likely to report skipping meals during the month for lack of funds establish a link between impatience and food consumption. Calibration exercises suggest that the hyperbolic discounting model is a better fit than the exponential model for explaining the monthly decline in caloric intake.[62] Those findings are reinforced by research on food purchases, which decline over the month even while food prices also decline over the month.[63] Compounding those effects is the fact that, to the extent that such cycles leave individuals in relative hunger at the end of each cycle, the cycle can be self-perpetuating. Studies find that individuals are, for example, more likely to plan to consume a high-calorie snack in the future if asked when they are hungry.[64]

While a timing effect in benefit delivery and program outcomes is perhaps clearest in the case of food stamps and food consumption, it is not limited to that case. Similar cycles have been found to result from the monthly delivery of other benefits, such as Social Security, for both food and other nondurable expenditures.[65] Such findings suggest direct policy implications, such as that paying food stamp and other benefits more frequently may improve policy outcomes. In at least one experience in another country, consumption smoothing among recipients appeared to improve when the frequency of benefit payments was increased.[66]

Such findings also suggest broader implications for policy beyond the timing of benefits. In general, the structure of benefits interacts with behavioral limitations to mediate outcomes. While the above examples show how self-control interacts with the timing of policy, other interactions of that type are easy to imagine. For example, limited computational capacity or bounded self-control might interact with the form of benefits—for example, whether they are delivered in cash or in kind—to lead individuals receiving cash benefits to have greater difficulty in planning or executing behavior in ways that are consistent with social goals. Such an effect might contribute, for example, to findings that food stamps may encourage food consumption more than cash transfers do.[67]

In addition to such challenges, a behavioral approach also highlights new opportunities for program design. In particular, policy design that is sensitive to behavioral tendencies can affect outcomes in ways that the standard model would not identify. What that means, in part, is that the form of benefits that is most useful to recipients may not be what the standard approach predicts. Programs can be designed in ways that, in addition to solving social problems, also address individuals' decisionmaking difficulties.

One instance in which the evidence seems to suggest that recipients take advantage of benefits in ways that the standard model would not suggest—although not necessarily by design—is the earned income tax credit. The EITC is relatively unusual for income support programs in that it offers recipients a choice of timing of benefits. The most common way for individuals to receive the EITC is to claim the credit on their federal income tax return and receive payment as part of their tax refund. However, many individuals who expect to claim the EITC on their tax return have the option to elect to have a portion of their anticipated EITC advanced to them in their paycheck, through a process of reverse withholding known as the Advance EITC.[68] Standard economic reasoning suggests that due to both time preferences and preferences for consumption smoothing, individuals should find that option attractive. In fact, the Advance EITC is strikingly unpopular. In recent years, only about 3 percent of households eligible to claim Advance EITC payments did so.[69]

That response is difficult to explain in the standard model. Transaction costs alone seem insufficient to explain observed take-up rates, and stigma is unlikely to play an important role. On the other hand, some of the behavioral barriers to take up highlighted above may play a role here. For example, claiming the EITC as a lump sum at tax time is, practically speaking, the default method of receiving benefits. There also is evidence that many eligible respondents are unaware of or do not understand the Advance EITC.[70] However, a field experiment that directly tested for the importance of those factors by providing information about the Advance EITC, supporting the choice through the employer, and encouraging a response one way or the other did not substantially raise participation in the Advance EITC.[71] Individuals seem to prefer to receive the EITC as a lump sum.

Preferences for the lump sum EITC are consistent with several behavioral explanations. To the extent that individuals treat their tax return and paycheck income as accruing to distinct mental accounts, for instance, they do not treat the opportunity to elect the advance EITC as a simple reordering of their stream of income but as a transfer of funds between those mental accounts. That is a transfer that individuals may be reluctant to make if, for example, they have earmarked their refund dollars for some particular expenditure. Some evidence is at least consistent with the view that individuals think of refunds and regular earnings as accruing to separate mental accounts. In surveys and interviews, individuals articulate clear plans for how they intend to use their EITC payment.[72] In addition, in surveys that ask low- and moderate-income individuals about how they view the trade-off between larger refunds and larger paychecks, many respondents express a definite preference for receiving part of their income as a tax refund.[73]

Preferences for taking the EITC as a lump sum may also derive from bounded self-control. Individuals with self-control problems may choose to forgo the Advance EITC option in order to use the EITC as a forced saving mechanism. Recipients can then use their tax return to, for example, purchase goods for which they otherwise would have had to save on their own, such as cars or appliances. Some survey evidence does suggest that individuals sometimes view the EITC in that way.[74] Other research also has found some evidence that EITC-eligible households frequently use their refund to buy consumer durables—big-ticket items such as furniture, appliances, or cars—suggesting that recipients are using the EITC as a saving mechanism to accumulate the funds necessary to purchase those items.[75] Most of those studies also find that many EITC recipients report using or planning to use their tax refund to pay down bills, such as utility bills or rent, which also is consistent with a response to difficulty with self-control.

While setting policy so that people are allowed to take the EITC as a lump sum and even to some extent encouraged to do so might appear to lead to welfare losses from the standard point of view, from the behavioral perspective it might be beneficial. To the extent that the lump sum EITC provides a commitment mechanism or reinforces mental accounting in ways that allow individuals opportunities to save that they might not otherwise have, policy might increase savings, so that rather than attempt to encourage use of the advanced option, policy might remain more neutral or even drop support of that option, as in some current proposals.[76] Policy might even seek to work more directly with behavioral tendencies to affect other outcomes, such as by capitalizing on the possibility that the EITC encourages saving.[77] Or policy could integrate the EITC into more formal asset-building strategies.[78]

More generally, the EITC example points to a broader implication for program design, which is that when policy is designed in ways that are sensitive to behavioral tendencies it might effect both the desired social outcomes as well as additional beneficial outcomes by addressing features of individual decisionmaking. Benefits might be designed in ways that directly or indirectly assist individuals with choice or with self-control. For example, some research has suggested that the timing of Supplemental Security Income benefits could be reordered in ways that might assist individuals with limited self-control to avoid episodes of drug abuse and the attendant health consequences.[79]

Finally, behavioral tendencies might lead to new levers by which policy can influence how individuals use benefits. Program design might be able to take advantage of behavioral tendencies in order to effect desired outcomes efficiently. For example, if recipients are sensitive to how benefits are presented or if reference-dependent preferences lead recipients to be sensitive to how benefits are framed, program design might be able to present or frame benefits in ways that are socially desirable.

There is some evidence that designating benefits in a particular way may lead to a labeling effect, whereby recipients tend to dispose of benefits in the ways suggested by their labels instead of treating benefits as fungible with other sources of income. That is consistent with mental accounting, with recipients posting labeled benefits to corresponding accounts for spending and consumption. There is some evidence from other countries that this may take place. For example, one study found that an unrestricted benefit labeled as a child benefit tended to raise spending on consumption goods for children more than spending on adults, at least in some families.[80] There also is some experimental evidence that individuals respond to income in ways suggested by labels.[81] As a result of such effects, the labeling and presentation of policies might be an element of program design that serves to encourage or discourage desired outcomes.

The potential implications of such findings are both narrow and broad. Narrowly, they suggests that program design should attend to how benefits are labeled as a possible way of effecting policy outcomes. For example, the labeling of a tax credit as a Child Tax Credit may not be a neutral feature of program design; the designation may have consequences for spending within the family and thereby for child welfare.[82] More broadly, such nonprice levers might be more generally available to policymakers as leverage in the design of policies to achieve important outcomes. These levers might go beyond simple labeling effects to include, for example, framing benefit schedules in terms of losses or gains or setting default delivery mechanisms to promote desired outcomes.

Work Incentives

Finally, even when income support policy successfully delivers benefits to targeted individuals and structures benefits so that recipients can use them to achieve desired outcomes, it also must address the special challenges associated with providing relief to the needy while preserving the incentives for those individuals to provide for themselves when possible. Although the primary objectives of income support and antipoverty policies are to ameliorate the particular conditions that they target—such as hunger, for example, or lack of adequate housing—most programs also have a common secondary goal of discouraging continued dependence on program benefits and encouraging self-support and employment. The challenge for policy, as noted above, is that those twin objectives are frequently and often inescapably at odds. The provision of means-tested benefits often creates a form of moral hazard, whereby the very benefits that forestall deprivation in poverty, once received, make the conditions of poverty less aversive and diminish the incentives to work and earn income. Even when benefits do not create moral hazard, they may interact with behavioral tendencies to discourage work, such as by indulging procrastination in searching for and taking work.

The exact nature and extent of the work disincentives associated with any given income support program depend on the specifics of program structure and goals, such as whether the program is available to working age adults, whether the program has work requirements or time limits, and how benefits are reduced as participants earn income. In general, however, making benefits available only to individuals who meet particular criteria creates incentives for individuals to change their behavior, within the framework established by program parameters, to meet those criteria. A particular concern in many instances is that individuals may intentionally reduce their labor supply in order to maximize the value of their benefits or to maintain or establish eligibility for benefits. In that respect the study of the labor supply response to income support programs is necessarily a behavioral endeavor, even before allowing for the psychological considerations introduced by behavioral economics. However, because designing policies to minimize adverse labor supply responses depends on an accurate understanding of what drives those responses and how they operate, relaxing traditional assumptions and taking a more empirical approach holds at least the potential to improve the ability of policymakers to manage such behavior.

The standard assumptions about individual preferences and decisionmaking processes lead to relatively straightforward conclusions about labor supply responses in the presence of income support policies—namely, that labor is a source of disutility, leisure is a source of positive utility, and that income from either earned or unearned sources supports consumption. The standard model further assumes, often implicitly, that beneficiaries are well informed about program rules when making decisions about the mix of earned income and benefits. The prescriptions that flow from this approach for policy design then depend on the way that benefits interact with labor income. When benefits are available in the absence of earned income or in addition to earned income, policy in general has to trade off the generosity of benefits against the fact that they will tend to reduce labor supply. Reducing benefits as labor income increases tends to discourage work; on the other hand, designing benefits to supplement labor income can encourage work.

A behavioral approach to the question of how income support policies affect labor supply builds on those basic implications and adds certain nuances that allow for different conclusions for program design. First, behavioral tendencies can create new challenges for program design because individuals may have a more complicated set of preferences with respect to work and leisure than the standard model assumes, and sometimes they may have difficulty expressing those preferences. If, for example, individuals possess only bounded self-control, they may have difficulty searching for and taking work even when they intend to do so, and the benefits that they qualify for by virtue of having only a marginal attachment to the labor force can undermine the willpower that they need to work more. The key implication for policy design is that in order to promote work effectively, policy sometimes has to address behavioral tendencies along with traditional moral hazard.

Second, sometimes behavioral tendencies afford new opportunities for program design. For example, when individuals are hampered by limits to attention and computational capacity, they may not understand the detailed terms of the programs for which they qualify. As a result, they will respond to their construal of the program parameters in forming their behavioral response rather than the true parameters; policymakers then may be able to shape that construal in ways that encourage work. In general, policy design might be able to take advantage of behavioral levers to promote work.

A possible example of the new kinds of challenges that a behavioral approach identifies for maintaining work incentives can be illustrated in the case of Temporary Assistance to Needy Families. TANF, the main federal cash welfare program, is an especially interesting case because it was born out of an explicit interest in work incentives. The Personal Responsibility and Work Opportunity Reconciliation Act of 1996, which created TANF, was motivated in large part by concerns that its predecessor program—Aid to Families with Dependent Children

(AFDC)—fostered dependency and discouraged work.[83] As a result, TANF imposes work requirements and time limits as measures to encourage work.[84] Time limits are a good example of the behavioral dimensions of such restrictions. While time limits are intended to mechanically cut off benefits to workers who would otherwise claim benefits for longer than allotted, they also are intended to influence the behavior of both recipients and potential recipients by changing the terms of the decision to claim benefits. Ultimately, it is how individuals view and respond to work incentives that determines how the incentives operate and how effective they are at encouraging work and mitigating moral hazard.

Under TANF, most individuals who qualify for welfare are limited to a cumulative lifetime total of sixty months of benefits. That means that welfare recipients face a potentially complex optimization problem in deciding whether and when to take benefits. Namely, prospective recipients who anticipate that the restriction will be binding must decide how to allocate their receipt of benefits over time. And all potential recipients have to incorporate a new source of uncertainty, whether or not they will exhaust their benefits, into their decisionmaking about claiming benefits and working. In the standard model, with perfectly optimizing, fully informed decisionmakers, the time limits simply act as a new constraint, and decisions about whether to work or claim benefits change accordingly as individuals re-optimize. In particular, for forward-looking individuals who view welfare benefits as insurance against negative shocks to their own employment or earnings prospects, time limits create a new incentive to put off applying for benefits in order to store up months of eligibility for possible later use.[85] Researchers have found some evidence of a behavioral response to time limits consistent with these incentives.[86]

Behavioral tendencies, however, are likely to interact with incentives like time limits in ways that change both their effectiveness and their welfare consequences. An important behavioral dimension to finding and taking work rather than claiming TANF benefits is that individuals may procrastinate in searching for and taking work. Some evidence suggests that welfare-eligible individuals may have such time-inconsistent preferences with respect to work and welfare and that they may lead individuals to be less likely to work.[87]

Consequently, policy design for programs such as TANF, in order to encourage work, must overcome not just the disincentives created by the program but also behavioral barriers to work. Time limits again provide an interesting example. One hypothesis about how the behavioral response to welfare time limits interacts with present-biased preferences suggests that such preferences can actually lead time limits to be more effective than in the standard model.[88] For beneficiaries with bounded self-control, time limits on welfare benefits could serve as a commitment device, allowing them to overcome the self-control problem that prevents them from returning to work. In the presence of time limits, workers may recognize that they have only limited access to welfare benefits, thus making working in the current period worthwhile.

Note, finally, that while the effects of time limits are similar under both models—in the standard model, recipients bank their months of eligibility; in the behavioral alternative, time limits serve as a commitment device—they represent starkly different outcomes for the welfare of recipients. Under the standard set of assumptions, time limits represent an additional constraint under which optimizing choices about working and earning must be made; as an added constraint, they necessarily reduce the welfare of recipients compared with an otherwise identical welfare regime without limits. In contrast, if self-control problems born of time-inconsistent preferences are at the root of some individuals' use of welfare, then time limits leave at least some welfare recipients better off.[89] This is an example of how, as discussed above, the moral hazard problem posed by income support policies can take on a fundamentally different character in the presence of behavioral tendencies.

The case of TANF and time limits is an example of the more general issue that behavioral tendencies may interact with or operate alongside the moral hazard created by income support programs. The principle, of course, is not limited to either TANF as a program or time limits as a design feature. One could imagine, for instance, that biased or otherwise inaccurate beliefs about labor market prospects also could inhibit work and that work requirements, counseling, or other support services might be an appropriate policy response. Similarly, the issue of behavioral tendencies complicating the design problem in programs like TANF is not the only implication that deviations from the standard model carry for policy design and work incentives. The other general issue is that behavioral tendencies might provide policymakers with additional tools and opportunities for encouraging work. The work incentives embedded in the EITC and how they are understood by eligible individuals are an example.

The EITC, in contrast to TANF, represents a fundamentally different approach to redistribution in which the benefits schedule itself is designed to encourage work. The EITC, which is essentially a subsidy to earned income, is designed in part to circumvent the difficulties associated with programs like TANF. Rather than providing benefits and imposing restrictions on the conditions under which they can be claimed, the EITC explicitly ties benefits to working and earning by making benefits a function of earned income.[90] The growth of the EITC in recent decades relative to traditional forms of welfare has been in no small part due to its more desirable work incentives.

Although generally the EITC encourages work more than programs such as TANF, it is not expected to uniformly promote an increase in labor supply. On one hand, the fact that the EITC is a subsidy to work creates an income effect that tends to discourage work. On the other hand, the EITC changes the effective wage rate, creating substitution effects. As the EITC phases in, thus supplementing wages, the substitution effect encourages work; as it phases out, decreasing the after-tax wage, the substitution effect discourages work. While standard economic theory suggests that the EITC may have these different effects on labor supply depending on the range of benefits, in practice researchers have not found that to be true. Instead, what they have found is that while the EITC does appear to have a positive impact on labor force participation, it does not appear to have a significant effect on the number of hours worked.[91] There are a number of competing explanations for why the participation effect is so clear while any effect on hours worked is not evident in the data.[92] One possibility is that individuals do not, in practice, have great flexibility in choosing the number of hours that they work. Another explanation is that hours worked may simply be poorly measured relative to participation—that the usual empirical methods and datasets may be inadequate to the task of detecting any impact of the EITC on the number of hours worked.

While those effects are real, behavioral tendencies also are likely to play a role in the muted response of hours worked to the EITC. The result may be due in part to the fact that the EITC follows a complicated schedule to which recipients can bring only limited attention and computational resources. What evidence is available does suggest that EITC-eligible individuals possess only imperfect knowledge of how the credit operates.[93] A direct experiment with providing information about the EITC schedule produced a labor supply response among some participants that was consistent with the incentives of the credit being understood only imperfectly.[94] The conflicting evidence on the impact of the EITC on labor force participation and hours worked also is consistent with evidence that individuals understand the work incentives of the EITC only in some approximate sense.[95] For instance, an increase in labor force participation with little effect on hours worked could be a result of workers understanding the average effects of the EITC on earnings but not the marginal effects. That is consistent with findings on behavioral responses to income taxes in general that suggest that people do not respond sharply to marginal tax rates.[96] Furthermore, any confusion about the parameters of the EITC may be heightened by the fact that low-income households face a generally bewildering tax schedule, owing in part to the phasing in and out of multiple credits like the EITC.[97] As a result, individuals may fail to distinguish between the differing substitution effects that operate in different regions of the EITC depending on the number of hours that they work, but they may respond to the increased returns to employment in choosing whether or not to work.

The behavioral insight for the design of programs like the EITC is the understanding that how individuals construe work incentives is mediated by behavioral tendencies such as imperfect optimization or bounded self-control and that policy design can influence that construal. So, in the case of the EITC, policy could in principle work to clarify the terms of the credit. But it may be advantageous, from the perspective of society (in terms of the consequences for work incentives), to keep the specific terms of the credit somewhat obscure. Similarly, in considering the design of possible expansions of the EITC or the introduction of new credits that might work similarly, the clarity of program parameters will in general not be a neutral feature of reforms in terms of their work incentives.

More generally, what a behavioral analysis of the benefit schedule of the EITC highlights is the fact that program design has available a set of behavioral levers that it might use to encourage work in conjunction with financial incentives or mechanical limits. Levers might include the presentation or framing of benefit schedules, as with the EITC. Another behavioral channel that might be important is through other-regarding preferences, in particular the influence of social norms. Social norms might influence work decisions and interact with the incentives created by income support policies.[98] Program design therefore might seek to encourage work by reinforcing pro-work social norms. For example, the general shift in income support policy in the 1990s in the United States—the replacement of AFDC with TANF, along with expansions of the EITC—might have encouraged work in part by reinforcing pro-work social norms.

7

Taxation and Revenue

Running a government is expensive. Correcting for market failures, providing public goods, guaranteeing social insurance, and redistributing income and sustaining antipoverty efforts—functions of government within the purview of public finance—all involve various expenditures. Increasing the expense are functions of government that are outside the scope of public finance, such as administering court systems, maintaining regulatory bodies, and other endeavors. In a typical year, the federal government's share of the U.S. economy is about 20 percent.[1] About one-fifth of federal spending is on Social Security; one-fifth on health programs, including Medicare and Medicaid; one-fifth on national defense; and the remaining two-fifths on everything else. Spending by state and local governments from their own sources amounts to roughly another 15 percent of total output, of which the largest single fraction, about one-third, is on education.[2]

In order to spend in this way, governments have to raise revenue. While there are other means, primarily borrowing by issuing debt, governments finance their operations mainly through taxation. Taxes take a variety of forms in the United States. At the federal level, the personal income tax raises close to half of total revenue. Another third or so comes from payroll taxes, the taxes that fund Social Security and Medicare. The rest is from other sources, such as corporate income taxes, excise taxes, estate and gift taxes, and so on. State and local governments also have income taxes, which account for about one-quarter of their revenue. In addition, state and local governments also rely heavily on consumption taxes, such as sales taxes on consumer goods, which raise about a third of their total revenue, as well as taxes on property, which account for another third. The remainder is from other sources.

Raising revenue in this way, through taxes on goods, income, and so on, changes the prices of nearly every economic activity that people engage in. Taxes on labor income lower the return to working, earning, and saving. Taxes on consumption change the relative prices of goods and services. Taxes on capital lower the return to accumulation. In some cases the change in price can be subtle. For instance, sales taxes often are in the neighborhood of 5 to 10 percent.[3] In other cases, it can be dramatic. At the federal level, current marginal income tax rates range from 10 percent up to 35 percent, and for many workers that is in addition to marginal payroll taxes of 15.3 percent. And effective marginal rates can be even higher when, for example, credits or deductions phase out. One calculation of effective marginal tax rates for labor income puts the rates at over 40 percent for workers across many income ranges.[4]

Because taxes change the terms of such choices, taxes affect how people act and behave. The standard economic analysis of taxation starts from understanding the relationship between taxes and behavior. The real consequences of taxation are largely a function of the magnitude and nature of the response to taxes. When taxes are imposed on income, do people work less? How much less? How are the impacts related to the level or rate of the tax? How are they related to its form and relationship with other elements of the tax code or broader policy? The questions are similar for effects on saving and investment, consumption, and so on. This margin of response—the elasticity of supply or demand with respect to the tax—is the key parameter for analysis.

Taking a behavioral perspective on the economic analysis of taxation may be important because behavioral tendencies will mediate the response to taxes. For example, due to limited computational capacity, individuals may respond to complex tax schedules only approximately or with error, or they may fail to understand the relationship of taxes to their behavior. Due to limited attention, individuals may fail to notice some taxes at all, in particular when they are hidden or obscure. The key implication is that individuals will respond to taxes as they perceive them, not necessarily as they are set. As a result, the relationship between taxes and behavior may become much less straightforward than in the standard model.

This relationship may be further complicated by the way that taxes might interact with nonstandard preferences. The impact of taxes on behavior might be determined in part by reference-dependence. For example, depending on how taxes are structured, they may be perceived as losses or as gains from some reference point, which might have consequences for behavior. In addition, responses to taxes might depend in part on other-regarding preferences. For example, taxes might activate or reinforce social norms.

The importance of such insights for understanding the economics of taxation and tax policy is likely to be substantial. It is not much of an exaggeration to say that all of the standard economic analysis of taxation is built around the analysis of how individuals respond to taxes. The fundamental question in this analysis is understanding the efficiency costs of taxation. While raising revenue, taxes impose a burden on society. When taxes change prices and so lead individuals to not undertake activities that they otherwise would have, economic efficiency is impaired (except in the case of externalities, as discussed in chapter 5). From the standard perspective, when individuals are responding optimally to taxes, the costs of taxation are a straightforward, rising function of the magnitude of their response.

Similarly, the relative magnitudes of responses to taxation determine the distributional features of taxes, or the incidence of taxes. That is, who bears the burden of the tax depends on who responds to the tax. The less individuals change their behavior in response to a tax, the more of the tax they typically end up paying.

The design of tax policy, in turn, is guided by the understanding of how taxes create these real effects. To design efficient taxes, policymakers can look for instances in which taxes do not elicit outsized responses. Policy also reflects some judgment about equity. Following from how we understand tax burdens, policymakers can design taxes to distribute those burdens according to social goals.

A behavioral perspective may complicate the analysis of tax impacts substantially. In allowing that individuals may fail to respond to taxes optimally, it breaks the straightforward link between observed behavior and inferences about welfare consequences. If, for example, individuals do not respond to taxes because they do not perceive them, then their lack of response may not represent their preferences, but rather reflect an error in choice. So while the lack of response mitigates the welfare loss due to forgone economic activity, it potentially creates welfare losses elsewhere due to the error. Likewise, behavioral tendencies in responding to taxation might also have consequences for who pays the tax. In the above example, the failure to notice a tax might, for instance, lead individuals to pay more of it than they otherwise would.

Because behavioral tendencies can change the way that taxes affect economic outcomes, they also have implications for the design of tax policy. The behavioral perspective identifies important design elements that policy must consider—for example, knowing that the presentation of taxes is no longer a neutral element of policy design, policy will have to reflect some judgment about how to set or accept the salience of taxes. It also identifies the tools and levers that tax policy might use to effect desired outcomes. For example, policy might take active steps to hide taxes, in order to mute response, or it may take steps to make taxes more salient, in order to generate a response. The course of action for policy design follows from conclusions about the welfare implications of such behavioral tendencies for tax efficiency and incidence.

In this chapter, we work through the behavioral approach to questions of taxation. We again divide the analysis according to our public finance framework, proceeding from the diagnosis of the problem, to judgments about objectives and trade-offs, to the prescription of policy solutions. Note, however, that within our framework taxation presents a special case since the policy problem—the underlying cause for government intervention—is usually taken to be a given revenue requirement: in order to fund the operations of government, the government must raise revenue.

Note also that this is a deliberately narrow statement of the problem; we confine ourselves, as is standard in public finance treatments of taxation, essentially to the implications of behavioral economics for the optimal tax problem and tax policy design. While governments levy taxes for a variety of reasons, not just to raise revenue, here we take a standard approach in public finance and consider the problem of taxation for the purposes of raising revenue in isolation. Any implications of behavioral economics for the use of taxes as an instrument of broader policy—such as corrective taxation or taxation as part of antipoverty efforts or income redistribution—are discussed separately in the chapters on those topics.

The significance of defining the problem this way for our exposition is that the diagnosis step becomes trivial—the justification for raising revenue is thus simply derivative of the justifications for any government interventions that require funding—and, more important for our purposes, it is unaffected by the introduction of behavioral economics concepts. Accordingly, we proceed directly to a discussion of the judgment dimension, followed by an analysis of the policy prescriptions that follow from the judgments made.

From that perspective and to those ends, we take a broad look at how the findings of behavioral economics interact with and modify the economic analysis of taxation. We begin with a review of how behavioral tendencies mediate the response of individuals to taxation; we go on to consider their implications for the welfare consequences of taxation; and we conclude with some implications for tax policy design. This approach yields potentially valuable insights for each of those issues:

—*Taxes and behavioral response.* Behavioral tendencies mediate how people respond to taxes. Inattention can lead to some taxes not being salient, and complexity of tax schedules can lead people to respond to taxes in error. Due to those effects, response to taxes might reflect a form of error rather than a simple preference. In addition, reference-dependence can mean that the framing of taxes has consequences for behavior, as can other-regarding preferences. Due to those effects, behavioral responses to taxes can be sensitive to contexts that the standard model would not identify.

—*Taxes and welfare.* The benefits associated with activities that taxes fund must be weighed against the efficiency costs that taxes impose on the economy by distorting prices. Taxes affect the distribution of economic outcomes as well, which impose trade-offs across individuals or groups. The optimal taxation problem weighs these costs and trade-offs: given a revenue requirement, tax policy seeks to maximize efficiency and meet social preferences for equity. Both distributional and efficiency outcomes depend on behavioral response, and allowing for the type of imperfect decisionmaking or nonstandard behaviors emphasized by behavioral economics can change the nature and terms of the trade-offs involved.

—*Tax policy.* From an economic perspective, the design of tax policy for the purpose of raising revenue is an attempt to apply the insights from the welfare analysis of the optimal taxation problem to practical problems associated with collecting revenue by various sources. Public finance can offer principles for tax policy design, evaluation of existing policies, and proposals for reform. Viewing tax policy through the lens of behavioral economics, we obtain new principles for tax policy design and new perspectives on existing and proposed features of taxation.

Optimal Taxation and Psychology

Taxation is necessary for society. Given some set of costly activities that are worthwhile for the government to undertake—for example, providing public goods such as national defense or providing social insurance to the elderly, sick, or unemployed—there is a need to raise revenue. The primary means of doing so is levying taxes, in a variety of forms: income taxes and taxes on wages, sales and excise taxes, taxes on capital gains and on estates, and so on.

The challenge that taxes pose for policy is that while they make beneficial expenditures possible, they also impose costs and trade-offs. At the most straightforward level, taxes redistribute welfare from those who pay taxes to those who benefit from what taxes fund. Taxes also create a drag on overall economic efficiency by creating wedges between the prices paid by consumers of goods and services and the prices received by suppliers. Moreover, taxes are costly to administer and enforce. The economic analysis of taxation seeks to identify the terms and nature of the trade-offs required, both to locate where the terms are more and less favorable and to inform judgments about when and under what conditions the benefits of taxes might be thought of as worth the costs.

From the perspective of public finance, the primary set of trade-offs is due to how individuals respond to the changing incentives created by taxes. When taxes affect prices, people react, creating consequences for social welfare. On one hand, the response dictates the efficiency costs of taxation—responses to taxes that move the economy away from its optimum cause a reduction in social welfare. On the other hand, the response determines the incidence of taxation—relative responses to taxes determine the distributional consequences of taxation. A secondary but not necessarily small set of costs from this perspective is due to both the practical costs associated with taxes, such as the costs of administering and complying with taxes, and the costs to society of unproductive tax avoidance behaviors.

In each of the trade-offs, behavior plays a key role. In the standard model, the terms of the trade-offs are delineated under the usual assumption of optimal decisionmaking and perfect self-interest. A behavioral perspective introduces new evidence and logic regarding how individuals respond to taxes and so changes the terms and forms of the trade-offs. Thus a behavioral perspective can inform our understanding of tax efficiency, incidence, compliance, and avoidance.

Behavioral Response and Welfare

The main approach to assessing the welfare consequences of taxes in public finance is to consider the nature of the welfare costs—both their magnitude and distribution—that arise because taxes discourage what would be socially productive economic activities. In general, taxes depress economic activity below its efficient level, leading to a welfare cost. In addition, because different groups are differentially sensitive to price changes, welfare costs are borne differentially across groups. As a result, when considering how and how much to tax, society must consider both the efficiency costs of taxation—usually called the excess burden of taxation, or the deadweight loss—and the distributional and equity consequences of taxation, or what is called tax incidence.

In the standard approach, public finance models deadweight loss and incidence as functions of elasticities, or parameterizations of the change in behavior in response to the tax. This approach allows statements about the efficiency costs of taxes on, for example, earned income in terms of the distortions that the taxes create in incentives to work and earn.[5] Similarly for commodity taxes, the magnitude of the deadweight losses of those taxes is a function of the relative decrease in consumption that they cause.[6] Likewise, the incidence of taxation can, in the standard approach, be identified in terms of the relative sensitivity of the response of affected parties to taxes.

Given the central role of individuals' response to taxes in determining their welfare consequences, a behavioral approach may change standard conclusions about taxes and welfare. A behavioral approach allows that how people respond to taxes may be less straightforward than the standard model supposes—their responses might reflect imperfect decisionmaking processes, nonstandard preferences, and so on. As a result, the efficiency and incidence consequences of their responses may be different from those in the standard model. The first step to a behavioral approach to issues of taxation and welfare is, then, to consider the ways in which behavioral tendencies mediate how individuals respond to taxes. The logic of tax efficiency and tax incidence can then be reconsidered from a behavioral perspective.

Psychology and Behavioral Response

The traditional approach to understanding the welfare consequences of taxation is to take the relevant price elasticities as sufficient for describing the response to a tax. So, for example, in the case of a commodity tax on good x, the formula for the own-price elasticity of demand, η_d, can be written as

$$\eta_d = \frac{\partial x}{\partial p_x} \cdot \frac{p_x}{x}$$

—that is, the elasticity is the percentage change in quantity demanded for a 1 percent change in the price. The own-price elasticity of supply, η_s, can be written analogously. In this model, the effect of taxes works through their impact on prices. So given the impact of taxes on prices, the formula given above summarizes the expected response.

This approach is straightforward as far as it goes, but it embeds a number of assumptions about behavior that often are left implicit. One key assumption is that individuals correctly perceive and understand the change in price due to taxes, so that their responses to taxes reveal something about their underlying preferences or the cost-benefit calculus involved in deciding whether or not to take an action. Standard assumptions about the form of preferences, such as reference-independence, also are common. Such assumptions allow this approach to abstract from responses due, for example, to the way that taxes are framed.

A behavioral approach to understanding how individuals respond to taxes calls those assumptions into question. Perhaps the major implication of behavioral economics for understanding people's response to taxes is the fact that individuals can no longer be assumed to perceive taxes correctly—even when they perceive net-of-tax prices correctly. Due to the effects of limited attention or computational capacity, individuals will respond not to the tax rate as it is set, but as they construe it. Furthermore, nonstandard preferences such as reference-dependence suggest that responses to taxation are likely to be unstable with respect to, for example, the way in which taxes are presented. And other-regarding preferences mean that preferences over the form and object of the tax itself can affect response. Behavioral aspects of tax response follow from these behavioral tendencies.

Inattention and Salience. Individuals respond only to taxes that they see or think about. Limited attention means that when taxes are not obvious or salient, they may be either fully or partially ignored. This conclusion contrasts with conclusions of the standard analysis, which typically assumes, often implicitly, that tax rates and other parameters are common knowledge. Even allowing for the costs associated with determining tax rates and tax bills, the benefits of holding and acting on accurate perceptions of taxes are likely to make the costs worth bearing except in the most extreme or trivial instances. As a consequence of inattention, an observed low elasticity of demand may be a consequence of individuals failing to notice a tax rather than of actually having preferences that make them insensitive to it.

Evidence suggests that salience effects are present with respect to both commodity and labor taxes. One recent study finds that individuals do not attend to sales taxes consistently and accurately, on the basis of two pieces of evidence.[7] The first was from an experiment run by the researchers in a grocery store, where price tags for a selected group of products were modified to include applicable sales taxes. Posting prices in that way led to reductions in demand, suggesting that individuals were failing to attend to the sales tax in the absence of the treatment. The second piece of evidence came from panel data on alcohol sales, comparing the effects of excise taxes imposed at the wholesale level, which are included in the posted price, with the effects of sales taxes, which are not. Consistent with the hypothesis that consumers do not fully attend to the costs of taxes not displayed in posted prices, alcohol consumption appears to be much more elastic with respect to changes in excise taxes than changes in sales taxes. A related piece of evidence comes from a different study on the effects of automated toll collection, which found that individuals paid less attention to tolls collected in that less salient manner than to tolls collected manually.[8]

These recent findings with respect to taxes specifically echo earlier findings from marketing research on how individuals respond to prices in general.[9] That research found behavior that is consistent with individuals failing to attend to prices, which suggests that individuals may not attend to taxes. For example, the research suggests that posting prices ending in $0.99—such as $9.99 as opposed to $10.00—can have material effects on demand.[10] That is consistent with individuals failing to attend to consumption taxes, which raise the price of many goods with this pricing feature. Other research finds evidence that individuals fail to attend to shipping costs relative to sale prices, a situation in some ways analogous to sales taxes.[11]

There is some evidence of salience effects in labor taxes as well. One finding consistent with individuals not attending fully to the income tax schedule is that taxpayers in general fail to bunch around the points in the income tax schedule where marginal tax rates change discretely.[12] The exception to this rule is that there appears to be bunching around the first such point, where the marginal tax rate goes from zero to a positive figure, which is presumably the portion of the schedule that is most salient. Another source of evidence for inattention comes from evidence on responses to changes in income tax withholding. Individuals may fail to perceive changes in withholding schedules.[13] Some studies find that changes in withholding schedules can lead to changes in spending even in the absence of a change in the tax rate.[14] That result—that behavior responds to mere changes in the way in which tax liability is presented—can be viewed as the labor tax analog to the effects of posting tax-inclusive prices for consumption goods described above. A related result was found in a laboratory experiment showing that subjects were more likely to plan to spend a hypothetical tax cut delivered as many small payments rather than one delivered as a lump sum.[15]

Complexity and Error. A different way in which individuals may respond to taxes imperfectly is to misperceive the magnitude or form of the tax. That is, even when individuals attend to the tax problem, they may respond to an inaccurate construal of the tax. Behavioral tendencies such as limited computational capacity and biased reasoning mean that when taxes are complex or obscure, responses may be based on inaccurate perceptions of taxes due to either outright error or adoption of rules of thumb. Put simply, a behavioral approach allows that tax schedules are complicated and that people make mistakes. Those mistakes, depending on the particular form that they take, might lead individuals to respond to taxes more or less than they would if they perceived tax schedules precisely. Note the functional distinction that this creates between salience and complexity, which are otherwise closely related concepts: while salience effects tend only to result in a response that is depressed relative to the response with perfectly optimizing behavior, complexity and error can have effects that go in either direction.

Errors can take a variety of forms. Individuals may respond to smoothed approximations of tax schedules or respond to local features of tax schedules while ignoring other elements.[16] Some evidence from laboratory experiments suggests that individuals do make such errors. For example, one study finds evidence that individuals may respond to average income tax rates rather than marginal rates.[17] Another study finds that individuals do not respond identically to income and consumption taxes with equivalent terms, as predicted by the standard model.[18] The effect could be due to errors or to differences in the time dimension of consumption and income taxation that interact with bounded self-control.

Other evidence consistent with a role for complexity and error in response to taxes comes from survey, observational, and field experiment data, primarily with respect to features of the income tax schedule. Evidence from those studies on whether individuals have and respond to accurate perceptions of marginal tax rates is more mixed, with some survey evidence consistent with misperception and some response estimates consistent with accurate perceptions.[19] Evidence on how individuals understand and respond to elements of the tax code beyond their marginal tax rate, however, generally suggests some degree of misperception or error. For example, the manner in which individuals report understanding and responding to the EITC is consistent with misperception.[20] Additional evidence comes from work that finds a response to an intervention providing information about the EITC schedule that suggests an imperfect understanding of the relevant tax schedule in the absence of the intervention.[21] Evidence on the way that individuals respond to loss of eligibility for the Child Tax Credit—by reducing labor supply in response—suggests imperfect understanding.[22] The finding that the response to the incentives to save provided by the Saver's Credit is sensitive to the presentation of the credit also indicates a type of error or misperception in responding to income taxes.[23] And evidence that some individuals fail to itemize income tax deductions when doing so would lower their tax bill is consistent with individuals responding in error to a complex tax code.[24]

Preferences. Finally, nonstandard preferences may interact with tax schedules to affect behavioral response. Individuals may perceive and evaluate taxes relative to reference points rather than in absolute terms; as a result, equivalent tax schemes may not generate identical responses if they are construed relative to different reference points. Individuals might, for example, consider changes to tax rates relative to the status quo or respond differentially to increases and decreases in taxes. That might lead to asymmetric responses to changes in tax rates depending on how increases or decreases are framed.

Evidence for the role of reference-dependence in responding to taxation comes from experimental work that provides the primary piece of evidence that framing and reference-dependence can influence how individuals respond to taxes.[25] That study finds that tax cuts presented as a "bonus" might be more likely to be spent than tax cuts presented as a "rebate." One interpretation sees the difference as result of reference-dependence—that when individuals perceive the tax cut as an outright gain (a "bonus") rather than as a restitution of a loss (a "rebate"), they are more likely to spend the tax cut. It is possible to interpret some of the cross-country evidence on the disposition of tax cuts as consistent with that finding.[26]

Behavioral economics also allows that individuals may hold preferences over the form or disposition of taxes that they might express in part through their response to taxation. That is, individuals may respond to a tax differently due to other-regarding preferences. For example, preferences for fairness or perceptions of fairness may create a barrier to downward wage adjustment to taxes, in a manner similar to the minimum wage. In addition, individuals may not mind paying taxes or may in fact seek to pay them when they believe either the taxes themselves or the activities that they fund to be worthwhile. For example, someone with preferences for redistribution may respond to progressive income taxes (say, in their decisions about how much to work) less than a perfectly self-interested individual.

TAX EFFICIENCY

Starting from a traditional approach to understanding tax efficiency, the cost of taxation can be written as a function of elasticities.[27] In a simple, partial equilibrium analysis, the formula for the excess burden of a tax is as follows:

$$EB = -\frac{1}{2} \cdot \frac{p \cdot q}{\frac{1}{\eta_d} - \frac{1}{\eta_s}} \cdot t^2,$$

where t is the tax rate, η_s is the elasticity of supply, and η_d is the elasticity of demand. A familiar set of results can be derived from this equation. First, the excess burden increases with more elastic market participants—that is, the greater the reduction in quantities transacted due to a tax, the larger the excess burden that it creates. Second, the excess burden increases with the square of the tax rate—as a result, the efficiency costs of taxes rise quickly with tax rates. These qualitative relationships are very general, and they hold for both labor and commodity taxes. That yields two rules of thumb about how to design tax policies so as to minimize distortions. The first is that taxes on inelastic goods are generally preferred for the way that they generate a smaller excess burden. The second is that holding the revenue requirement constant, lower tax rates on wider tax bases lead to less excess burden than higher rates on narrower bases.

Because a behavioral approach modifies our understanding of how individuals respond to taxes, it is likely to affect the validity and generality of those conclusions. For the reasons laid out above, observed elasticities may sometimes conflate preferences with salience or with errors due to complexity. Furthermore, those elasticities may depend on reference points or other elements of the choice environment usually taken to be neutral for response and welfare. They also may reflect other-regarding preferences. The relationship between excess burden and elasticity is likely to be complicated as a result. In addition, the relationship between the tax rate and the excess burden becomes less straightforward because tax rates and elasticities are probably no longer plausibly independent factors in the calculation of excess burden. For example, as tax rates rise, their salience rises, and elasticities may change.

Hidden Taxes. Changes to efficiency results may occur because of the effects of tax salience. Some taxes can be partially hidden from those who face them, leading individuals to fail to fully react to those taxes. Note that there are a number of different ways that a tax might be considered hidden, not all of which are likely to affect an individual's response and welfare. For example, when taxes are in some way built into prices so that individuals do not realize that they are paying a tax, that tax might be said to be hidden. Value-added taxes could be considered to be largely hidden from consumers. But taxes hidden in this sense still provoke a response to the extent that they increase prices; therefore, while they may have interesting political properties due to the failure of individuals to perceive them, economically there is little effect on tax efficiency. (See box 7-1 for a brief discussion on this point about behavioral economics and political economy.)

Here we are concerned with taxes that are hidden in the sense that individuals may easily fail to attend to them, so that they fail to take account of the tax in making decisions about working, consuming, or saving. Sales taxes, for example, which typically are not included in prices posted to consumers, may be hidden in this sense. When taxes are hidden in this way, the observed elasticity in the excess burden formula is smaller (in absolute value) for a behavioral individual than it would be for a perfectly optimizing agent.

What does the lack of response mean in terms of the excess burden of the tax? It is tempting, based on the partial equilibrium analysis of excess burden calculations, to say that the lack of response to a tax is good from the perspective of social welfare—that there is less distortion due to less elastic responses and that therefore the social cost of taxation is mitigated. But that conclusion depends heavily on taking a partial equilibrium perspective; it ignores that error on the part of the individual has to be accounted for somewhere.

When individuals fail to respond to a tax because it is not salient, in general there will be two, potentially offsetting, effects. On one hand, it will mitigate the welfare loss that comes through the traditional channel, because the change in quantity will be less than when taxes are fully salient. On the other hand, it can lead directly to a loss of social welfare through a new channel, in that the mistake of failing to account for the tax can move individuals away from their private optimum.[28] That is, when an individual fails to re-optimize in response to the tax, it can impose a welfare cost relative to full optimization. The nature and extent of the cost may depend on how the error propagates and the dimensions along which individuals compensate. The welfare implications may depend on the width of the choice brackets that individuals employ in making decisions about taxed activities. How much inattention to sales taxes matters might depend, for example, on whether individuals adjust their budget constraint at the register or at the end of the month. Welfare costs also might depend on how choices are made across domains—for example, if individuals spend more money for failing to perceive a tax, that money might come out of savings. In general, what happens in the next period or along other margins of adjustment is likely to be important.

Note finally that an additional complicating factor for the welfare analysis of salience is that part of the choice context that attention to taxes is sensitive to is the tax rate itself. High taxes are more likely to be salient, while modest taxes are more likely to escape notice. As a result, the observed elasticity not only differs from the elasticity that would obtain under full salience, it also varies in a way that may create an interdependence between the tax rate and the response parameter in the calculation of excess burden. For instance, it may be the case that, other things being equal, the excess burden rises with the tax rate in excess of its square because in addition to entering the calculation directly, the rising tax rate also leads to a greater degree of tax salience and thus to a more pronounced behavioral response. In particular, new nonlinearities in the tax rate become possible, as tax levels may cross thresholds from levels that generally are not salient to levels that generally are salient.

Taken together, these considerations introduce considerable nuance to the usual rules of thumb about taxes and efficiency. Most significant, it is no longer necessarily the case that a low elasticity response to a tax indicates that the tax is relatively efficient. A depressed behavioral response could represent true preferences, but it also could represent a lack of salience. That is, low elasticity could signal a choice error that is itself potentially costly to welfare. Likewise, the desirable efficiency feature of low tax rates on broad tax bases becomes somewhat complicated. Changes in the tax rate affect the salience of the tax, which in turn has welfare implications. That imposes a trade-off between the magnitude of a tax and the degree to which the tax can be hidden that creates an additional constraint on welfare outcomes.

Tax Mistakes. Other changes to the standard conclusions about tax efficiency come from the fact that individuals may construe taxes imperfectly, especially when tax schedules are complex. Tax mistakes are related to hidden taxes, but they have at least two distinguishing features. First, while failure to attend to taxes pushes the response in one direction only (toward underresponse), tax mistakes can in principle cause a response to be greater than or less than the response expected from perfectly optimizing individuals. Second, whereas tax salience is a relatively general, single feature, tax mistakes can take many forms. There is only one way to ignore a tax, but there are a lot of ways to get it wrong: miscalculating taxes, mistaking average for marginal tax rates, failing to connect taxes with the benefits that they fund, and so on. As a result of the variation in both the causes and outcomes of tax mistakes, final judgments about their welfare consequences depend on the nature of the specific error.

Despite the need to consider the welfare consequences of particular tax mistakes individually, the general logic of the case of hidden taxes still applies. On one hand, excess burden calculations change due to the introduction of elasticities

Box 7-1. *Behavioral Political Economy*

Many interesting findings from behavioral economics studies of taxes have to do not with the way that behavioral economics mediates responses to taxes, but instead how behavioral insights explain preferences for features of the tax code.[a] Those studies are closely related to the behavioral public finance analysis of taxation, but they are distinct in that they are not really about how behavioral economics informs the efficiency or incidence of taxation. What they reveal instead are the behavioral dimensions to political support for taxes and features of taxes.

For example, early identification of apparently imperfect decisionmaking with respect to taxes comes from a qualitative finding that support for a feature of the tax code like a tax credit may depend on whether it is framed as a credit for those who qualify or as a penalty for those who do not qualify.[b] Subsequent studies have examined more carefully, for example, through laboratory experiments, how support for levels or features of taxes can be sensitive to behavioral tendencies. For example, individuals may fail to perceive their total tax burden when they face multiple schedules, as they do with separate payroll and income taxes.[c] The result might lead individuals to support higher total overall tax burdens. Errors in perception about how taxes operate can affect support for reform.[d] Similarly, perceptions of fairness could affect the level or form of taxes that individuals are willing to support as voters.

Behavioral tendencies may not only affect direct support for elements of taxes but also may constrain and influence political outcomes with respect to taxes. For example, when taxes are not salient but expenditures are, that may lead to expansion of the size of government through a form of fiscal illusion, for which there is scattered evidence.[e] Similarly, reference-dependence may influence the feasibility of different forms of deficit reduction if individuals are less willing to accept tax increases than they are to forgo tax cuts.[f]

More broadly, what these examples illustrate is that the psychology of individuals and the ways in which decisionmaking deviates from the standard economic assumptions influence conclusions for economic policy on multiple levels. The objective of this book is to understand the importance of behavioral economics

based on misconstrued taxes, which can be mistakenly high or low. On the other hand, overall welfare calculations change due to the fact that the tax causes people to err and moves them away from their optimum. The implications of tax mistakes for welfare in any particular case depend on the nature of the specific mistake. Take, for example, the case of individuals responding to average income tax rates rather than marginal rates. With a progressive rate structure, average tax rates are below the marginal rate, and so in general individuals making that through the channel of public finance analysis. But as we see here, a behavioral political economy analysis is possible, as well.

While throughout this volume we have largely set aside issues related to political economy, we have done so for emphasis and focus, not because there are no interesting and important behavioral issues to explore in this area. Behavioral political economy analysis also can be important for topics other than taxation. Take externalities, for example, specifically the problem of global warming. Given both the time dimension of the problem—most of the external costs are far in the future, while the actions that produce them take place today—and the uncertain nature of the outcomes, behavioral tendencies such as time-inconsistent preferences, limited computational capacity, and biased reasoning are likely to play a role in the political support garnered by policy alternatives. Similarly, biases and errors in reasoning might play a role in support for the level and form of redistribution, or for support for alternative reforms in social insurance programs, and so on.

a. Joel Slemrod, "Old George Orwell Got It Backward: Some Thoughts on Behavioral Tax Economics," CESifo Working Paper 2777 (Munich: Ifo Institute for Economic Research, 2009); Edward J. McCaffery and Jonathan Baron, "Thinking about Tax," *Psychology, Public Policy, and Law*, vol. 12, no. 1 (2006), pp. 106–35.

b. Thomas C. Schelling, "Economic Reasoning and the Ethics of Policy," *Public Interest*, no. 63 (Spring 1981), pp. 37–61.

c. Edward J. McCaffery and Jonathan Baron, "The Humpty Dumpty Blues: Disaggregation Bias in the Evaluation of Tax Systems," *Organizational Behavior and Human Decision Processes*, vol. 91, no. 2 (2003), pp. 230–42.

d. Joel Slemrod, "The Role of Misconceptions in Support for Regressive Tax Reform," *National Tax Journal*, vol. 59, no. 1 (2006), pp. 57–75.

e. Rupert Sausgruber and Jean-Robert Tyran, "Testing the Mill Hypothesis of Fiscal Illusion," *Public Choice*, vol. 122, no. 1–2 (2005), pp. 39–68; Brian E. Dollery and Andrew C. Worthington, "The Empirical Analysis of Fiscal Illusion," *Journal of Economic Surveys*, vol. 10, no. 3 (1996), pp. 261–97.

f. Charles Schultze, "Is There a Bias toward Excess in U.S. Government Budgets or Deficits?" *Journal of Economic Perspectives*, vol. 6, no. 2 (1992), pp. 25–43.

mistake underrespond to the true tax rate and earn more and supply more labor than they would if they correctly understood the tax schedule. Underresponse works through tax efficiency to reduce the excess burden of the income tax.[29] Weighing against this improvement, however, is the fact that it represents a costly error for the individuals who make the mistake.

Another important type of tax mistake with possibly special consequences for efficiency is the potential failure of individuals with limited computational capacity to respond to benefit taxes as such rather than as taxes for general revenue. When taxes raise revenues that directly benefit taxpayers, such as the Social Security payroll tax or unemployment taxes, payers' response to those taxes or fees depends on how they understand the link between the taxes that they pay now and the benefits that they will later enjoy. An optimal response to the tax considers that net effect. The standard way of modeling the incidence and efficiency of benefit taxes is usually as analogous to the welfare consequences of mandated benefits.[30] But due to limits to computational capacity, the connection between taxes and benefits is not obvious or automatic. As a result, it cannot be assumed that merely implementing a benefit tax leads to a tax being perceived as such by those on whom it falls, and the welfare economics of benefit taxes therefore changes. So, for example, imperfectly optimizing individuals may ignore the claim to Social Security benefits that they accrue by paying the Social Security payroll tax.[31] That error may make those taxes more distortionary than they would be otherwise.

Like hidden taxes, tax mistakes add a behavioral nuance to tax efficiency calculations that complicate the trade-offs that society and policymakers must weigh in setting tax policy. As above, observed elasticities can no longer be taken to reveal preferences about responses to taxes because they may be due in part to error. In general, that creates new trade-offs for policy, whereby the optimal tax problem must not only consider the efficiency costs of taxation but also make a judgment regarding whether to respect preferences revealed by elasticities or to consider the potential influence of salience or error.[32] Optimal tax policy can set tax parameters not only to minimize the excess burden of taxation but also to minimize the private welfare costs due to inattention or mistakes.

Tax Preferences. Different changes to the calculation of the excess burden of taxes come from allowing individuals to hold nonstandard preferences. When individuals hold preferences that are different from those assumed by the standard model, their response to taxes may be different and so the welfare costs of taxes may be different too. On one hand, tax behavior may reflect reference-dependent preferences, leading the response parameter to be unstable with respect to reference points; as a result, the excess burden of taxation will be unstable with respect to those reference points. On the other hand, to the extent that the response to taxation reflects other-regarding preferences, that too may result in excess burden calculations that differ from those in the standard model.

Note that any effect on the efficiency costs of taxes due to nonstandard preferences is fundamentally different in character from results having to do with salience or error. In the case of nonstandard preferences, no additional welfare term is introduced by the private error of individuals. Any effects on efficiency of nonstandard preferences operate simply by the way that they change how individuals respond to taxes. The result of individuals holding preferences that differ from those that the standard model presumes is simply a different response parameter and a correspondingly different efficiency cost.

For example, in the case of reference-dependent preferences, one result for tax efficiency might be that loss-gain asymmetry in preferences can translate into loss-gain asymmetry in excess burden. That is, the magnitude of the response to a tax might depend on what it is evaluated in reference to or whether the tax represents a loss or a gain relative to some reference point. If so, the simple framing or presentation of taxes as losses or gains may have some effect on the efficiency costs of those taxes.

When individuals are not, in practice, perfectly self-interested, that too may have effects for the welfare costs of taxation, lowering the excess burden of taxation when individuals believe that what the taxes fund—or the tax system itself—contributes to social outcomes for which they have a preference. So, for example, individuals with strong preferences for redistribution may not exhibit as strong a behavioral response to a progressive income tax as would be attributed to them in a model that assumed perfect self-interest, with the result that such a tax could lead to a smaller excess burden than would be expected.

Tax Incidence

In addition to understanding the magnitude of the social welfare costs associated with taxation, tax policy also is interested in the distribution of the burden of taxation. That is, who pays taxes? Producers or consumers? Capital or labor? Employers or workers? The central incidence result in public finance is that the distribution of the costs of taxation is a function of the relative elasticities of the demand and supply side of the relevant market. The simplest case of partial equilibrium tax incidence is given by the formula below for the case in which the statutory incidence of taxation falls on the supply side of the market:[33]

$$\frac{dp^d}{dt} = \frac{\eta_s}{\eta_s - \eta_d},$$

where p^d is the price paid in the market by the demand side and dp^d/dt is the change in that price for a one-unit change in the tax rate. This highlights the two key results of the standard incidence analysis: First, taxes are borne by the relatively inelastic side of the market—that is, those actors whose behavior is relatively insensitive to prices tend to pay more of the tax. Second, the economic incidence of a tax is determined by how individuals respond to the tax, not by the legal incidence of the tax. That is, from the perspective of economic welfare—setting aside administrative issues—the assignment of the legal responsibility to remit a tax is a neutral feature of tax policy.

Because tax incidence depends on elasticities in this way, allowing for behavioral tendencies to influence the way in which individuals respond to taxes has corresponding consequences for incidence calculations, much as it did for efficiency. Note, however, that complications of direct effects on welfare due to behavioral tendencies are less central in determining the incidence of taxes than they are for efficiency. As a result, distinguishing among the particular causes of nonstandard responses to taxes—inattention, error, or preferences—is of less importance. That said, behavioral tendencies could change conclusions about incidence in fundamental ways.

First, to the extent that behavioral tendencies affect the response to taxes in a way that alters the relative elasticities of market participants, they will affect the incidence of the tax. Consider, for example, the case of tax salience and sales taxes. If individuals as consumers fail to attend to sales taxes, they become functionally insensitive to those taxes, and, other things being equal, they bear a larger share of the burden of the taxes than they would if they were perfect optimizers.[34] Similarly, when tax mistakes lead individuals to be more or less sensitive to taxes, they may pay a lesser or greater share of the tax, respectively. And when nonstandard preferences alter responses to taxes, they too tend to have corresponding effects for incidence.

Second, the influence of behavioral tendencies on how individuals respond to taxes can cause the standard result that the legal incidence of taxes is unrelated to the economic incidence of taxes to fail to hold. That is because behavioral tendencies provide a mechanism whereby the legal incidence of taxation can affect the response to taxes. In the case of hidden taxes or tax mistakes, in which legal incidence has consequences for the salience of the tax or for the propensity of individuals to respond to the tax in error, they will affect incidence. For instance, the incidence of the employer and employee portions of the payroll tax may actually be different if imperfectly optimizing workers respond differentially due to, say, the differential salience of the two parts of the tax. Nonstandard preferences might also have consequences for the neutrality of legal incidence if they affect how individuals behave in response to a tax. For example, if the legal incidence of taxes suggests or reinforces social norms about who ought to bear the burden of the tax, it might affect behavioral response and incidence.[35]

Tax Compliance and Avoidance

Another margin of adjustment to taxation with potentially significant welfare consequences includes behaviors to comply with or avoid taxes. Other things being equal, an efficient tax is one that people comply with; avoidance is a form of distortion, and along with the enforcement and administrative costs associated with combating avoidance, it can reduce efficiency. Therefore, important trade-offs for tax policy are related not only to the behavioral response that comes from reductions in taxed activity—consuming fewer goods and services, working fewer hours, and so on—but also to the response that taxes generate in terms of compliance and avoidance behaviors. Part of what can make a tax inefficient in practice is if individuals can easily avoid the tax or if the costs of monitoring and administering the tax are high.

Part of the reason that such costs get comparatively less treatment in the economics of taxation is because the policy implications are somewhat mechanical. In the standard model, individuals weigh the costs and benefits of complying with tax laws and regulations against the costs and benefits of avoidance and make a decision about how fully to comply with or how aggressively to avoid their tax liability. The costs of avoiding or failing to comply are the expected penalties and costs of noncompliance or the costs associated with shifting or other avoidance behaviors. The benefits are what the individual clears in net from engaging in the activity. The optimal level of activity therefore depends on factors such as the probability of an audit and the magnitude of any sanctions relative to the gains.[36] In response, policy can set fines and penalties high enough and with the right probability of enforcement to deter avoidance and balance the costs of enforcement against the benefits of improved revenue collection.

This aspect of tax efficiency becomes somewhat more interesting in a behavioral world, where the decision to comply or not is complicated by behavioral tendencies and the implications for policy trade-offs therefore become less straightforward. A variety of psychological factors might interact with the decision to pay taxes.[37] If individuals make errors or exhibit failures of self-control in assessing the costs and benefits associated with avoidance behaviors and possible consequences, that may affect their decisions about compliance. The same may be true if individuals have nonstandard preferences.

A variety of empirical evidence suggests a possible role for behavioral factors in the analysis of tax compliance. In particular, the relatively high levels of tax compliance observed in the United States, specifically with respect to the income tax, often is judged to be an imperfect fit with the standard model.[38] Given the actual, relatively modest probability of audits and the magnitude of the associated penalties, the hypothesis that individuals come at that decision in an optimal fashion or from a position of perfect self-interest can be difficult to support.

A number of features of behavioral decisionmaking might contribute to higher-than-expected tax compliance. For example, if individuals interpret the outcomes of compliance and avoidance decisions as losses and gains relative to a reference point, or if they have difficulty evaluating small probabilities of enforcement accurately, that could explain high rates of compliance.[39] Individuals might perceive the probabilities of audits to be higher than they are, and the penalties themselves might be obscure or complex in ways that lead individuals to perceive them to be larger than they are. The loss of paying the penalty might loom large relative to the potential gains from avoidance. Such types of decisionmaking errors or nonstandard preferences might push in the direction of compliance.

One particular behavioral tendency that is likely to be of special importance for tax compliance is other-regarding preferences, which might lead individuals to comply with taxes at a higher rate than they would under perfect self-interest. Individuals might care about outcomes in ways that lead them to comply with taxes, they also might care about process or fairness in ways that support compliance, or they may be sensitive to social norms that reinforce tax compliance. Individuals therefore may have intrinsic motivations for complying with taxes. There is some evidence consistent with social influences on tax compliance. Scattered effects of such influences are found in laboratory experiments, such as a greater willingness to comply with taxes when their burdens are believed to be more evenly distributed or when their disposition is determined in more participatory ways.[40] Some survey evidence also suggests similar preferences over process;[41] for example, one study finds evidence consistent with conditional cooperation in tax compliance.[42] Field tests of normative appeals with respect to tax compliance have not demonstrated much success to date, however.[43]

The bottom line for the judgments that tax policy must reflect with respect to compliance and efficiency is that behavioral tendencies might in some ways lead trade-offs associated with delivering compliance to be more favorable than in the standard framework. There is a significant caveat to that interpretation, however, which is the possibility for motivational crowding out.[44] Motivational crowding out occurs when strengthening extrinsic incentives causes intrinsic incentives to weaken. In the case of tax compliance, to the extent that latent other-regarding preferences push individuals in the direction of compliance, policymakers must be careful not to impose extrinsic motivations, such as penalties and fines, at levels or in forms that are likely to crowd out intrinsic motivations. The possibility of crowding out might make the returns to increased enforcement activities smaller than would be assumed in the standard model.

Tax Policy Design

Given the need for revenue to fund the various functions of government and given some understanding of the welfare consequences of taxation, the goal of tax policy is to raise sufficient revenue in ways that have desirable welfare properties. That includes setting the form and parameters of tax policy so as to raise taxes efficiently, in the sense that the taxes minimize the social costs due to distortions. It also requires implementing tax policy so that the burden of taxes is distributed in ways that correspond to social goals and preferences for equity and incidence.

And, finally, it is a matter of designing and implementing tax policy to promote compliance, minimize distortions due to avoidance and evasion, and minimize enforcement costs. The welfare analysis of taxation generates lessons for how tax policy design can achieve those goals, and a behavioral approach to understanding the welfare consequences of taxation leads to corresponding revisions for tax policy design.

The standard model identifies features of tax policy that have desirable properties along the lines of efficiency, equity, and compliance. They usually are summarized in broad terms as rules of thumb for tax design. For example, taxing relatively inelastic goods or activities tends to be efficient. Similarly, establishing low tax rates on wide tax bases generally is more efficient than setting higher rates on narrower bases. In practical terms, that often calls for tax simplicity and a tax base that has few exclusions and exceptions. For incidence, the main implication for policy is its relative neutrality. That is, while policy can be mindful of the way in which relative elasticities determine incidence, it cannot in general determine economic incidence by setting legal incidence. Finally, under some standard assumptions, avoidance is fully captured by the relevant measures of elasticity, and so again, taxes on activities for which there is less response and fewer margins for avoidance may be preferred.

Because behavioral economics changes conclusions about how features of taxes translate into welfare outcomes, it also changes such rules of thumb for tax policy design. For the practical purposes of tax policy design, the key change is that the way in which individuals respond to a tax is in the policymaker's choice set to some degree.[45] That complicates standard design principles substantially. For tax efficiency it means, on one hand, that policymakers might be able to manipulate elasticities in desirable ways, but is complicated by the fact that, on the other hand, policy can no longer take observed elasticities as indicative of the true social costs of taxation. For tax incidence, it means that policy elements such as setting legal incidence are no longer necessarily neutral for economic incidence. For compliance, behavioral tendencies create new opportunities to foster compliance, but they also mean that avoidance costs cannot be judged on elasticities alone.[46]

Tax policy can thus be designed with respect to how imperfect decisionmakers respond to taxes: that individuals fail to attend to taxes that are not salient, that they make mistakes construing taxes and prices, and that they evaluate taxes according to reference-dependent and other-regarding preferences. That creates both challenges and opportunities. The challenge is that some of the old rules of thumb for tax policy are no longer valid. Interpreting response to taxes is not straightforward—for example, for a variety of reasons, individuals may fail to respond to taxes, and that failure does not necessarily indicate preferences that make those taxes efficient. It may reflect costly errors on the part of individuals, and policy must reflect that possibility. In addition, legal incidence is no longer a neutral matter for policy, and so tax policy must take into consideration the implications of legal incidence for economic incidence.

The opportunity for tax policy is that it can make use of behavioral observations to achieve the ends of tax policy. For example, policy might actively consider the salience implications in selecting between an excise and a sales tax in order to achieve policy goals. The opportunities presented follow from two, related, observations: on one hand, individuals do not respond to taxes and prices the way that the standard model would predict; on the other hand, individuals do respond to nonprice factors in ways that the standard model would not predict. In general, individual response to tax policy is a joint product of the taxes and prices and the nonprice elements of the choice context. All of those levers are available for setting tax policy to achieve desired ends.

Those observations apply to tax policy in general. For concreteness, we discuss specific implications for three classes of taxes: commodity taxes, labor taxes, and capital taxes.

Commodity Taxes

One important class of taxes in the United States is what can be broadly referred to as commodity taxes, which are taxes levied on the transaction of goods and services. Sales and excise taxes are the largest and most common of these types of taxes. An important source of revenue for many state and local governments, sales taxes typically are collected at the point of retail sale, and they often are expressed as a percent of the purchase price. The base of sales taxes often is very broad—reflected in the way that they typically are defined by their exclusions, such as food—and rates typically are modest. Excise taxes, used by both the federal and state governments, typically are imposed at the wholesale level, and they are often imposed per unit of sale. Excise taxes target narrow categories of products, such as gasoline or alcohol, and sometimes they can be larger in magnitude than sales taxes.

In some ways commodity taxes are those for which the practical design implications of the optimal taxation problem are the most straightforward. From the perspective of efficiency, the goal of these taxes is to minimize the distortion that they cause, and that distortion is completely captured by the reduction in the consumption of taxed goods caused by the tax. For that reason, commodity taxes are most efficient when located on relatively inelastic goods. Taxes on goods such as cigarettes, for example, while serving multiple ends, are sometimes argued to be relatively efficient for that reason. With regard to incidence, commodity taxes tend to be borne by the relatively inelastic side of the market, a fact to which policy should attend but cannot, in general, influence. So, for example, whether any particular good is taxed through an excise tax and collected at the wholesale level or taxed through a sales tax and collected at the retail level should in general not matter for who ultimately pays the tax.

From a behavioral point of view, as discussed at length above, theoretical considerations of optimal commodity taxes are less straightforward; as a result, translating the implications of behavioral tendencies into practical design rules is more complicated. While there are potentially many behavioral dimensions to commodity taxation, the key issue is likely to be the taxes' salience and the degree to which they are hidden from individuals. Tax policy parameters can affect the salience of taxes, which can affect how efficiently the taxes collect revenue and the distribution of their burden.

The opportunity for commodity taxes with respect to their salience is that policy may be able to manipulate salience in ways that lead the taxes to have less of an impact on social welfare. For example, sales taxes might be less salient to consumers than excise taxes because of the way that excise taxes are reflected in the prices posted to the consumer. The challenge is in knowing which is preferable from the perspective of overall social welfare. While making taxes less salient reduces the deadweight loss of the tax, it also raises the welfare costs of the private errors that individuals commit in ignoring the tax.

One implication is that as a general rule, taxing goods that appear to be inelastic to taxation will not always be optimal for tax efficiency. That is because failure to respond does not necessarily reflect preferences but can instead reflect failure to perceive a tax that is not salient. The result is that locating a tax where individuals do not respond might magnify the error that individuals make in failing to respond, which can have welfare costs distinct from the deadweight loss of the tax. The relationship between how individuals respond to taxes and where taxes might be efficiently located thus becomes less straightforward. Tax policy has to consider not just the observed elasticity but also the potential for and possible magnitude of error.

Another implication for policy is that the usual preference for low tax rates on a large tax base may also be more nuanced when we allow for the effects of salience. In particular, there is likely to be an interaction between tax level and tax salience. For example, if lack of attention to taxes is bad for tax efficiency and low tax rates are easier to ignore, then there is a trade-off between keeping taxes low to keep them efficient and making them high enough to be salient. Rather than imposing many low-rate taxes, policy might favor paying the fixed costs of attention just once on a single, higher-rate tax.

Finally, the effects of salience for behavioral response open a new channel by which tax policy might be able to set commodity taxes so as to manipulate their incidence. In general, lowering salience tends to increase the portion of the tax paid by the group from whom it is hidden. So, for example, the decision to post tax-inclusive or tax-exclusive prices might matter for the incidence of the tax. Taxes that are included in prices to the consumer—such as by levying the tax at the wholesale level, as with excise taxes; or requiring that taxes be posted in prices, as with gas taxes; or both, as with a value-added tax—minimize the degree to which they are hidden from consumers. Increasing the salience of taxes in this way may also work to shift the tax burden away from consumers and to producers, as consumers become more responsive to after-tax prices.

Labor Taxes

Taxes on labor, including income taxes and payroll taxes, are the centerpiece of the American tax system, at least at the federal level. The personal income tax is levied directly on individual earnings and collected through a combination of withholding, direct payments, and annual tax filing. The signature feature of the income tax may be its complexity. It is calculated as a function of income, but the translation from earned income to taxable income involves numerous adjustments, due, for example, to exemptions and deductions. The tax itself also is complex, due both to the nonlinear rate schedule that makes the tax progressive—there currently are six tax brackets—and to the existence of a variety of adjustments made directly to the tax bill, such as tax credits. Payroll taxes, such as those that fund Social Security and Medicare, are distinct from income taxes and typically are calculated in a more straightforward manner. Perhaps the most interesting institutional feature of payroll taxes is the way that liability is nominally split between employers and workers.

The standard results from optimal tax theory apply directly to the design of efficient and equitable income and labor tax systems. Perhaps the main goal of these taxes is to raise revenue in the most efficient manner possible, which is largely identified with designing the taxes to produce relatively small responses in labor supply and taxable earnings. In part, this is strictly about efficiency—not generating disincentives to participate in the labor market or to supply work hours. It also is partly about compliance, where the goal is to minimize effects on tax avoidance or evasion behaviors. For incidence, the central implication of policy is that collection policies—for instance, the split in the liability of the payroll tax—are neutral.

From a behavioral point of view, results for efficiency, incidence, and compliance are modified by the behavioral tendencies of individuals; as a result, so are the implications for policy design. Tax policy can affect the degree and nature of the complexity of taxes in ways that change how individuals respond to them. For example, complexity can lead individuals to hold mistaken impressions of their marginal tax rate that offset aspects of the tax code that have negative welfare effects. Complexity is related to salience effects, as with commodity taxes, but more multidimensional. In addition, nonstandard preferences play a role in how individuals respond to labor taxes, and tax policy can be set to meet or work through preferences to achieve desirable outcomes. For example, compliance with income taxes might be a function of perceptions of fairness, which policy can seek to promote.

Perhaps the major implication of behavioral economics for the design of efficient income taxes comes from the fact that imperfectly optimizing individuals can no longer be assumed to perceive taxes correctly. Individuals respond not to the tax rate as it is set but as they construe it. While, as noted above, the welfare consequences of complexity are not clear-cut, it does raise questions about whether policymakers could be improving welfare outcomes by deliberately setting the parameters of tax policy in ways that manipulate complexity in order to achieve outcomes. For example, the complexity of the tax code might make it difficult for individuals to respond to income taxes precisely. That effect could possibly help with efficiency if it causes individuals to not understand their marginal tax rates and therefore to supply more labor than they otherwise would. For that reason, tax policy design might seek to leave this feature of the tax code opaque or vague.

There may be opportunities for tax policy to improve efficiency by improving understanding in special cases. Consider the case of taxes—such as the Social Security payroll tax—that fund an identifiable benefit. The efficiency of those taxes depends to some extent on consumers making the connection between the taxes and the benefits that they fund. Were individuals perfect optimizers, they could be assumed to make that connection and to respond accordingly. With behavioral agents it cannot be assumed that merely implementing a benefit tax leads to the tax being perceived as such by those on whom it falls. As a result, policymakers might profitably take actions to make that connection more salient or easier to understand. In this case, then, individuals in the current system—which has a dedicated set of taxes for programs such as Social Security—might be more likely to make that connection than those in an alternative system in which payroll taxes are folded into the income tax. Promoting this connection to individuals is likely to make them more apt to treat the tax as a mandated benefit, with possibly desirable consequences for efficiency.

Another practical implication of complexity for the design of efficient labor taxes is that there is likely to be heterogeneity in response to complexity, which policymakers may have to take into account. That is, the effect of complexity is different for groups that interact with the tax schedule in different ways. For example, the self-employed and wage earners might respond differently—having higher or lower elasticities—to income taxes, due just to self-selection across employment status. The self-employed may also, because of the different administrative features of the way that they pay taxes—for example, paying estimated taxes on a quarterly basis rather than paying through paycheck withholding—find different aspects of taxes more or less salient or complex. The government should design a tax code that reflects such possible interactions between complexity and response. A similar argument might apply to other provisions of the tax code—such as tax benefits for retirement saving—that serve primarily to reduce the tax burden of those sufficiently sophisticated to take advantage of them.

Finally, efficiency in income tax design might be promoted or diminished to the extent that features of taxes meet nonstandard preferences, such as reference-dependence or other-regarding preferences. To the extent that behavioral responses to taxes such as income taxes reflect not just preferences over labor and leisure, for example, but also perceptions of how taxes are administered or what taxes are used for, other-regarding preferences might influence behavioral response. Policy therefore might consciously seek to design such taxes in ways that meet those preferences. For example, the complexity of the income tax might undermine perceptions of fairness in ways that might impact efficiency. Reference-dependence also is likely to play a role in the response to income taxes. For example, paying income taxes through paycheck withholding instead of by making estimated quarterly payments, in addition to having consequences for enforcement, might matter for behavioral response to the extent that paychecks with and without withholding set different reference points. Policy could, for example, manipulate the frequency or structure of estimated payments to alter such effects.

A behavioral approach to labor tax policy also has some potential implications for how policy can be set to distribute the burden of such taxes in ways that meet social goals. In particular, as with commodity taxes, when individuals display behavioral tendencies, then policy may be able to affect the incidence of taxes through the assignment of legal incidence. For example, the split of the payroll tax across employers and workers may have some consequences for who ultimately bears the tax. In addition, the complexity of the income tax might contribute to workers bearing the burden of that tax, if it leads workers to be less sensitive to tax rates.

The design of labor taxes also might seek to reflect insights from behavioral economics in order to meet the goal of promoting compliance and discouraging avoidance. Imperfect understanding of penalties and audit probabilities might contribute to compliance, and tax policy might find it effective to work with that tendency. In addition, other-regarding preferences might lead individuals to have intrinsic motivations to comply with taxes. Policy might seek to activate or reinforce such preferences, such as by communicating prescriptive social norms about tax compliance. Finally, when individuals hold such preferences, the question arises of how hard to lean on extrinsic motivations to comply with taxes—audits and punitive actions—because the behavioral model allows for the possibility that the effects of extrinsic motivations will be offset by a corresponding diminution in the force of intrinsic motivations to comply. Policies encouraging compliance need to be designed with that effect in mind.

A final and overarching point for tax policy design is that while policymakers might be able to use behavioral responses to taxes to improve tax policy outcomes, firms and employers can take actions too. For example, while individuals might find it difficult to optimize with respect to complex income taxes, firms might set terms of employment in ways that are optimal for the typical worker.[47] The direct manipulation of the complexity of the income tax schedule by tax authorities might then be less effective, because actions by firms can offset such effects.

Capital Taxes

Governments at various levels in the United States also tax capital accumulation in some forms. Capital gains taxes and taxes on dividends tax wealth accumulation and income from wealth. Capital gains and dividends are taxed like income, but in some cases according to schedules that are different from those for earned income. Estate taxes, which are levied on an estate directly, also tax accumulated wealth. Property taxes, which are levied on the value of housing and land and are imposed on owners, are an important source of revenue for state and local governments.

Setting aside substantial economic questions related to the special dynamic consequences of these taxes, from a general perspective they and commodity and labor taxes face a similar suite of design issues. Given a judgment on the part of policymakers to collect revenue in this way, policy seeks to implement the taxes in a manner that has desirable consequences for welfare. From the perspective of efficiency, the central task of the taxes is to not discourage saving, investing, and accumulating wealth. There also is the matter of encouraging compliance, which for these taxes may be a particular problem.

The behavioral analysis stresses that how individuals respond to these taxes and therefore the consequences of the taxes for welfare are mediated by behavioral tendencies. One aspect of that is the complexity of such taxes. Many of the behavioral tendencies that lead individuals to misjudge the magnitude or other properties of taxes in other domains also occur with capital taxes. Behavioral response to capital taxes might also be affected by bounded self-control. These taxes involve a substantial time dimension, in ways that other taxes do not. The activity that generates the tax liability can be separated from the realization of that liability by long periods of time.

Policy with respect to capital taxes therefore might work with or through behavioral tendencies to mitigate the effects of their distortion of incentives to accumulate wealth. For example, difficulties that individual have with planning and saving even in the absence of taxes could mean that taxes on capital and wealth accumulation might magnify those difficulties and further impair saving.

That would be an additional barrier for policy to overcome in designing such taxes. On the other hand, policy might be able to take advantage of the fact that the implications of tax liability are far in the future to reduce the salience of those taxes for short-sighted individuals, in ways that might mitigate the welfare consequences of the taxes.

Another important dimension to the efficiency of capital taxes is that the scope for avoidance is substantial, and behaviorally informed design might be able to address that issue. For example, a substantial portion of the response to the estate tax might be due to avoidance activities.[48] To the extent that other-regarding preferences play a role in tax compliance, policy might attempt to operate along the available dimensions to improve compliance—for instance, by improving perceptions of fairness.

A

Preference, Choice, and Welfare

A s an additional step in integrating insights from psychology into public finance along the lines described in chapter 2, we introduce a highly simplified model for thinking through what those insights imply for preference and choice and, by extension, for public finance. Note that the purpose of this appendix is to clarify this relationship for the interested reader; the text itself, with the exception of appendix B, does not employ the notation developed here.

There are two components to this model. The first includes the implications of behavioral tendencies for preference and choice. Imperfect optimization, bounded self-control, and nonstandard preferences mean that choice no longer reveals preference. The second includes the implications of choice behavior for how we think about welfare. The possibility that choice does not consistently reveal preference poses a challenge for evaluating welfare.

Preference and Choice

Perhaps the core insight of economics with respect to choice is that when the standard assumptions about individual choice hold, choice reveals preference. Findings from behavioral economics suggest that those assumptions often do not hold and that as a result choice may not reveal preference. We present a way to capture that aspect of choice and to compare how individuals make choices in the behavioral and in the standard model.

Setup

Let x = an action (such as consuming a good) that individuals choose to engage
in or not.

Let b = the subjective valuation of x; in other words b = u(x).

Let c = the objective costs associated with x, denominated in the same units as b.

STANDARD MODEL

In the standard model, individuals choose x when the benefits outweigh the
costs: $b > c$.

Different individuals value actions differently, so b is distributed f(b). For
example, if x is consumption of donuts, high b individuals are those who love
donuts. Furthermore, individuals optimize perfectly, have unbounded self-
control, and hold standard preferences.

The key implication of this is that choice reveals preference: x iff $b > c$.

BEHAVIORAL MODEL

In a behavioral model, people are imperfect optimizers, have bounded self-
control, and hold nonstandard preferences. We can represent those tendencies
by saying that the choice of x now reflects the following decision criterion:

$$\beta(b) > c,$$

where $\beta(\cdot)$ is a transformation of the benefits, b, due to behavioral tendencies. So,
for example, overconfidence about likely good outcomes might lead individuals
to choose as though b were higher than its true value or procrastination might
lead individuals to choose as though b were lower than its true value. When we
make the simplifying assumption that c (the costs of x) are perceived without
error, even by behavioral agents, then

$\beta(b) > b$ when behavioral tendencies lead individuals to overvalue x

$\beta(b) < b$ when behavioral tendencies lead individuals to undervalue x.

For example, when x is consumption of donuts, $\beta(b)$ might be greater than
b due to failure of self-control or ignorance of the deleterious effects of donut
consumption on health. This is a deliberately simple and flexible way to allow for
behavioral tendencies; richer representations are clearly possible. The key feature
of behavioral choice, which this model does capture, is that choice no longer
necessarily reveals preference.

Choice of x occurs where $\beta(b) > c$.

Because, in general, $\beta(b) \neq b$, it may be the case that individuals choose x when $b < c$ and, conversely, that individuals fail to choose x when $b > c$. There is some true b that represents welfare, but in general it cannot be inferred from observable patterns of choice. Moreover, notice that markets under these conditions operate on $\beta(b)$, not b.

We can allow in this model that choice can be sensitive to features that do not matter in the standard model, such as framing or presentation effects. We call them nudges, following Thaler and Sunstein.[1] In general, nudges affect the form of $\beta(\cdot)$. But to reflect their importance, we can write that slightly less generally as $\beta(b, n)$, where n are nudges. Written that way, we get:

$$\text{Choice of } x \text{ occurs where } \beta(b, n) > c,$$

where different nudges—default rules, framing effects, appeals to social norms, and so on—can affect the choice of x, even when they do not alter the underlying costs and benefits of that choice.

Choice and Welfare

The failure of choice to reveal preference can create difficulties for public finance as well as for economic analysis more generally. What can we infer about welfare when choice does not reveal preference? That is, how do we infer b when people choose according to $\beta(b)$? Or, if under different nudges we observe different revealed preferences $\beta(b, n)$, what do we take to be the true value of b? In considering social welfare, what b do we put in the social welfare function for people?

One way to model this indeterminacy that is useful for our purposes is to disaggregate the process of choice. Behavioral economists sometimes do so by referring to distinct conceptions of utility, where within any given individual we might think of there being what amount to multiple selves, each revealing different preferences through different processes.[2] For example, we might think of time inconsistency as resulting from conflicts between a short-run self, the procrastinating self, whose preferences are revealed by choice, and long-run self, the patient self, whose preferences are revealed by what individuals intended to choose ex ante or what they wish that they had chosen ex post. And we can think about other choice inconsistencies in a similar fashion.

To represent this, consider a model that generalizes slightly from the above model of choice, where

$$\beta(b) = \text{the utility revealed by choice}$$
$$\theta(b) = \text{the utility implied by intentions}$$
$$b = \text{hedonic utility.}$$

In the standard model the following identity holds: $b = \theta(b) = \beta(b)$. In the behavioral model, that identity can be broken at either point: Where people choose in error, for example, the utility revealed by choices, $\beta(b)$, will not correspond to the utility that they experience, b. Where individuals fail to exhibit self-control, the utility implied by their intentions, $\theta(b)$, may not correspond to the utility revealed by their choices, $\beta(b)$.

Finally, in some circumstances revealed preferences for x may not be consistent, even apart from choice errors or failures of self-control. We might write in those cases that

$$\beta'(b) \neq \beta(b),$$

where $\beta'(b)$ and $\beta(b)$ are different revealed preferences for the same x under different circumstances of choice, for example, choice under alternative frames. That may occur, for example, where utility is specified with respect to reference points, where utility may be greater or lesser depending on the reference point that individuals employ.

Extensions of this model can incorporate choice where a stable b fails to exist.

B

Choice, Welfare, and Policy

Building on the notation and model of preference, choice, and welfare introduced in appendix A, we can formalize slightly some of the implications of behavioral economics for public finance. This material is, again, supplementary; the chapters in part 2 of this volume employ the thinking that it reflects (as described in the text of chapter 3) but not the notation.

There are three parts to this, following the three sections in the body of chapter 3. The first concerns how behavioral economics interacts with market failures. That individuals choose in nonstandard ways in general alters the consequences of market failures. The second deals with what behavioral economics implies for policy judgments, in particular that it identifies a new set of judgments with respect to intrapersonal preference conflicts that policy must reflect. The third relates to what behavioral economics means for policy design, in particular how to think about nudges.

Policy Problems and Choice

Standard Model

In the standard model individual choice operates according to standard assumptions even when markets fail. So if there are, say, negative public health externalities to the consumption of donuts, x, the consequences of those externalities (excess consumption, from a social point of view) follow from the fact that individuals consider the costs, c, and benefits, b, to themselves and consume accordingly.

Behavioral Model

The effects of market failures become less determinate because the response of individuals to market structure or conditions becomes more variable. Individuals may consume donuts in excess of the social optimum even in the absence of external costs due to, say, difficulties with self-control that lead $\beta(b)$ to be greater than b. Conversely, even if there are external costs associated with donut consumption, individuals may or may not consume them in excess of the social optimum if $\beta(b)$ is for some reason less than b.

Policy Judgments and Welfare

For making policy judgments with respect to welfare, the benefit b to the individual is of interest. If policy is to reflect social welfare judgments, policymakers sometimes have to make judgments about b. We argue that policy judgments can proceed much as they do when assigning welfare weights across individuals in making judgments about, for example, redistribution. Here, policy judgments assign weights to alternative possible conceptions of a single individual's preferences.

The difficulty for economic analysis when b is of interest is how to infer b when choice no longer can be assumed to reveal preference—that is, how to infer b when people choose according to $\beta(b)$? Or, if under different nudges we observe different revealed preferences $\beta(b, n)$, what should we infer about b? Put another way, in considering social welfare, what b do we put in the social welfare function for people?

Standard Model

In the standard model, choices are consistent:

$$b = \theta(b) = \beta(b).$$

As a result, social welfare analysis can assume that preferences are revealed by choice.

Behavioral Model

In the behavioral model, that is no longer necessarily the case. For example, we might want policy to reflect the possibility that individuals may choose in error or inconsistently. That might be represented as the opening of a wedge between the utility that is revealed by choice and true, hedonic utility. So,

$$b \neq \theta(b) = \beta(b), \text{ so that } b \neq \beta(b).$$

In making judgments about policy, it generally is not possible to recover b. Policy can infer $\beta(b)$ based on observed choices, as it can in the standard model. Policy can also make an inference of b, call it b^p, based on other data or reasoning. Policy can then reflect weights on alternative inferences, $\lambda b^p + (1 - \lambda)\beta(b)$. Where policy is confident in nonchoice inferences of b, it can set $\lambda = 1$. Where policy has no basis to contradict choice, it can set $\lambda = 0$. This allows for intermediate cases.

Similarly, we might want policy to reflect the possibility that individuals may fail to exhibit self-control. This type of inconsistency might be represented as a wedge between the utility reflected by intentions and the utility revealed by choice. So,

$$b = \theta(b) \neq \beta(b), \text{ so that } b \neq \beta(b).$$

Again, in making judgments about policy, it is not necessary to recover b. Instead, policy can reflect weights on alternative inferences, $\lambda b^p + (1 - \lambda)\beta(b)$. For example, in this case policymakers may take data on stated intentions, $\theta(b)$, as containing information about true preferences, b, and operate on some convex combination of those and preferences revealed by choice: $\lambda\theta(b) + (1 - \lambda)\beta(b)$.

A final important case is where we observe inconsistent realizations of $\beta(b)$ or $\theta(b)$, even for the same choice, x, so that $\beta'(b) \neq \beta(b)$.

Here, policy can reflect weights on alternative revelations, $\lambda\beta'(b) + (1 - \lambda)\beta(b)$.

Policy Design and Choice

Finally, as discussed above, when policy seeks to alter or manage the behavior of individuals, in general it has to contend with their behavioral tendencies.

Standard Model

We can affect choice with policies like taxes and subsidies, t, for $t > |b - c|$.

So, for instance, if we want to discourage the consumption of donuts, we can add a tax on donuts. A corollary of this point is that only policies that materially change the costs and benefits associated with the action are effective in changing behavior. For example, a policy that instead of taxing donuts mandated that calories be labeled more prominently on the box would not be effective.

Moreover, we can generally assume that policies that operate in this fashion, by changing relative costs and benefits, are efficient, in the sense that they affect the right people—the people whose welfare is affected the least by changing their behavior. That is, taxes or subsidies discourage or encourage activity on the margin, given the distribution $f(b)$. In the donut example, the policy can be seen as efficient in that those who are discouraged from consuming donuts by the tax are those who in fact value donuts the least among those who were originally consuming them; those who continue to consume donuts are those who value them the most.

Behavioral Model

A behavioral approach changes how we understand the operation of policy in a number of ways. On one hand, individuals can no longer be assumed to perceive policies accurately. So when a cost is increased by a tax t, instead of choosing x when $b > c + t$, the condition becomes

$$\beta(b) > c + \tau(t),$$

where $\tau(\cdot)$ is a transformation of the tax that is due to behavioral tendencies. This captures the general tendency of individuals to respond to policies imperfectly. For example, the salience of a tax might determine $\tau(\cdot)$.

On the other hand, features of the choice context that do not materially affect the costs and benefits of the choice—nudges—can influence choice. It is important to note that nudges are frequently in the policymaker's choice set. In addition to setting t, policy can affect n. So, for example, when x is donuts, n might be the way in which calories are labeled on the box. So that by manipulating the nudge, we can change how individuals make the decision to consume donuts even without changing the relative costs and benefits associated with their consumption.

Written this way, individuals take action x when $\beta(b, n) > c + \tau(t)$.

Taken together, the result is that the response to policy is a joint outcome of policy parameters and nudges. That may lead to surprising outcomes: in some cases, price levers may be ineffective, as when taxes are not salient; in other cases, nudges can be extremely effective, as with defaults in program enrollment.

Finally, because $\beta(b, n)$ is not generally distributed as b, policies that target b may influence the wrong people. That is, policies that operate through $\beta(b, n)$ can generate responses among individuals in the wrong part of the b distribution. For example, if the individuals who are very responsive to some particular policy to discourage the consumption of donuts are for some reason individuals with high values of b, the policy will lead to larger welfare losses than in the standard case. In this way, behavioral tendencies will affect the efficiency of policy.

Notes

Chapter One

1. See Katherine Baicker, Sendhil Mullainathan, and Joshua Schwartzstein, "Insuring the Health of Behavioral Consumers," unpublished paper (2010), for an analysis of the issues in this section.

2. Box 4-2 in chapter 4 discusses some examples of such behavior. For example, there is some evidence of framing effects in health behaviors: Daniel J. O'Keefe and Jakob D. Jensen, "The Relative Persuasiveness of Gain-Framed and Loss-Framed Messages for Encouraging Disease Detection Behaviors: A Meta-Analytic Review," *Journal of Communication*, vol. 59, no. 2 (2009), pp. 296–316. Another example finds evidence of status quo bias over treatment options: Haiden A. Huskamp and others, "The Impact of a Three-Tier Formulary on Demand Response for Prescription Drugs," *Journal of Economics and Management Strategy*, vol. 14, no. 3 (2005), pp. 729–53.

3. It also suggests a different form of overuse, one that comes from psychological over-weighting of benefits rather than from a gap in price.

4. Richard H. Thaler and Cass R. Sunstein, *Nudge: Improving Decisions about Health, Wealth, and Happiness* (Yale University Press, 2008).

5. Raj Chetty, Adam Looney, and Kory Kroft, "Salience and Taxation: Theory and Evidence," *American Economic Review*, vol. 99, no. 4 (2009), pp. 1145–77.

6. Hunt Allcott and Sendhil Mullainathan, "Behavior and Energy Policy," *Science*, vol. 327, no. 5970 (March 5, 2010), pp. 1204–05.

7. Jonathan Gruber and Botond Koszegi, "Tax Incidence When Individuals Are Time-Inconsistent: The Case of Cigarette Excise Taxes," *Journal of Public Economics*, vol. 88, no. 9–10 (2004), pp. 1959–87.

8. B. Douglas Bernheim and Antonio Rangel, "Behavioral Public Economics: Welfare and Policy Analysis with Nonstandard Decision-Makers," in *Behavioral Economics and Its Applications*, edited by Peter Diamond and Hannu Vartianen (Princeton University Press, 2007); B. Douglas Bernheim and Antonio Rangel, "Beyond Revealed Preference: Choice-

Theoretic Foundations for Behavioral Welfare Economics," *Quarterly Journal of Economics,* vol. 124, no. 1 (February 2009), pp. 51–104.

9. Esther Duflo and others, "Saving Incentives for Low- and Middle-Income Families: Evidence from a Field Experiment with H&R Block," *Quarterly Journal of Economics,* vol. 121, no. 4 (2006), pp. 1311–46.

10. Eric P. Bettinger and others, "The Role of Simplification and Information in College Decisions: Results from the H&R Block FAFSA Experiment," Working Paper 15361 (Cambridge, Mass.: National Bureau of Economic Research, September 2009).

11. Jeffrey Kling and others, "Misperception in Choosing Medicare Drug Plans," unpublished paper (2008).

12. Bruce D. Meyer, "Lessons from the U.S. Unemployment Insurance Experiments," *Journal of Economic Literature,* vol. 33, no. 1 (March 1995), pp. 91–131.

13. Ibid.

14. Justine S. Hastings and Jeffrey M. Weinstein, "Information, School Choice, and Academic Achievement: Evidence from Two Experiments," *Quarterly Journal of Economics,* vol. 123, no. 4 (2008), pp. 1373–1414.

Chapter Two

1. Matthew Rabin, "Psychology and Economics," *Journal of Economic Literature,* vol. 36, no. 1 (1998), pp. 11–46; Sendhil Mullainathan and Richard Thaler, "Behavioral Economics," in *International Encyclopedia of Social and Behavioral Sciences,* edited by Neil J. Smelser and Paul B. Baltes (Oxford: Pergamon Press, 2001), pp. 1094–1100; Daniel Kahneman, "Maps of Bounded Rationality: Psychology for Behavioral Economics," *American Economic Review,* vol. 93, no. 5 (2003), pp. 1449–75; Colin F. Camerer, "Behavioral Economics," in *Advances in Economics and Econometrics: Theory and Applications, Ninth World Congress,* vol. 2, edited by Richard Blundell, Whitney K. Newey, and Torsten Persson (Cambridge University Press, 2006), pp. 181–214; Stefano DellaVigna, "Psychology and Economics: Evidence from the Field," *Journal of Economic Literature,* vol. 47, no. 2 (2009), pp. 315–72.

2. Sheena S. Iyengar and Mark R. Lepper, "When Choice Is Demotivating: Can One Desire Too Much of a Good Thing?" *Journal of Personality and Social Psychology,* vol. 79, no. 6 (2000), pp. 995–1006.

3. Sheena S. Iyengar, Gur Huberman, and Wei Jiang, "How Much Choice Is Too Much? Contributions to 401(k) Retirement Plans," in *Pension Design and Structure: New Lessons from Behavioral Finance,* edited by Olivia S. Mitchell and Steve Utkus (Oxford University Press, 2004), pp. 83–95.

4. Robyn A. LeBoeuf and Eldar Shafir, "Decision Making," in *The Cambridge Handbook of Thinking and Reasoning,* edited by Keith J. Holyoak and Robert G. Morrison (Cambridge University Press, 2005), pp. 243–65.

5. Daniel Kahneman, *Attention and Effort* (Englewood Cliffs, N.J.: Prentice Hall, 1973); Harold Pashler, *Attention* (Philadelphia: Taylor and Francis Press, 1998); Harold Pashler, James C. Johnston, and Eric Ruthruff, "Attention and Performance," *Annual Review of Psychology,* vol. 52, no. 1 (2001), pp. 629–51.

6. Neville Moray, "Attention in Dichotic Listening: Affective Cues and the Influence of Instructions," *Quarterly Journal of Experimental Psychology,* vol. 11, no. 1 (1959), pp. 56–60.

7. Xavier Drèze, Stephen J. Hoch, and Mary E. Purk, "Shelf Management and Space Elasticity," *Journal of Retailing,* vol. 70, no. 4 (1994), pp. 301–26.

8. Raj Chetty, Adam Looney, and Kory Kroft, "Salience and Taxation: Theory and Evidence," *American Economic Review*, vol. 99, no. 4 (2009), pp. 1145–77; Amy Finkelstein, "E-Z Tax: Tax Salience and Tax Rates," *Quarterly Journal of Economics*, vol. 124, no. 3 (2009), pp. 969–1010.

9. Daniel M. Wegner and others, "Paradoxical Effects of Thought Suppression," *Journal of Personality and Social Psychology*, vol. 53, no. 1 (1987), pp. 5–13.

10. Colin Camerer, George Loewenstein, and Martin Weber, "The Curse of Knowledge in Economic Settings: An Experimental Analysis," *Journal of Political Economy*, vol. 97, no. 5 (1989), pp. 1232–54.

11. Daniel J. Simons and Christopher F. Chabris, "Gorillas in Our Midst: Sustained Inattentional Blindness for Dynamic Events," *Perception*, vol. 28, no. 9 (1999), pp. 1059–74.

12. Amos Tversky, "Elimination by Aspects: A Theory of Choice," *Psychological Review*, vol. 79, no. 4 (1972), pp. 281–99; Xavier Gabaix and others, "Costly Information Acquisition: Experimental Analysis of a Boundedly Rational Model," *American Economic Review*, vol. 96, no. 4 (2006), pp. 1043–68.

13. Timothy D. Willson and others, "Focalism: A Source of Durability Bias in Affective Forecasting," *Journal of Personality and Social Psychology*, vol. 78, no. 5 (2000), pp. 821–36.

14. Iyengar and Lepper, "When Choice Is Demotivating: Can One Desire Too Much of a Good Thing?"

15. Amos Tvesky and Eldar Shafir, "Choice under Conflict: The Dynamics of Deferred Decision," *Psychological Science*, vol. 3, no. 6 (1992), pp. 358–61.

16. Christopher K. Hsee, "The Evaluability Hypothesis: An Explanation for Preference Reversals between Joint and Separate Evaluations of Alternatives," *Organizational Behavior and Human Decision Processes*, vol. 67, no. 3 (1996), pp. 247–57; Christopher K. Hsee and others, "Preference Reversals between Joint and Separate Evaluations of Options: A Review and Theoretical Analysis," *Psychological Bulletin*, vol. 125, no. 5 (1999), pp. 576–90.

17. Eldar Shafir, "Choosing Versus Rejecting: Why Some Options Are Both Better and Worse Than Others," *Memory and Cognition*, vol. 21, no. 4 (1993), pp. 546–56.

18. Hilke Plassmann and others, "Marketing Actions Can Modulate Neural Representations of Experienced Pleasantness," *Proceedings of the National Academy of Sciences*, vol. 105, no. 3 (2008), pp. 1050–54.

19. Dan Ariely, George Loewenstein, and Drazen Prelec, "'Coherent Arbitrariness': Stable Demand Curves without Stable Preferences," *Quarterly Journal of Economics*, vol. 118, no. 1 (2003), pp. 73–105; Dan Ariely, George Loewenstein, and Drazen Prelec, "Tom Sawyer and the Construction of Value," *Journal of Economic Behavior and Organization*, vol. 60, no. 1 (2006), pp. 1–10.

20. Joel Huber, John W. Payne, and Christopher Puto, "Adding Asymmetrically Dominated Alternatives: Violations of Regularity and the Similarity Hypothesis," *Journal of Consumer Research*, vol. 9, no. 1 (1982), pp. 90–98; John R. Doyle and others, "The Robustness of the Asymmetrically Dominated Effect: Buying Frames, Phantom Alternatives, and In-Store Purchases," *Psychology and Marketing*, vol. 16, no. 3 (1999), pp. 225–43.

21. Itamar Simonson, "Choice Based on Reasons: The Case of Attraction and Compromise Effects," *Journal of Consumer Research*, vol. 16, no. 2 (1989), pp. 158–74.

22. Jeffrey B. Liebman and Richard J. Zeckhauser, "Schmeduling," unpublished working paper, Harvard University, 2004.

23. Richard J. Herrnstein and Drazen Prelec, "Melioration: A Theory of Distributed Choice," *Journal of Economic Perspectives*, vol. 5, no. 3 (1991), pp. 137–56.

24. Emmanuel Saez, "Do Taxpayers Bunch at Kink Points?" *American Economic Journal: Economic Policy*, vol. 2, no. 3 (2010), pp. 180–212.

25. Xavier Gabaix and David Laibson, "Shrouded Attributes, Consumer Myopia, and Information Suppression in Competitive Markets," *Quarterly Journal of Economics*, vol. 121, no. 2 (2006), pp. 505–40.

26. Jeffrey Kling and others, "Misperception in Choosing Medicare Drug Plans," unpublished paper, 2008.

27. Richard H. Thaler, "Mental Accounting and Consumer Choice," *Marketing Science*, vol. 4, no. 3 (1985), pp. 199–214; Richard H. Thaler, "Mental Accounting Matters," *Journal of Behavioral Decision Making*, vol. 12, no. 3 (1999), pp. 183–206.

28. Suzanne Fogel, "Income Source Effects," unpublished manuscript, DePaul University, 2008; Hal R. Arkes and others, "The Psychology of Windfall Gains," *Organizational Behavior and Human Decision Processes*, vol. 59, no. 3 (1994), pp. 331–47.

29. Chip Heath and Jack B. Soll, "Mental Budgeting and Consumer Decisions," *Journal of Consumer Research*, vol. 23, no. 1 (1996), pp. 40–52.

30. Amos Tversky and Daniel Kahneman, "The Framing of Decisions and the Psychology of Choice," *Science*, vol. 211, no. 4481 (January 30, 1981), pp. 453–58.

31. Peter Kooreman, "The Labeling Effect of a Child Benefit System," *American Economic Review*, vol. 90, no. 3 (June 2000), pp. 571–83.

32. Drazen Prelec and George Loewenstein, "The Red and the Black: Mental Accounting of Savings and Debt," *Marketing Science*, vol. 17, no. 1 (1998), pp. 4–28.

33. Daniel Read, George Loewenstein, and Matthew Rabin, "Choice Bracketing," *Journal of Risk and Uncertainty*, vol. 19, no. 1–3 (1999), pp. 171–97.

34. John T. Gourville, "Pennies-a-Day: The Effect of Temporal Reframing on Transaction Evaluation," *Journal of Consumer Research*, vol. 24, no. 4 (1998), pp. 395–408.

35. Daniel Kahneman and Amos Tversky, "Prospect Theory: An Analysis of Decision under Risk," *Econometrica*, vol. 47, no. 2 (1979), pp. 263–91; Michael H. Birnbaum, "New Paradoxes of Risky Decision Making," *Psychological Review*, vol. 115, no. 2 (2008), pp. 463–501.

36. Amos Tversky and Daniel Kahneman, "Availability: A Heuristic for Judging Frequency and Probability," *Cognitive Psychology*, vol. 5, no. 2 (1973), pp. 207–32.

37. Amos Tversky and Daniel Kahneman, "Judgment under Uncertainty: Heuristics and Biases," *Science*, vol. 185, no. 4157 (1974), pp. 1124–31.

38. Kahneman and Tversky, "Prospect Theory: An Analysis of Decision under Risk."

39. Thomas Gilovich, Robert Vallone, and Amos Tversky, "The Hot Hand in Basketball: On the Misperception of Random Sequences," *Cognitive Psychology*, vol. 17, no. 3 (July 1985), pp. 295–314.

40. Howard Kunreuther, "Causes of Underinsurance against Natural Disasters," *Geneva Papers on Risk and Insurance*, vol. 9, no. 31 (1984), pp. 206–20.

41. David Dunning, Chip Heath, and Jerry M. Suls, "Flawed Self-Assessment: Implications for Health, Education, and the Workplace," *Psychological Science in the Public Interest*, vol. 5, no. 3 (2004), pp. 69–106; Don Moore and Paul Healy, "The Trouble with Overconfidence," *Psychological Review*, vol. 115, no. 2 (2008), pp. 502–17.

42. Ola Svenson, "Are We All Less Risky and More Skillful Than Our Fellow Drivers?" *Acta Psychologica*, vol. 47, no. 2 (February 1981), pp. 143–48.

43. Colin Camerer and Dan Lovallo, "Overconfidence and Excess Entry: An Experimental Approach," *American Economic Review*, vol. 89, no. 1 (March 1999), pp. 306–18; Ulrike Malmendier and Geoffrey Tate, "Who Makes Acquisitions? CEO Overconfidence and the Market's Reaction," *Journal of Financial Economics*, vol. 89, no. 1 (2008), pp. 20–43.

44. David Armor and Shelley Taylor, "When Predictions Fail: The Dilemma of Unrealistic Optimism," in *Heuristics and Biases: The Psychology of Intuitive Judgment*, edited by Thomas Gilovich, Dale Griffin, and Daniel Kahneman (Cambridge University Press, 2002), pp. 334–47.

45. Johannes Spinnewijn, "Unemployed but Optimistic: Optimal Insurance Design with Biased Beliefs," unpublished working paper, 2009.

46. Linda Babcock and George Loewenstein, "Explaining Bargaining Impasse: The Role of Self-Serving Biases," *Journal of Economic Perspectives*, vol. 11, no. 1 (1997), pp. 109–26.

47. Shane Frederick, "Cognitive Reflection and Decision Making," *Journal of Economic Perspectives*, vol. 19, no. 4 (Fall 2005), pp. 25–42.

48. Donald A. Redelmeier and Eldar Shafir, "Medical Decision Making in Situations with Multiple Alternatives," *JAMA*, vol. 274, no. 4 (1995), pp. 302–05.

49. Barry Schwartz and others, "Maximizing Versus Satisficing: Happiness Is a Matter of Choice," *Journal of Personality and Social Psychology*," vol. 83, no. 5 (2002), pp. 1178–97; Ap Dijksterhuis and others, "On Making the Right Choice: The Deliberation-without-Attention Effect," *Science*, vol. 311, no. 5763 (February 17, 2006), pp. 1005–07.

50. Kris N. Kirby and Richard J. Herrnstein, "Preference Reversals Due to Myopic Discounting of Delayed Reward," *Psychological Science*, vol. 6, no. 2 (1995), pp. 83–89.

51. Stefano DellaVigna and Ulrike Malmendier, "Paying Not to Go to the Gym," *American Economic Review*, vol. 96, no. 3 (2006), pp. 694–719.

52. Shane Frederick, George Loewenstein, and Ted O'Donoghue, "Time Discounting and Time Preference: A Critical Review," *Journal of Economic Literature*, vol. 40, no. 2 (2002), pp. 351–401.

53. Katherine L. Milkman, Todd Rogers, and Max H. Bazerman, "I'll Have the Ice Cream Soon and the Vegetables Later: A Study of Online Grocery Purchases and Order Lead Time," *Marketing Letters*, vol. 21, no. 1 (2010), pp. 17–35; Daniel Read, George Loewenstein, and Shobana Kalyanaraman, "Mixing Virtue and Vice: Combing the Immediacy Effect and the Diversification Heuristic," *Journal of Behavioral Decision Making*, vol. 12, no. 4 (1999), pp. 257–273.

54. Dan Ariely and Klaus Wertenbroch, "Procrastination, Deadlines, and Performance," *Psychological Science*, vol. 13, no. 3 (2002), pp. 219–24.

55. Nava Ashraf, Dean Karlan, and Wesley Yin, "Tying Odysseus to the Mast: Evidence from a Commitment Savings Product in the Philippines," *Quarterly Journal of Economics*, vol. 121, no. 2 (2006), pp. 635–72.

56. Ted O'Donoghue and Matthew Rabin, "Doing It Now or Later," *American Economic Review*, vol. 89, no. 1 (1999), pp. 103–24.

57. Kurt Lewin, *Field Theory in Social Science* (New York: Harper, 1951).

58. Howard Leventhal, Robert Singer, and Susan Jones, "Effects of Fear and Specificity of Recommendation upon Attitudes and Behavior," *Journal of Personality and Social Psychology*, vol. 2, no. 1 (1965), pp. 20–29.

59. Derek J. Koehler and Connie S. K. Poon, "Self-Predictions Overweight Strength of Current Intentions," *Journal of Experimental Social Psychology*, vol. 42, no. 4 (2006), pp. 517–24.

60. Eric P. Bettinger and others, "The Role of Simplification and Information in College Decisions: Results from the H&R Block FAFSA Experiment," Working Paper 15361 (Cambridge, Mass.: National Bureau of Economic Research, September 2009); Brigitte C. Madrian and Dennis F. Shea, "The Power of Suggestion: Inertia in 401(k) Participation and Savings Behavior," *Quarterly Journal of Economics*, vol. 116, no. 4 (2001), pp. 1149–87.

61. Baba Shiv and Alexander Fedorikhin, "Heart and Mind in Conflict: The Interplay of Affect and Cognition in Consumer Decision Making," *Journal of Consumer Research*, vol. 26, no. 3 (1999), pp. 278–92.

62. Saul Shiffman and Andrew J. Waters, "Negative Affect and Smoking Lapses: A Prospective Analysis," *Journal of Consulting and Clinical Psychology*, vol. 72, no. 2 (2004), 192–201.

63. George Loewenstein, "Out of Control: Visceral Influences on Behavior," *Organizational Behavior and Human Decision Processes*, vol. 65, no. 3 (1996), pp. 272–92.

64. George Loewenstein, Ted O'Donoghue, and Matthew Rabin, "Projection Bias in Predicting Future Utility," *Quarterly Journal of Economics*, vol. 118, no. 4 (2003), pp. 1209–48.

65. Daniel Read and Barbara van Leeuwen, "Predicting Hunger: The Effects of Appetite and Delay on Choice," *Organizational Behavior and Human Decision Processes*, vol. 76, no. 2 (1998), pp. 189–205.

66. Michael Conlin, Ted O'Donoghue, and Timothy J. Vogelsang, "Projection Bias in Catalog Orders," *American Economic Review*, vol. 97, no 4 (2007), pp. 1217–49.

67. Gary S. Becker and Kevin M. Murphy, "A Theory of Rational Addiction," *Journal of Political Economy*, vol. 96, no. 4 (1988), pp. 675–700.

68. Jonathan Gruber and Botond Koszegi, "Is Addiction 'Rational'? Theory and Evidence," *Quarterly Journal of Economics*, vol. 116, no. 4 (2001), pp. 1261–1303.

69. B. Douglas Bernheim and Antonio Rangel, "Addiction and Cue-Triggered Decision Processes," *American Economic Review*, vol. 94, no. 5 (2004), pp. 1558–90.

70. David Laibson, "Golden Eggs and Hyperbolic Discounting," *Quarterly Journal of Economics*, vol. 112, no. 2 (1997), pp. 443–77.

71. Richard H. Thaler and H. M. Shefrin, "An Economic Theory of Self-Control," *Journal of Political Economy*, vol. 89, no. 2 (1981), pp. 392–406.

72. George Loewenstein and Ted O'Donoghue, "Animal Spirits: Affective and Deliberative Processes in Human Behavior," working paper, Department of Social and Decision Sciences, Carnegie Mellon University, 2004.

73. Yaacov Trope and Nira Liberman, "Temporal Construal," *Psychological Review*, vol. 110, no. 3 (2003), pp. 403–21.

74. Daniel Kahneman, Jack L. Knetsch, and Richard Thaler, "Experimental Tests of the Endowment Effect and the Coase Theorem," *Journal of Political Economy*, vol. 98, no. 6 (December 1990), pp. 1325–48.

75. David Genesove and Christopher Mayer, "Loss Aversion and Seller Behavior: Evidence from the Housing Market," *Quarterly Journal of Economics,* vol. 116, no. 4 (2001), pp. 1233–60.

76. Daniel Kahneman, Jack L. Knetsch, and Richard H. Thaler, "The Endowment Effect, Loss Aversion, and Status Quo Bias," *Journal of Economic Perspectives,* vol. 5, no. 1 (Winter 1991), pp. 193–206; Botond Koszegi and Matthew Rabin, "Reference-Dependent Consumption Plans," *American Economic Review*, vol. 99, no. 3 (2009), pp. 909–36.

77. Botond Koszegi and Matthew Rabin, "A Model of Reference-Dependent Preferences," *Quarterly Journal of Economics*, vol. 121, no. 4 (November 2006), pp. 1133–65.

78. Kathryn Zeiler and Charles R. Plott, "The Willingness to Pay/Willingness to Accept Gap, the Endowment Effect, Subject Misconceptions, and Experimental Procedures for Eliciting Valuations," *American Economic Review*, vol. 95, no. 3 (2005), pp. 530–45; Andrea Isoni, Graham Loomes, and Robert Sugden, "The Willingness to Pay/Willingness to Accept Gap, the 'Endowment Effect', Subject Misconceptions, and Experimental Procedures for Eliciting Valuations: A Reassessment," *American Economic Review*, forthcoming.

79. Kahneman and Tversky, "Prospect Theory: An Analysis of Decision under Risk"; Amos Tversky and Daniel Kahneman, "Loss Aversion in Riskless Choice: A Reference-Dependent Model," *Quarterly Journal of Economics*, vol. 106, no. 4 (November 1991), pp. 1039–61.

80. Nicholas Epley, Dennis Mak, and Lorraine Chen Idson, "Bonus or Rebate? The Impact of Income Framing on Spending and Saving," *Journal of Behavioral Decision Making*, vol. 19, no. 3 (2006): 213–27.

81. Matthew Rabin, "Risk Aversion and Expected-Utility Theory: A Calibration Theorem," *Econometrica*, vol. 68, no. 5 (September 2000), pp. 1281–92; Matthew Rabin and Richard H. Thaler, "Risk Aversion," *Journal of Economic Perspectives*, vol. 15, no. 1 (Winter 2001), pp. 219–32.

82. Justin Sydnor, "(Over)Insuring Modest Risks," *American Economic Journal: Applied Economics*, forthcoming.

83. Tversky and Kahneman, "The Framing of Decisions and the Psychology of Choice."

84. William Samuelson and Richard Zeckhauser, "Status Quo Bias in Decision Making," *Journal of Risk and Uncertainty*, vol. 1, no. 1 (1988), pp. 7–59.

85. Raymond S. Hartman, Michael J. Doane, and Chi-Keung Woo, "Consumer Rationality and the Status Quo," *Quarterly Journal of Economics*, vol. 106, no. 1 (February 1991), pp. 141–62.

86. Ernst Fehr and Urs Fischbacher, "The Nature of Human Altruism," *Nature*, vol. 425, no. 6960 (2003), pp. 785–91.

87. Hessel Oosterbeek, Randolph Sloof, and Gijs van de Kuilen, "Differences in Ultimatum Game Experiments: Evidence from a Meta-Analysis," *Experimental Economics*, vol. 7, no. 2 (2004), pp. 171–88.

88. James Andreoni and John Miller, "Giving According to GARP: An Experimental Test of the Consistency of Preferences for Altruism," *Econometrica*, vol. 70, no. 2 (2002), pp. 737–53.

89. James Andreoni, "Philanthropy," in *Handbook of Giving, Reciprocity and Altruism*, edited by Serge-Christophe Kolm and Jean Mercier Ythier (Amsterdam: North Holland, 2006), pp. 1201–69.

90. Thomas R. Palfrey and Jefferey E. Prisbrey, "Anomalous Behavior in Public Goods Experiments: How Much and Why?" *American Economic Review*, vol. 87, no. 5 (1997), pp. 829–46.

91. Eric J. Brunner, "Free Riders or Easy Riders? An Examination of the Voluntary Provision of Public Radio," *Public Choice*, vol. 97, no. 4 (1998), pp. 587–604; Eric Brunner and Jon Sonstelie, "School Finance Reform and Voluntary Fiscal Federalism," *Journal of Public Economics*, vol. 87, no. 9–10 (2003), pp. 2157–85.

92. Matthew Rabin, "Incorporating Fairness into Game Theory and Economics," *American Economic Review*, vol. 83, no. 5 (1993), pp. 1281–1302.

93. Daniel Kahneman, Jack L. Knetsch and Richard Thaler, "Fairness as a Constraint on Profit Seeking: Entitlements in the Market," *American Economic Review*, vol. 76, no. 4 (1986), pp. 728–41.

94. Ernst Fehr and Klaus M. Schmidt, "A Theory of Fairness, Competition, and Cooperation," *Quarterly Journal of Economics*, vol. 114, no. 3 (1999), pp. 817–68; Ernst Fehr and Simon Gachter, "Fairness and Retaliation: The Economics of Reciprocity," *Journal of Economic Perspectives*, vol. 14, no. 3 (2000), pp. 159–81.

95. Joel Sobel, "Interdependent Preferences and Reciprocity," *Journal of Economic Literature*, vol. 43, no. 2 (2005), pp. 392–436.

96. Jon Elster, "Social Norms and Economic Theory," *Journal of Economic Perspective*, vol. 3, no. 4 (1989), pp. 99–117.

97. James Andreoni and B. Douglas Bernheim, "Social Image and the 50-50 Norm: A Theoretical and Experimental Analysis of Audience Effects," *Econometrica*, vol. 77, no. 5 (2009), pp. 1607–36.

98. Robert B. Cialdini, Raymond R. Reno, and Carl A. Kallgren, "A Focus Theory of Normative Conduct: Recycling the Concept of Norms to Reduce Littering in Public Places," *Journal of Personality and Social Psychology*, vol. 58, no. 6 (1990), pp. 1015–26.

99. Noah J. Goldstein, Robert B. Cialdini, and Vladas Griskevicius, "A Room with a Viewpoint: Using Social Norms to Motivate Environmental Conservation in Hotels," *Journal of Consumer Research*, vol. 35, no. 3 (2008), pp. 472–82.

100. Ian Ayres, Sophie Raseman, and Alice Shih, "Evidence from Two Large Field Experiments that Peer Comparison Feedback Can Reduce Residential Energy Usage," Working Paper 15386 (Cambridge, Mass.: National Bureau of Economic Research, September 2009); P. Wesley Schultz and others, "The Constructive, Destructive, and Reconstructive Power of Social Norms," *Psychological Science*, vol. 18, no. 5 (2007), pp. 429–34.

101. Robert H. Frank, "Positional Externalities Cause Large and Preventable Welfare Losses," *American Economic Review*, vol. 95, no. 2 (2005), pp. 137–41; Sara J. Solnick and David Hemenway, "Are Positional Concerns Stronger in Some Domains than in Others?" *American Economic Review*, vol. 95, no. 2 (2005), pp. 147–51.

102. Erzo F. P. Luttmer, "Neighbors as Negatives: Relative Earnings and Well-Being," *Quarterly Journal of Economics*, vol. 120, no. 3 (2005), pp. 963–1002.

103. George A. Akerlof and Rachel E. Kranton, *Identity Economics: How Our Identities Shape Our Work, Wages, and Well-Being* (Princeton University Press, 2010).

104. Robyn A. LeBoeuf, Eldar Shafir, and Julia Belyavsky Bayuk, "The Conflicting Choices of Alternating Selves," *Organizational Behavior and Human Decision Processes*, vol. 111, no. 1 (2010), pp. 48–61; Daniel J. Benjamin, James J. Choi, and A. Joshua Strickland, "Social Identity and Preferences," *American Economic Review*, vol. 100, no. 4 (2010), pp. 1913–28.

105. Steven D. Levitt and John A. List, "Homo Economicus Evolves," *Science*, vol. 319, no. 5865 (2008), pp. 909–10.

106. John A. List, "Does Market Experience Eliminate Market Anomalies?" *Quarterly Journal of Economics*, vol. 118, no. 41 (2003), pp. 41–71.

107. Gary S. Becker, "Irrational Behavior and Economic Theory," *Journal of Political Economy*, vol. 70, no. 1 (1962), pp. 1–13.

108. Thomas Russell and Richard Thaler, "The Relevance of Quasi-Rationality in Competitive Markets," *American Economic Review*, vol. 75, no. 5 (December 1985), pp. 1071–82.

109. Ernst Fehr and Jean-Robert Tyran, "Individual Irrationality and Aggregate Outcomes," *Journal of Economic Perspectives*, vol. 19, no. 4 (2005), pp. 43–66.

Chapter Three

1. Jonathan Gruber, *Public Finance and Public Policy* (New York: Worth Publishers, 2007); Harvey S. Rosen and Ted Gayer, *Public Finance* (Boston: McGraw-Hill, 2008).

Chapter Four

1. Michael Holland, quoted in "They Said It," *Science*, vol. 300, no. 5617 (April 11, 2003), p. 247.

2. Joint Committee on Taxation, "Estimates of Federal Tax Expenditures for Fiscal Years 2009–2013" (Government Printing Office, 2010).

3. Board of Trustees, *2009 Annual Report of the Board of Trustees of the Federal Old-Age and Survivors Insurance and Federal Disability Insurance Trust Funds* (Social Security Administration, 2009).

4. William G. Gale, John Karl Scholz, and Ananth Seshadri, "Are All Americans Saving 'Optimally' for Retirement?" unpublished working paper, 2009; Jonathan Skinner, "Are You Sure You're Saving Enough for Retirement?" *Journal of Economic Perspectives*, vol. 21, no. 3 (2007), pp. 59–80; Laurence Kotlikoff, "Is Conventional Financial Planning Good for Your Financial Health?" Boston University working paper, 2006; John Karl Scholz, Ananth Seshadri, and Surachai Khitatrakun, "Are Americans Saving 'Optimally' for Retirement?" *Journal of Political Economy*, vol. 114, no. 4 (2006), pp. 607–43; Eric M. Engen, William G. Gale, and Cori R. Uccello, "The Adequacy of Retirement Saving," *Brookings Papers on Economic Activity*, no. 2 (1999), pp. 65–188.

5. Shlomo Benartzi and Richard H. Thaler, "Heuristics and Biases in Retirement Savings Behavior," *Journal of Economic Perspectives*, vol. 21, no. 3 (2007), pp. 81–104.

6. B. Douglas Bernheim, Jonathan Skinner, and Steven Weinberg, "What Accounts for the Variation in Retirement Wealth among U.S. Households?" *American Economic Review*, vol. 91, no. 4 (September 2001), pp. 832–57.

7. Esther Duflo and others, "Saving Incentives for Low- and Middle-Income Families: Evidence from a Field Experiment with H&R Block," *Quarterly Journal of Economics*, vol. 121, no. 4 (2006), pp. 1311–46.

8. Brigitte C. Madrian and Dennis F. Shea, "The Power of Suggestion: Inertia in 401(k) Participation and Savings Behavior," *Quarterly Journal of Economics*, vol. 116, no. 4 (2001), pp. 1149–87.

9. Sheena S. Iyengar, Gur Huberman, and Wei Jiang, "How Much Choice Is Too Much? Contributions to 401(k) Retirement Plans," in *Pension Design and Structure: New Lessons from Behavioral Finance*, edited by Olivia S. Mitchell and Steve Utkus (Oxford University Press, 2004), pp. 83–95.

10. Dean Karlan and others, "Getting to the Top of Mind: How Reminders Increase Saving," Working Paper 16205 (Cambridge, Mass.: National Bureau of Economic Research, 2010).

11. Laurent E. Calvet, John Y. Campbell, and Paolo Sodini, "Measuring the Financial Sophistication of Households," *American Economic Review*, vol. 99, no. 2 (2009), pp. 393–98.

12. Lisa Meulbroek, "Company Stock in Pension Plans: How Costly Is It?" *Journal of Law and Economics*, vol. 48, no. 2 (2005), pp. 443–74; Shlomo Benartzi, "Excessive Extrapolation and the Allocation of 401(k) Accounts to Company Stock," *Journal of Finance*, vol. 56, no. 5 (2001), pp. 1747–64.

13. James J. Choi, David Laibson, and Brigitte C. Madrian, "Why Does the Law of One Price Fail? An Experiment on Index Mutual Funds," *Review of Financial Studies*, vol. 23 (2010), pp. 1405–32.

14. Shlomo Benartzi and Richard H. Thaler, "Naive Diversification Strategies in Defined Contribution Saving Plans," *American Economic Review*, vol. 91, no. 1 (March 2001), pp. 79–98.

15. Shlomo Benartzi and Richard H. Thaler, "Risk Aversion or Myopia? Choices in Repeated Gambles and Retirement Investments," *Management Science*, vol. 45, no. 3 (1999), pp. 364–81; Jeffrey R. Brown, Nellie Liang, and Scott Weisbenner, "Individual Account Investment Options and Portfolio Choice: Behavioral Lessons from 401(k) Plans," *Journal of Public Economics*, vol. 91, no. 10 (2007), pp. 1992–2013; James J. Choi, David Laibson, and Brigitte C. Madrian, "Mental Accounting in Portfolio Choice: Evidence from a Flypaper Effect," *American Economic* Review, vol. 99, no. 5 (2009), pp. 2085–95.

16. Esther Duflo and Emmanuel Saez, "The Role of Information and Social Interactions in Retirement Plan Decisions: Evidence from a Randomized Experiment," *Quarterly Journal*

of Economics, vol. 118, no. 3 (2003), pp. 815–42; Marcelo Pinheiro, "Loyalty, Peer Group Effects, and 401(k)," *Quarterly Review of Economics and Finance*, vol. 48, no. 1 (2008), pp. 94–122; Jeffrey R. Brown and others, "Neighbors Matter: Causal Community Effects and Stock Market Participation," *Journal of Finance*, vol. 63, no. 3 (2008), pp. 1509–31.

17. David Laibson, Andrea Repetto, Jeremy Tobacman, "Self-Control and Saving for Retirement," *Brookings Papers on Economic Activity*, no. 1 (1998), pp. 91–196.

18. Alexander L. Brown, Zhikang Eric Chua, and Colin F. Camerer, "Learning and Visceral Temptation in Dynamic Saving Experiments," *Quarterly Journal of Economics*, vol. 124, no. 1 (2009), pp. 197–231.

19. Nava Ashraf, Dean Karlan, and Wesley Yin, "Tying Odysseus to the Mast: Evidence from a Commitment Savings Product in the Philippines," *Quarterly Journal of Economics*, vol. 121, no. 2 (2006), pp. 635–72.

20. John Ameriks, Andrew Caplin, and John Leahy, "Wealth Accumulation and the Propensity to Plan," *Quarterly Journal of Economics*, vol. 118, no. 3 (2003), pp. 1007–47; Annamaria Lusardi, "Planning and Saving for Retirement," unpublished working paper, 2003.

21. Amy Finkelstein and James Poterba, "Selection Effects in the United Kingdom Individual Annuities Market," *Economic Journal*, vol. 112, no. 476 (2002), pp. 28–50.

22. Olivia S. Mitchell and others, "New Evidence on the Money's Worth of Individual Annuities," *American Economic Review*, vol. 89, no. 5 (1999), pp. 1299–1318.

23. Jeffrey R. Brown, Marcus D. Casey, and Olivia S. Mitchell, "Who Values the Social Security Annuity? New Evidence on the Annuity Puzzle," Working Paper 13800 (Cambridge, Mass.: National Bureau of Economic Research, 2008).

24. Jeffrey R. Brown, "Rational and Behavioral Perspectives on the Role of Annuities in Retirement Planning," Working Paper 13537 (Cambridge, Mass.: National Bureau of Economic Research, October 2007); Wei-Yin Hu and Jason S. Scott, "Behavioral Obstacles to the Annuity Market," unpublished paper, 2007.

25. Jeffrey R. Brown and others, "Why Don't People Insure Late Life Consumption? A Framing Explanation of the Under-Annuitization Puzzle," *American Economic Review*, vol. 98, no. 2 (2008), pp. 304–09.

26. Robert S. Gazzale and Lina Walker, "Behavioral Biases in Annuity Choice: An Experiment," Williams College Economics Department Working Paper Series (March 25, 2009).

27. Congressional Budget Office, "Social Security and Private Saving: A Review of the Empirical Evidence" (July 1998).

28. Gary V. Englehardt and Jonathan Gruber, "Social Security and the Evolution of Elderly Poverty," in *Public Policy and the Income Distribution*, edited by Alan Auerbach, David Card, and John Quigley (New York: Russell Sage Foundation, 2006), pp. 259–87.

29. Martin Feldstein, "The Optimal Level of Social Security Benefits," *Quarterly Journal of Economics*, vol. 100, no. 2 (1985), pp. 303–20; Ayse Imrohoroglu, Selahattin Imrohoroglu, and Douglas H. Jones, "Time-Inconsistent Preferences and Social Security," *Quarterly Journal of Economics*, vol. 118, no. 2 (2003), pp. 745–84.

30. Pinheiro, "Loyalty, Peer Group Effects, and 401(k)."

31. Richard H. Thaler, "Psychology and Savings Policies," *American Economic Review*, vol. 84, no. 2 (1994), pp. 186–92.

32. Madrian and Shea, "The Power of Suggestion: Inertia in 401(k) Participation and Savings Behavior."

33. Gabriel D. Carroll and others, "Optimal Defaults and Active Decisions," *Quarterly Journal of Economics*, vol. 124, no. 4 (2009), pp. 1639–74; James Choi, David Laibson, and

Brigitte C. Madrian, "Reducing the Complexity Costs of 401(k) Participation through Quick Enrollment," in *Developments in the Economics of Aging*, edited by David A. Wise (University of Chicago Press, 2009).

34. J. Mark Iwry and David C. John, "Pursuing Universal Retirement Security through Automatic IRAs," Retirement Security Project Paper 2009-3 (Brookings, July 2009).

35. Office of Management and Budget, *Budget of the United States Government, Fiscal Year 2011* (2010).

36. Duflo and others, "Saving Incentives for Low- and Middle-Income Families: Evidence from a Field Experiment with H&R Block."

37. Office of Management and Budget, *Budget of the United States Government, Fiscal Year 2011*.

38. Peter Tufano, Daniel Schneider, and Sondra Beverly, "Leveraging Tax Refunds to Encourage Saving," Retirement Security Project Policy Brief 2005-8 (Washington: Retirement Security Project, August 2005).

39. Sondra Beverly, Daniel Scheider, and Peter Tufano, "Splitting Tax Refunds and Building Savings: An Empirical Test," in *Tax Policy and the Economy*, vol. 20, edited by James M. Poterba (MIT Press, 2006), pp. 111–61.

40. Richard H. Thaler and Shlomo Benartzi, "Save More Tomorrow: Using Behavioral Economics to Increase Employee Savings," *Journal of Political Economy*, vol. 112, no. 1, (2004), pp. 164–87.

41. Leonard E. Burman and others, "Effects of Public Policies on the Disposition of Pre-Retirement Lump-Sum Distributions: Rational and Behavioral Influences," working paper, December 2007.

42. William G. Gale and others, "Increasing Annuitization in 401(k) Plans with Automatic Trial Income," Hamilton Project Discussion Paper 2008-02 (Brookings, June 2008).

43. Brown and others, "Why Don't People Insure Late Life Consumption?"

44. Social Security Administration, *Annual Statistical Supplement to the Social Security Bulletin: 2009* (Government Printing Office, 2010).

45. Courtney Coile and others, "Delays in Claiming Social Security Benefits," *Journal of Public Economics*, vol. 84, no. 3 (2002), pp. 357–85.

46. Peter Diamond and Botond Koszegi, "Quasi-Hyperbolic Discounting and Retirement," *Journal of Public Economics*, vol. 87, no. 9–10 (2003), pp. 1839–72.

47. David Fetherstonhaugh and Lee Ross, "Framing Effects and Income Flow Preferences in Decisions about Social Security," in *Behavioral Dimensions of Retirement Economics*, edited by Henry J. Aaron (Brookings, 1999), pp. 187–213; Jeffrey B. Liebman and Erzo F.P. Littmer, "The Perception of Social Security Incentives for Labor Supply and Retirement: The Median Voter Knows More Than You'd Think," working paper, April 7, 2009.

48. Jonathan Gruber and Peter Orszag, "Does the Social Security Earnings Test Affect Labor Supply and Benefits Receipt?" *National Tax Journal*, vol. 56, no. 4 (2003), pp. 755–73.

49. Giovanni Mastrobuoni, "Do Better-Informed Workers Make Better Retirement Choices? A Test Based on the Social Security Statement," unpublished working paper, April 2006; Howell W. Jackson, "Accounting for Social Security Benefits," in *Behavioral Public Finance*, edited by Edward J. McCaffery and Joel Slemrod (New York: Russell Sage Foundation, 2006), pp. 261–303.

50. Henrik Cronqvist and Richard H. Thaler, "Design Choices in Privatized Social-Security Systems: Learning from the Swedish Experience," *American Economic Review*, vol. 94, no. 2 (2004), pp. 424–28.

51. Carmen DeNavas-Walt, Bernadette D. Proctor, and Jessica C. Smith, *Income, Poverty, and Health Insurance Coverage in the United States: 2009* (Government Printing Office, 2010).

52. Congressional Budget Office, "H.R. 4872, Reconciliation Act of 2010 (Final Health Care Legislation)," March 20, 2010.

53. Kenneth J. Arrow, "Uncertainty and the Welfare Economics of Medical Care," *American Economic Review*, vol. 53 (1963), pp. 941–73; Michael Rothschild and Joseph Stiglitz, "Equilibrium in Competitive Insurance Markets: An Essay on the Economics of Imperfect Information," *Quarterly Journal of Economics*, vol. 90, no. 4 (1976), pp. 629–49.

54. Eric J. Johnson and others, "Framing, Probability Distortions, and Insurance Decisions," *Journal of Risk and Uncertainty*, vol. 7, no. 1 (1993), pp. 35–51.

55. George Loewenstein, "Hot-Cold Empathy Gaps and Medical Decisionmaking," *Health Psychology*, vol. 24, no. 4 (2005), pp. S49–S56; Peter A. Ubel and others, "Misimagining the Unimaginable: The Disability Paradox and Health Care Decisionmaking," *Health Psychology*, vol. 24, no. 4 (2005), pp. S57–S62; Paul Dolan and Daniel Kahneman, "Interpretations of Utility and Their Implications for the Valuation of Health," *Economic Journal*, vol. 118, no. 525 (2008), pp. 215–34.

56. William Samuelson and Richard Zeckhauser, "Status Quo Bias in Decisionmaking," *Journal of Risk and Uncertainty*, vol. 1, no. 1 (1988), pp. 7–59.

57. Paul Slovic and others, "Preference for Insuring against Probable Small Losses: Insurance Implications," *Journal of Risk and Insurance*, vol. 44, no. 2 (1977), pp. 237–58.

58. Alvaro Sandroni and Francesco Squintani, "Overconfidence, Insurance, and Paternalism," *American Economic Review*, vol. 97, no. 5 (2007), pp. 1994–2004.

59. Colin Camerer, George Loewenstein and Martin Weber, "The Curse of Knowledge in Economic Settings: An Experimental Analysis," *Journal of Political Economy*, vol. 97, no. 5 (1989), pp. 1232–54.

60. Benjamin Handel, "Adverse Selection and Switching Costs in Health Insurance Markets: When Nudging Hurts," unpublished working paper, November 12, 2009.

61. David M. Cutler, Amy Finkelstein, and Kathleen McGarry, "Preference Heterogeneity in Insurance Markets: Explaining a Puzzle of Insurance," *American Economic Review*, vol. 98, no. 2 (2008), pp. 157–62; Alma Cohen and Peter Siegelman, "Testing for Adverse Selection in Insurance Markets," *Journal of Risk and Insurance,* vol. 77, no. 1 (2010), pp. 39–84.

62. Amy Finkelstein and Kathleen McGarry, "Multiple Dimensions of Private Information: Evidence from the Long-Term Care Insurance Market," *American Economic Review*, vol. 96, no. 4 (2006), pp. 938–58.

63. Hanming Fang, Michael P. Keane, and Dan Silverman, "Sources of Advantageous Selection: Evidence from the Medigap Insurance Market," *Journal of Political Economy*, vol. 116, no. 2 (2008), pp. 303–50.

64. Lisa Dubay, John Holahan, and Allison Cook, "The Uninsured and the Affordability of Health Insurance Coverage," *Health Affairs*, vol. 26, no. 1 (2007), pp. w22–w30; Julie L. Hudson and Thomas M. Selden, "Children's Eligibility and Coverage: Recent Trends and a Look Ahead," *Health Affairs*, vol. 26, no. 5 (2007), pp. w618–w629.

65. Jonathan Gruber and Ebonya Washington, "Subsidies to Employee Health Insurance Premiums and the Health Insurance Market," *Journal of Health Economics*, vol. 24, no. 2 (2005), pp. 253–76.

66. Helen Levy and Thomas DeLeire, "What Do People Buy When They Don't Buy Health Insurance and What Does That Say about Why They Are Uninsured?" *Inquiry*, vol. 45, no. 4 (2008), pp. 365–79; M. Kate Bundorf and Mark V. Pauly, "Is Health Insurance

Affordable for the Uninsured?" *Journal of Health Economics*, vol. 25, no. 4 (July 2006), pp. 650–73.

67. Jeffrey Kling and others, "Misperception in Choosing Medicare Drug Plans," unpublished working paper, July 2009.

68. Jason T. Abaluck and Jonathan Gruber, "Choice Inconsistencies among the Elderly: Evidence from Plan Choice in the Medicare Part D Program," Working Paper 14759 (Cambridge, Mass.: National Bureau of Economic Research, February 2009).

69. Joachim Winter and others, "Medicare Prescription Drug Coverage: Consumer Information and Preferences," *Proceedings of the National Academy of Sciences*, vol. 103, no. 20 (2006), pp. 7929–34.

70. Richard G. Frank and Karine Lamiraud, "Choice, Price Competition, and Complexity in Markets for Health Insurance," *Journal of Economic Behavior and Organization*, vol. 71, no. 2 (2009), pp. 550–62; Jessica Greene and others, "Comprehension and Choice of a Consumer-Directed Health Plan," *American Journal of Managed Care*, vol. 14, no. 6 (2008), pp. 369–76.

71. Mark V. Pauly, "The Economics of Moral Hazard," *American Economic Review*, vol. 58, no. 3 (1968), pp. 531–37; Richard Zeckhauser, "Medical Insurance: A Case Study of the Trade-Off between Risk Spreading and Appropriate Incentives," *Journal of Economic Theory*, vol. 2, no. 1 (1970), pp. 10–26.

72. Joseph P. Newhouse and others, "Some Interim Results from a Controlled Trial of Cost Sharing in Health Insurance," *New England Journal of Medicine*, vol. 305, no. 25 (1981), pp. 1501–07.

73. Robert H. Brook and others, "Does Free Care Improve Adults' Health? Results from a Randomized Controlled Trial," *New England Journal of Medicine*, vol. 309, no. 23 (1983), pp. 1426–34.

74. Amitabh Chandra, Jonathan Gruber, and Robin McKnight, "Patient Cost-Sharing and Hospitalization Offsets in the Elderly," *American Economic Review*, vol. 100, no. 1 (2010), pp. 193–213.

75. John Hsu and others, "Unintended Consequences of Caps on Medicare Drug Benefits," *New England Journal of Medicine*, vol. 354, no. 22 (2006), pp. 2349–59; Cary P. Gross and others, "Relation between Medicare Screening Reimbursement and Stage at Diagnosis for Older Patients with Colon Cancer," *JAMA*, vol. 296, no. 23 (2006), pp. 2815–22.

76. Michael E. Chernew, Allison B. Rosen, and A. Mark Fendrick, "Value-Based Insurance Design," *Health Affairs*, vol. 26, no. 2 (2007), pp. w195–w203; Niteesh K. Choudhry and others, "Should Patients Receive Secondary Prevention Medications for Free after a Myocardial Infarction? An Economic Analysis," *Health Affairs*, vol. 26, no. 1 (2007), pp. 186–94; Dana P. Goldman, Geoffrey F. Joyce, and Pinar Karaca-Mandic, "Varying Pharmacy Benefits with Clinical Status: The Case of Cholesterol-Lowering Therapy," *American Journal of Managed Care*, vol. 12, no. 1 (2006), pp. 21–28.

77. Jeffrey Liebman and Richard Zeckhauser, "Simple Humans, Complex Insurance, Subtle Subsidies," in *Using Taxes to Reform Health Insurance: Pitfalls and Promises*, edited by Henry Aaron and Leonard Burman (Brookings, 2008).

78. Gruber and Washington, "Subsidies to Employee Health Insurance Premiums and the Health Insurance Market"; Michael Chernew, Kevin Frick, and Catherine G. McLaughlin, "The Demand for Health Insurance Coverage by Low-Income Workers: Can Reduced Premiums Achieve Full Coverage?" *Health Services Research*, vol. 32, no. 4 (1997), pp. 453–70.

79. *Patient Protection and Affordable Care Act*, Public Law 111-148, 111 Cong., March 23, 2010, sec. 1511.

80. Massachusetts Division of Health Care Finance and Policy, "Health Care in Massachusetts: Key Indicators," May 2010.

81. Kling and others, "Misperception in Choosing Medicare Drug Plans."

82. Michael Chernew and Dennis P. Scanlon, "Health Plan Report Cards and Insurance Choice," *Inquiry*, vol. 35, no. 1 (Spring 1998), pp. 9–22; Leemore Dafny and David Dranove, "Do Report Cards Tell Consumers Anything They Don't Already Know? The Case of Medicare HMOs," *RAND Journal of Economics*, vol. 39, no. 3 (2008), pp. 790–821.

83. Dahlia K. Remler and Sherry A. Glied, "What Other Programs Can Teach Us: Increasing Participation in Health Insurance Programs," *American Journal of Public Health*, vol. 93, no. 1 (2003), pp. 67–74.

84. Amy Davidoff, Alshadye Yemane, and Emerald Adams, "Health Coverage for Low-Income Adults: Eligibility and Enrollment in Medicaid and State Programs: 2002," Kaiser Family Foundation Policy Brief (Washington: February 2005); Dubay, Holahan, and Cook, "The Uninsured and the Affordability of Health Insurance Coverage"; Hudson and Selden, "Children's Eligibility and Coverage: Recent Trends and a Look Ahead."

85. Marianne Bertrand, Sendhil Mullainathan, and Eldar Shafir, "Behavioral Economics and Marketing in Aid of Decisionmaking among the Poor," *Journal of Public Policy and Marketing*, vol. 25, no. 1 (2006), pp. 8–23.

86. Janet Currie and Jonathan Gruber, "Health Insurance Eligibility and Child Health: Lessons from Recent Expansions of the Medicaid Program," *Quarterly Journal of Economics*, vol. 111, no. 2 (1996), pp. 431–66; Janet Currie, "The Take-Up of Social Benefits," in *Public Policy and the Income Distribution*, edited by Alan J. Auerbach, David Card, and John M. Quigley (New York: Russell Sage Foundation, 2006), pp. 80–148.

87. Stan Dorn, *Automatic Enrollment Strategies: Helping State Coverage Expansions Achieve Their Goals*, prepared by the Urban Institute for the State Coverage Initiatives Program of Academy Health (Washington: August 2007); Robert Nelb, "Effortless Enrollment: Using Existing Information to Automatically Enroll Eligible Families in Medicaid and SCHIP," Hamilton Project Economic Policy Innovation Prize paper (Brookings, May 2009).

88. Stan Dorn and others, "Nine in Ten: Using the Tax System to Enroll Eligible, Uninsured Children into Medicaid and SCHIP," Urban Institute Working Paper (Washington: Urban Institute, January 2009).

89. Eric P. Bettinger and others, "The Role of Simplification and Information in College Decisions: Results from the H&R Block FAFSA Experiment," Working Paper 15361 (Cambridge, Mass.: National Bureau of Economic Research, September 2009).

90. Anna Aizer, "Public Health Insurance, Program Take-Up, and Child Health," *Review of Economics and Statistics*, vol. 89, no. 3 (2007), pp. 400–15.

91. Mark G. Duggan, "Hospital Ownership and Public Medical Spending," *Quarterly Journal of Economics*, vol. 115, no. 4 (2000), pp. 1343–73.

92. Mark deWolf and Katherine Klemmer, "Job Openings, Hires, and Separations Fall during the Recession," *Monthly Labor Review*, vol. 133, no. 5 (May 2010), pp. 36–44.

93. Jonathan Gruber, "The Consumption Smoothing Benefits of Unemployment Insurance," *American Economic Review*, vol. 87, no. 1 (1997), pp. 192–205.

94. Jonathan Gruber, "The Wealth of the Unemployed," *Industrial and Labor Relations Review*, vol. 55, no. 1 (2001), pp. 79–94.

95. Martin Feldstein and James Poterba, "Unemployment Insurance and Reservation Wages," *Journal of Public Economics*, vol. 23, no. 1–2 (1984), pp. 141–67; Lawrence H. Summers, "Why Is Unemployment So Very High near Full Employment?" *Brookings Papers on Economic Activity*, no. 2 (1986), pp. 339–82; Edward Balls, Lawrence F. Katz, and Lawrence

H. Summers, "Britain Divided: Hysteresis and the Regional Dimension of Britain's Unemployment Problem," Harvard University working paper, 1991; Laurence Ball and Robert Moffitt, "Productivity Growth and the Phillips Curve," Working Paper 8421 (Cambridge, Mass.: National Bureau of Economic Research, 2001); Vincent Hogan, "Wage Aspirations and Unemployment Persistence," *Journal of Monetary Economics*, vol. 51, no. 8 (2004), pp. 1623–43.

96. Colin Camerer and others, "Labor Supply of New York City Cabdrivers: One Day at a Time," *Quarterly Journal of Economics*, vol. 112, no. 2 (1997), pp. 407–41; Henry S. Farber, "Reference-Dependent Preferences and Labor Supply: The Case of New York City Taxi Drivers," *American Economic Review*, vol. 98, no. 3 (2008), pp. 1069–82; Alexandre Mas, "Pay, Reference Points, and Police Performance," *Quarterly Journal of Economics*, vol. 121, no. 3 (2006), pp. 783–821.

97. Johannes Spinnewijn, "Unemployed but Optimistic: Optimal Insurance Design with Biased Beliefs," unpublished working paper, 2009.

98. Alan B. Krueger and Andreas Mueller, "Job Search and Unemployment Insurance: New Evidence from Time Use Data," *Journal of Public Economics*, vol. 94, no. 3–4 (2010), pp. 298–307.

99. M. Daniele Paserman, "Job Search and Hyperbolic Discounting: Structural Estimation and Policy Evaluation," *Economic Journal*, vol. 118, no. 531 (2008), pp. 1418–52; Stefano DellaVigna and M. Daniele Paserman, "Job Search and Impatience," *Journal of Labor Economics*, vol. 23, no. 3 (2005), pp. 527–88.

100. Martin Neil Baily, "Some Aspects of Optimal Unemployment Insurance," *Journal of Public Economics,* vol. 10, no. 3 (1978), pp. 379–402; Raj Chetty, "Moral Hazard versus Liquidity and Optimal Unemployment Insurance," *Journal of Political Economy*, vol. 116, no. 2 (2008), pp. 173–234.

101. Bruce D. Meyer, "Unemployment Insurance and Unemployment Spells," *Econometrica*, vol. 58, no. 4 (1990), pp. 757–82; Lawrence F. Katz and Bruce D. Meyer, "The Impact of the Potential Duration of Unemployment Benefits on the Duration of Unemployment," *Journal of Public Economics*, vol. 41, no. 1 (1990), pp. 45–72.

102. David Card, Raj Chetty, and Andrea Weber, "Cash-On-Hand and Competing Models of Intertemporal Behavior: New Evidence from the Labor Market," *Quarterly Journal of Economics*, vol. 122, no. 4 (2007), pp. 1511–60.

103. David Card, Raj Chetty, and Andrea Weber, "The Spike at Benefit Exhaustion: Leaving the Unemployment System or Starting a New Job?" *American Economic Review*, vol. 97, no. 2 (2007), pp. 113–18.

104. Dan A. Black and others, "Is the Threat of Reemployment Services More Effective than the Services Themselves? Evidence from Random Assignment in the UI System," *American Economic Review*, vol. 93, no. 4 (2003), pp. 1313–27; Steven M. Director and Frederick J. Englander, "Requiring Unemployment Insurance Recipients to Register with the Public Employment Service," *Journal of Risk and Insurance*, vol. 55, no. 2 (1988), pp. 245–58.

105. Bruce Meyer, "Lessons from the U.S. Unemployment Insurance Experiments," *Journal of Economic Literature*, vol. 33, no. 1 (1995), pp. 91–131; G. Kirby and others, *Responses to Personal Reemployment Accounts (PRAs): Findings from the Demonstration States* (Washington: Mathematica Policy Research, 2008).

106. Reid Cramer, "AutoSave: A Proposal to Reverse America's Savings Decline and Make Savings Automatic, Flexible, and Inclusive," New America Foundation discussion draft, July 2006.

107. Martin Feldstein and Daniel Altman, "Unemployment Insurance Savings Accounts," Working Paper 6860 (Cambridge, Mass.: National Bureau of Economic Research, 1998);

Joseph E. Stiglitz and Jungyoll Yun, "Integration of Unemployment Insurance with Retirement Insurance," *Journal of Public Economics*, vol. 89, no. 11–12 (2005), pp. 2037–67; Jeffrey R. Kling, "Fundamental Restructuring of Unemployment Insurance: Wage-Loss Insurance and Temporary Unemployment Accounts," Hamilton Project Discussion Paper 2006-05 (Brookings, September 2006).

108. Meyer, "Lessons from the U.S. Unemployment Insurance Experiments"; Kirby and others, *Responses to Personal Reemployment Accounts (PRAs)*.

109. Carl Davidson and Stephen A Woodbury, "Wage-Rate Subsidies for Dislocated Workers," Upjohn Institute Staff Working Paper 95-31 (Kalamazoo, Mich.: January 1995); Lori G. Kletzer and Robert E. Litan, "A Prescription to Relieve Worker Anxiety," Brookings Institution Policy Brief 73 (March 2001); Robert J. LaLonde, "The Case for Wage Insurance," Council Special Report 30 (Washington: Council on Foreign Relations, September 2007).

110. Howard Bloom and others, *Testing a Reemployment Incentive for Displaced Workers: The Earnings Supplement Project* (Ottawa, Ontario: Social Research and Demonstration Corporation, May 1999).

111. Robert J. LaLonde, "The Promise of Public Sector-Sponsored Training Programs," *Journal of Economic Perspectives*, vol. 9, no. 2 (1995), pp. 149–68; Christopher J. O'Leary, "Evaluating the Effectiveness of Labor Exchange Services," in *Labor Exchange Policy in the United States*, edited by David E. Balducchi, Randall W. Eberts, and Christopher J. O'Leary (Kalamazoo, Mich.: W. E. Upjohn Institute for Employment Research, 2004), pp. 135–78.

Chapter Five

1. Al Gore, *An Inconvenient Truth: The Planetary Emergency of Global Warming and What We Can Do about It* (New York: Rodale, 2006).

2. Nicholas Stern and others, *The Economics of Climate Change* (Cambridge University Press, 2007); Martin L. Weitzman, "On Modeling and Interpreting the Economics of Catastrophic Climate Change," *Review of Economics and Statistics*, vol. 91, no. 1 (2009), pp. 1–19; Congressional Budget Office, *Potential Impacts of Climate Change in the United States* (May 2009).

3. Alan H. Sanstad and Richard B. Howarth, "Consumer Rationality and Energy Efficiency," *Proceedings of the ACEEE 1994 Summer Study on Energy Efficiency in Buildings*, vol. 1 (Washington: American Council for an Energy-Efficient Economy, 1994); Hunt Allcott and Sendhil Mullainathan, "Behavior and Energy Policy," *Science*, vol. 327, no. 5970 (2010), pp. 1204–05.

4. Clive Seligman and John M. Darley, "Feedback as a Means of Decreasing Residential Energy Consumption," *Journal of Applied Psychology*, vol. 62, no. 4 (1977), pp. 363–68; Wokje Abrahamse and others, "A Review of Intervention Studies Aimed at Household Energy Conservation," *Journal of Environmental Psychology*, vol. 25, no. 3 (2005), pp. 273–91.

5. Dean Mountain, "The Impact of Real-Time Feedback on Residential Electricity Consumption: The Hydro One Pilot" (Ontario: Mountain Economic Consulting and Associates, 2006).

6. Hunt Allcott, "Rethinking Real Time Electricity Pricing," MIT working paper, 2009.

7. Sarah Darby, "The Effectiveness of Feedback on Energy Consumption. A Review for DEFRA of the Literature on Metering, Billing, and Direct Displays," unpublished manuscript, Environmental Change Institute, University of Oxford, April 2006.

8. Michael S. Rosenwald, "For Hybrid Drivers, Every Trip Is a Race for Fuel Efficiency," *Washington Post,* May 26, 2008, p. A1.

9. Richard P. Larrick and Jack B. Soll, "The MPG Illusion," *Science,* vol. 320, no. 5883 (2008), pp. 1593–94.

10. Willett Kempton and Laura Montgomery, "Folk Quantification of Energy," *Energy,* vol. 7, no. 10 (1982), pp. 817–27.

11. Shahzeen Z. Attari and others, "Public Perceptions of Energy Consumption and Savings," *Proceedings of the National Academy of Sciences,* vol. 107, no. 37 (2010), pp. 16054–59.

12. Jerry A. Hausman, "Individual Discount Rates and the Purchase and Utilization of Energy-Using Durables," *Bell Journal of Economics,* vol. 10, no. 1 (1979), pp. 33–54.

13. Timothy Brennan, "Consumer Preference Not to Choose: Methodological and Policy Implications," *Energy Policy,* vol. 35, no. 3 (March 2007), pp. 1616–27.

14. Adam B. Jaffe and Robert N. Stavins. "The Energy Paradox and the Diffusion of Conservation Technology," *Resource and Energy Economics,* vol. 16, no. 2 (1994), pp. 91–122.

15. Hannah Choi Granade and others, "Unlocking Energy Efficiency in the U.S. Economy" (New York: McKinsey and Company, 2009).

16. Ian Ayres, Sophie Raseman, and Alice Shih, "Evidence from Two Large Field Experiments that Peer Comparison Feedback Can Reduce Residential Energy Usage," Working Paper 15386 (Cambridge, Mass.: National Bureau of Economic Research, September 2009); P. Wesley Schultz and others, "The Constructive, Destructive, and Reconstructive Power of Social Norms," *Psychological Science,* vol. 18, no. 5 (2007), pp. 429–34.

17. Jessica M. Nolan and others, "Normative Social Influence Is Underdetected," *Personality and Social Psychology Bulletin,* vol. 34, no. 7 (2008), pp. 913–23.

18. Noah J. Goldstein, Robert B. Cialdini, and Vladas Griskevicius, "A Room with a Viewpoint: Using Social Norms to Motivate Environmental Conservation in Hotels," *Journal of Consumer Research,* vol. 35, no. 3 (2008), pp. 472–82.

19. Gwendolyn Brandon and Alan Lewis, "Reducing Household Energy Consumption: A Qualitative and Quantitative Field Study," *Journal of Environmental Psychology,* vol. 19, no. 1 (1999), pp. 75–85; Dora L. Costa and Matthew E. Kahn, "Energy Conservation 'Nudges' and Environmentalist Ideology: Evidence from a Randomized Residential Electricity Field Experiment," Working Paper 15939 (Cambridge, Mass.: National Bureau of Economic Research, April 2010).

20. Micheline Maynard, "Say 'Hybrid' and Many People Will Hear 'Prius,'" *New York Times,* July 4, 2007, p. A1.

21. Erez Yoeli, "Does Social Approval Stimulate Prosocial Behavior? Evidence from a Field Experiment in the Residential Electricity Market," University of Chicago working paper, May 18, 2009.

22. Lars Osterberg and Terrence Blaschke, "Adherence to Medication," *New England Journal of Medicine,* vol. 353, no. 5 (2005), pp. 487–97.

23. Andrew Caplin and Kfir Eliaz, "AIDS Policy and Psychology: A Mechanism-Design Approach," *RAND Journal of Economics,* vol. 34, no. 4 (2003), pp. 631–46.

24. Edward Lazear, "Intergenerational Externalities," *Canadian Journal of Economics/Revue canadienne d'économique,* vol. 16, no. 2 (May 1983), pp. 212–28.

25. Cara B. Ebbeling, Dorota B. Pawlak, and David S. Ludwig, "Childhood Obesity: Public-Health Crisis, Common Sense Cure," *The Lancet,* vol. 360, no. 9331 (2002), pp. 473–82.

26. George Loewenstein and Ted O'Donoghue, "Animal Spirits: Affective and Deliberative Processes in Human Behavior," working paper, Department of Social and Decision Sciences, Carnegie Mellon University, 2004.

27. C. Peter Herman, Marion P. Olmsted, and Janet Polivy, "Obesity, Externality, and Susceptibility to Social Influence: An Integrated Analysis," *Journal of Personality and Social Psychology*, vol. 45, no. 4 (1983), pp. 926–34; John M. de Castro, "Eating Behavior: Lessons from the Real World of Humans," *Nutrition*, vol. 16, no. 10 (2000), pp. 800–13; Brian Wansink, "Environmental Factors That Increase the Food Intake and Consumption Volume of Unknowing Consumers," *Annual Review of Nutrition*, vol. 24 (July 2004), pp. 455–79.

28. Nicholas A. Christakis and James H. Fowler, "The Spread of Obesity in a Large Social Network over 32 Years," *New England Journal of Medicine*, vol. 357, no. 4 (2007), pp. 370–79.

29. Josef Falkinger, "Limited Attention as a Scarce Resource in Information-Rich Economies," *Economic Journal*, vol. 118, no. 532 (2008), pp. 1596–1620.

30. Heather Schofield and Sendhil Mullainathan, "The Psychology of Nutrition Messages," in *Beyond Health Insurance: Public Policy to Improve Health*, vol. 19, *Advances in Health Economics and Health Services Research*, edited by Michael Grossman and others, (Bingley, U.K.: Emerald Group Publishing, 2008), pp. 145–172.

31. Ilana Ritov and Jonathan Baron, "Reluctance to Vaccinate: Omission Bias and Ambiguity," *Journal of Behavioral Decision Making*, vol. 3, no. 4 (1990), pp. 263–77; David Asch and others, "Omission Bias and Pertussis Vaccination," *Medical Decision Making*, vol. 14, no. 2 (1994), pp. 118–23.

32. Bruno S. Frey, *Not Just for the Money: An Economic Theory of Personal Motivation* (Cheltenham, U.K.: Edward Elgar, 1997); Bruno S. Frey and Reto Jegen, "Motivation Crowding Theory," *Journal of Economic Surveys*, vol. 15, no. 5 (2001), pp. 589–611.

33. Roland Benabou and Jean Tirole, "Incentives and Prosocial Behavior," *American Economic Review*, vol. 96, no. 5 (2006), pp. 1652–78; Stephan Meier, "A Survey on Economic Theories and Field Evidence on Pro-Social Behavior," in *Economics and Psychology: A Promising New Cross-Disciplinary Field*, edited by Bruno S. Frey and Alois Stutzer (MIT Press, 2007), pp. 51–88.

34. Carl Mellstrom and Magnus Johannesson, "Crowding Out in Blood Donation: Was Titmuss Right?" *Journal of the European Economic Association*, vol. 6, no. 4 (2008), pp. 845–63.

35. Uri Gneezy and Aldo Rustichini, "A Fine Is a Price," *Journal of Legal Studies*, vol. 29, no. 1 (2000), pp. 1–17.

36. Daniel Kahneman, Jack L. Knetsch, and Richard H. Thaler, "Experimental Tests of the Endowment Effect and the Coase Theorem," *Journal of Political Economy*, vol. 98, no. 6 (1990), pp. 1325–48.

37. Arthur C. Pigou, *The Economics of Welfare* (London: Macmillan, 1920).

38. Raj Chetty, Adam Looney, and Kory Kroft, "Salience and Taxation: Theory and Evidence," *American Economic Review*, vol. 99, no. 4 (2009), pp. 1145–77.

39. Dan Ariely, "Eyes off the Price," *New York Times*, July 19, 2008.

40. Erin T. Mansur, "Upstream versus Downstream Implementation of Climate Policy," Working Paper 16116 (Cambridge, Mass.: National Bureau of Economic Research, June 2010).

41. Corinna Fischer, "Feedback on Household Electricity Consumption: A Tool for Saving Energy?" *Energy Efficiency*, vol. 1, no. 1 (2008), pp. 79–104.

42. Sara Murray and Sudeep Reddy, "Capital Takes Bag Tax in Stride," *Wall Street Journal*, September 20, 2010.

43. Robert B. Cialdini, "Crafting Normative Measures to Protect the Environment," *Current Directions in Psychological Science*, vol. 12, no. 4 (2003), pp. 105–09.

44. Hunt Allcott, "Social Norms and Energy Conservation," MIT working paper, February 25, 2010.

45. Timothy Brennan, "'Night of the Living Dead' or 'Back to the Future'? Electric Utility Decoupling, Reviving Rate-of-Return Regulation, and Energy Efficiency," Resources for the Future Discussion Paper 08-27 (August 2008).

46. National Highway Traffic Safety Administration, *Final Regulatory Impact Analysis, Corporate Average Fuel Economy for MY 2012–MY 2016 Passenger Cars and Light Trucks* (Washington: March 2010).

47. David Hirshleifer, Sonya Seongyeon Lim, and Siew Hong Teoh, "Disclosure to a Credulous Audience: The Role of Limited Attention," unpublished working paper, 2002.

48. Peter C. Reiss and Matthew W. White, "What Changes Energy Consumption? Prices and Public Pressures," *RAND Journal of Economics*, vol. 39, no. 3 (2008), pp. 636–63.

49. Ronald H. Coase, "The Problem of Social Cost," *Journal of Law and Economics*, vol. 3, no. 1 (1960), pp. 1–44.

50. Daniel Kahneman, Jack L. Knetsch, and Richard H. Thaler, "Experimental Tests of the Endowment Effect and the Coase Theorem," *Journal of Political Economy*, vol. 98, no. 6 (1990), pp. 1325–48.

51. Lester Thurow, "The Income Distribution as a Pure Public Good," *Quarterly Journal of Economics*, vol. 85, no. 2 (1971), pp. 327–36.

52. Theodore Bergstrom, Lawrence Blume, and Hal Varian, "On the Private Provision of Public Goods," *Journal of Public Economics*, vol. 29, no. 1 (1986), pp. 25–49.

53. Robert Sugden, "Reciprocity: The Supply of Public Goods through Voluntary Contributions," *Economic Journal*, vol. 94, no. 376 (1984), pp. 772–87; James Andreoni, "Impure Altruism and Donations to Public Goods: A Theory of Warm Glow Giving," *Economic Journal*, vol. 100, no. 401 (1990), pp. 464–77.

54. Gerald Marwell and Ruth E. Ames, "Economists Free Ride; Does Anyone Else? Experiments on the Provision of Public Goods IV," *Journal of Public Economics*, vol. 15, no. 3 (1981), pp. 295–310; John O. Ledyard, "Public Goods: A Survey of Experimental Research," in *Handbook of Experimental Economics,* edited by John Kagel and Alvin Roth (Princeton University Press, 1995), pp. 111–94; James Andreoni, "Cooperation in Public-Goods Experiments: Kindness or Confusion?" *American Economic Review*, vol. 85, no. 4 (1995), pp. 891–904.

55. Thomas R. Palfrey and Jefferey E. Prisbrey, "Anomalous Behavior in Public Goods Experiments: How Much and Why?" *American Economic Review*, vol. 87, no. 5 (1997), pp. 829–46; Jacob K. Goeree, Charles A. Holt, and Susan K. Laury, "Private Costs and Public Benefits: Unraveling the Effects of Altruism and Noisy Behavior," *Journal of Public Economics*, vol. 83, no. 2 (2002), pp. 255–76.

56. Ernst Fehr and Simon Gachter, "Cooperation and Punishment in Public Goods Experiments," *American Economic Review*, vol. 90, no. 4 (2000), pp. 980–94.

57. Eric J. Brunner, "Free Riders or Easy Riders? An Examination of the Voluntary Provision of Public Radio," *Public Choice*, vol. 97, no. 4 (1998), pp. 587–604; Eric Brunner and Jon Sonstelie, "School Finance Reform and Voluntary Fiscal Federalism," *Journal of Public Economics*, vol. 87, no. 9-10 (2003), pp. 2157–85.

58. James Andreoni, "Philanthropy," in *Handbook of Giving, Reciprocity, and Altruism*, edited by Serge-Christophe Kolm and Jean Mercier Ythier (Amsterdam: North Holland, 2006), pp. 1201–69.

59. James Andreoni, Brian Erard, and Jonathan Feinstein, "Tax Compliance," *Journal of Economic Literature*, vol. 36 (1998), pp. 818–60.

60. Peter G. Warr, "Pareto Optimal Redistribution and Private Charity," *Journal of Public Economics*, vol. 19, no. 1 (1982), pp. 131–38.

61. James Andreoni, "Giving with Impure Altruism: Applications to Charity and Ricardian Equivalence," *Journal of Political Economy*, vol. 97, no. 6 (1989), pp. 1447–58.

62. James Andreoni, "An Experimental Test of the Public-Goods Crowding-Out Hypothesis," *American Economic Review*, vol. 83, no. 5 (1993), pp. 1317–27; Gary E. Bolton and Elena Katok, "An Experimental Test of the Crowding Out Hypothesis: The Nature of Beneficent Behavior," *Journal of Economic Behavior and Organization*, vol. 37, no. 3 (1998), pp. 315–31.

63. Richard Steinberg, "Does Government Spending Crowd Out Donations? Interpreting the Evidence," *Annals of Public and Cooperative Economics*, vol. 62, no. 4 (1991), pp. 591–617; A. Abigail Payne, "Does the Government Crowd Out Private Donations? New Evidence from a Sample of Non-Profit Firms," *Journal of Public Economics*, vol. 69, no. 3 (1998), pp. 323–45.

64. Dan Ariely, Anat Bracha, and Stephan Meier, "Doing Good or Doing Well? Image Motivation and Monetary Incentives in Behaving Prosocially," *American Economic Review*, vol. 99, no. 1 (2009), pp. 544–55.

65. Bruno S. Frey and Felix Oberholzer-Gee, "The Cost of Price Incentives: An Empirical Analysis of Motivation Crowding-Out," *American Economic Review*, vol. 87, no. 4 (1997), pp. 746–55.

66. Paul A. Samuelson, "The Pure Theory of Public Expenditure," *Review of Economics and Statistics*, vol. 36, no. 4 (1954), pp. 387–89.

67. Catherine C. Eckel, Philip J. Grossman, and Rachel M. Johnston, "An Experimental Test of the Crowding Out Hypothesis," *Journal of Public Economics*, vol. 89, no. 8 (2005), pp. 1543–60.

68. John Peloza and Piers Steele, "The Price Elasticities of Charitable Contributions: A Meta Analysis," *Journal of Public Policy and Marketing*, vol. 24, no. 2 (2005), pp. 260–72.

69. Catherine C. Eckel and Philip J. Grossman, "Rebate Versus Matching: Does How We Subsidize Charitable Giving Matter?" *Journal of Public Economics*, vol. 87, no. 3–4 (2003), pp. 681–701; Catherine C. Eckel and Philip J. Grossman, "Subsidizing Charitable Contributions: A Natural Field Experiment Comparing Matching and Rebate Subsidies," *Experimental Economics*, vol. 11, no. 3 (2008), pp. 234–52.

70. Dean Karlan and John A. List, "Does Price Matter in Charitable Giving? Evidence from a Large-Scale Natural Field Experiment," *American Economic Review*, vol. 97, no. 5 (2007), pp. 1774–93.

71. Craig E. Landry and others, "Toward an Understanding of the Economics of Charity: Evidence from a Field Experiment," *Quarterly Journal of Economics*, vol. 121, no. 2 (2006) pp. 747–82.

72. Jen Shang and Rachel Croson, "A Field Experiment in Charitable Contribution: The Impact of Social Information on the Voluntary Provision of Public Goods," *Economic Journal*, vol. 119, no. 540 (2009), pp. 1422–39; Stefano DellaVigna, John A. List, and Ulrike Malmendier, "Testing for Altruism and Social Pressure in Charitable Giving," Working Paper 15629 (Cambridge, Mass.: National Bureau of Economic Research, December 2009).

73. Enrico Moretti, "Human Capital Externalities in Cities," in *Handbook of Regional and Urban Economics,* vol. 4, edited by J. Vernon Henderson and Jacques-Francois Thisse (Amsterdam: Elsevier, 2004), pp. 2243–91.

74. David Card, "Estimating the Return to Schooling: Progress on Some Persistent Econometric Problems," *Econometrica*, vol. 69, no. 5 (2001), pp. 1127–60.

75. James J. Heckman and Paul A. LaFontaine, "The American High School Graduation Rate: Trends and Levels," *Review of Economics and Statistics*, vol. 92, no. 2 (2010), pp. 244–62.

76. John Bound, Michael Lovenheim, and Sarah Turner, "Why Have College Completion Rates Declined? An Analysis of Changing Student Preparation and Collegiate Resources," *American Economic Journal: Applied Economics*, vol. 2, no. 3 (2010), pp. 129–57; William G. Bowen, Matthew M. Chingos, and Michael S. McPherson, *Crossing the Finish Line: Completing College at America's Public Universities* (Princeton University Press, 2009).

77. Philip Oreopoulos, "Do Dropouts Drop out Too Soon? Wealth, Health, and Happiness from Compulsory Schooling," *Journal of Public Economics*, vol. 91, no. 11-12 (December 2007), pp. 2213–29.

78. Joshua Angrist and Victor Lavy, "The Effects of High-Stakes High School Achievement Awards: Evidence from a Randomized Trial," *American Economic Review*, vol. 99, no. 4 (September 2009), pp. 1384–1414; Lorraine Dearden and others, "Conditional Cash Transfers and School Dropout Rates," *Journal of Human Resources*, vol. 44, no. 4 (2008), pp. 827–57; Thomas Dee, "Conditional Cash Penalties in Education: Evidence from the Learnfare Experiment," Working Paper 15126 (Cambridge, Mass.: National Bureau of Economic Research, July 2009).

79. James Riccio and others, *Toward Reduced Poverty across Generations: Early Findings from New York City's Conditional Cash Transfer Program* (New York: MDRC, March 2010).

80. Roland G. Fryer Jr., "Financial Incentives and Student Achievement: Evidence from Randomized Trials," Working Paper 15898 (Cambridge, Mass.: National Bureau of Economic Research, April 2010).

81. Edward L. Deci, "Effects of Externally Mediated Rewards on Intrinsic Motivation," *Journal of Personality and Social Psychology*, vol. 18, no. 1 (1971), pp. 105–15; Alfie Kohn, *Punished by Rewards: The Trouble with Gold Stars, Incentive Plans, A's, Praise, and Other Bribes* (Boston: Houghton Mifflin, 1993).

82. Amanda Pallais, "Small Differences That Matter: Mistakes in Applying to College," MIT working paper, February 2009.

83. Susan M. Dynarski and Judith E. Scott-Clayton, "The Cost of Complexity in Federal Student Aid: Lessons From Optimal Tax Theory and Behavioral Economics," *National Tax Journal*, vol. 59, no. 2 (2006), pp. 319–56; Susan M. Dynarski and Judith E. Scott-Clayton, "Complexity and Targeting in Federal Student Aid: A Quantitative Analysis," in *Tax Policy and the Economy*, vol. 22, edited by James M. Poterba (University of Chicago Press, 2008), pp. 109–50.

84. Eric P. Bettinger and others, "The Role of Simplification and Information in College Decisions: Results from the H&R Block FAFSA Experiment," Working Paper 15361 (Cambridge, Mass.: National Bureau of Economic Research, September 2009).

85. U.S. Department of Education, "Obama Administration Announces Streamlined College Aid Application," press release, June 24, 2009.

86. Cecilia E. Rouse, "Private School Vouchers and Student Achievement: An Evaluation of the Milwaukee Parental Choice Program," *Quarterly Journal of Economics*, vol. 113, no. 2 (1998), pp. 553–602; Caroline M. Hoxby, "School Choice and School Productivity: Could School Choice Be a Tide That Lifts All Boats?" in *The Economics of School Choice*, edited by Caroline M. Hoxby (University of Chicago Press, 2003), pp. 287–342; Julie Berry Cullen, Brian A. Jacob, and Steven Levitt, "The Effect of School Choice on Participants: Evidence from Randomized Lotteries," *Econometrica*, vol. 74, no. 5 (2006), pp. 1191–1230.

87. Clive R. Belfield and Henry M. Levin, "The Effects of Competition between Schools on Educational Outcomes: A Review for the United States," *Review of Educational Research*, vol. 72 (2002), pp. 279–341; David N. Figlio and Cecilia Elena Rouse, "Do Accountability

and Voucher Threats Improve Low-Performing Schools?" *Journal of Public Economics*, vol. 90, no. 1-2 (2006), pp. 239–55; Justine S. Hastings, Thomas J. Kane, and Douglas O. Staiger, "Heterogeneous Preferences and the Efficacy of Public School Choice," unpublished working paper, May 2009.

88. Jesse M. Rothstein, "Good Principals or Good Peers? Parental Valuation of School Characteristics, Tiebout Equilibrium, and the Incentive Effects of Competition among Jurisdictions," *American Economic Review*, vol. 96, no. 4 (2006), pp. 1333–50; Brian A. Jacob and Lars Lefgren, "What Do Parents Value in Education? An Empirical Investigation of Parents' Revealed Preferences for Teachers," *Quarterly Journal of Economics*, vol. 122, no. 4 (2007), pp. 1603–37.

89. Clara Hemphill and Kim Nauer, "The New Marketplace: How Small-School Reforms and School Choice Have Reshaped New York City's High Schools" (Center for New York City Affairs, June 2009).

90. Justine S. Hastings and Jeffrey M. Weinstein, "Information, School Choice, and Academic Achievement: Evidence from Two Experiments," *Quarterly Journal of Economics*, vol. 123, no. 4 (2008), pp. 1373–1414.

Chapter Six

1. Carmen DeNavas-Walt, Bernadette D. Proctor, and Jessica C. Smith, *Income, Poverty, and Health Insurance Coverage in the United States: 2009* (Government Printing Office, 2010).

2. Thomas Piketty and Emmanuel Saez, "Income Inequality in the United States, 1913–1998," *Quarterly Journal of Economics*, vol. 118, no. 1 (2003), pp. 1–39; updated figures through 2008 available at http://elsa.berkeley.edu/~saez/.

3. Wilfred T. Masumura and John J. Hisnanick, *Dynamics of Economic Well-Being: Moving Up and Down the Income Ladder, 1998 to 1999*, Current Population Reports P70-100 (U.S. Census Bureau, 2005).

4. DeNavas-Walt, Proctor, and Smith, *Income, Poverty, and Health Insurance Coverage in the United States: 2009*.

5. Julia B. Isaacs, "International Comparisons of Economic Mobility," in *Getting Ahead or Losing Ground: Economic Mobility in America*, edited by Julia B. Isaacs, Isabel V. Sawhill, and Ron Haskins (Brookings, 2007), pp. 36–44.

6. Abram Bergson, "A Reformulation of Certain Aspects of Welfare Economics," *Quarterly Journal of Economics*, vol. 52, no. 2 (1938), pp. 310–34; Paul A. Samuelson, *Foundations of Economic Analysis* (Harvard University Press, 1947).

7. Lionel Robbins, "Interpersonal Comparisons of Utility: A Comment," *Economic Journal*, vol. 48, no. 192 (1938), pp. 635–41.

8. James J. Heckman, "Skill Formation and the Economics of Investing in Disadvantaged Children," *Science*, vol. 312, no. 5782 (June 30, 2006), pp. 1900–02.

9. S. V. Subramanian and Ichiro Kawachi, "Income Inequality and Health: What Have We Learned So Far?" *Epidemiologic Reviews*, vol. 26, no. 1 (2004), pp. 78–91; Michael Marmot, "The Influence of Income on Health: Views of an Epidemiologist," *Health Affairs*, vol. 21, no. 2 (2002), pp. 31–46.

10. James Andreoni, "Philanthropy," in *Handbook of Giving, Reciprocity, and Altruism*, edited by Serge-Christophe Kolm and Jean Mercier Ythier (Amsterdam: North Holland, 2006), pp. 1201–69.

11. James Andreoni and John Miller, "Giving According to GARP: An Experimental Test of the Consistency of Preferences for Altruism," *Econometrica*, vol. 70, no. 2 (2002), pp.

737–53; Ernst Fehr and Urs Fischbacher, "The Nature of Human Altruism," *Nature*, vol. 425, no. 6960 (2003), pp. 785–91.

12. Lester Thurow, "The Income Distribution as a Pure Public Good," *Quarterly Journal of Economics*, vol. 85, no. 2 (1971), pp. 327–36.

13. Michael J. Boskin and Eytan Sheshinkski, "Optimal Redistributive Taxation When Individual Welfare Depends upon Relative Income," *Quarterly Journal of Economics*, vol. 92, no. 4 (1978), pp. 589–601; Ronald Wendner and Lawrence H. Goulder, "Status Effects, Public Goods Provision, and Excess Burden," *Journal of Public Economics*, vol. 92, no. 10–11 (2008), pp. 1968–85.

14. Robert H. Frank, "Positional Externalities Cause Large and Preventable Welfare Losses," *American Economic Review*, vol. 95, no. 2 (2005), pp. 137–41.

15. Erzo F. P. Luttmer, "Neighbors as Negatives: Relative Earnings and Well-Being," *Quarterly Journal of Economics*, vol. 120, no. 3 (2005), pp. 963–1002.

16. Sara J. Solnick and David Hemenway, "Are Positional Concerns Stronger in Some Domains than in Others?" *American Economic Review*, vol. 95, no. 2 (2005), pp. 147–51.

17. Daniel Kahneman, Jack L. Knetsch and Richard Thaler, "Fairness as a Constraint on Profit Seeking: Entitlements in the Market," *American Economic Review*, vol. 76, no. 4 (September 1986), pp. 728–41; Matthew Rabin, "Incorporating Fairness into Game Theory and Economics," *American Economic Review*, vol. 83, no. 5 (1993), pp. 1281–1302.

18. Ernst Fehr and Klaus Schmidt, "Theories of Fairness and Reciprocity: Evidence and Economic Applications," in *Advances in Economics and Econometrics: Theory and Applications*, edited by Mathias Dewatripont, Lars P. Hansen, and Stephen J. Turnovsky (Cambridge University Press, 2003), pp. 208–57.

19. Christina Fong, "Social Preferences, Self-Interest, and the Demand for Redistribution," *Journal of Public Economics*, vol. 82, no. 2 (2001), pp. 225–46; Alberto Alesina and Eliana La Ferrara, "Preferences for Redistribution in the Land of Opportunities," *Journal of Public Economics*, vol. 89, no. 5 (2005), pp. 897–931.

20. Marianne Bertrand, Sendhil Mullainathan, and Eldar Shafir, "A Behavioral-Economics View of Poverty," *American Economic Review*, vol. 94, no. 2 (2004), pp. 419–23.

21. Abhijit Banerjee and Sendhil Mullainathan, "The Shape of Temptation: Implications for the Economic Lives of the Poor," Working Paper 15973 (Cambridge, Mass.: National Bureau of Economic Research, May 2010).

22. Marianne Bertrand, Sendhil Mullainathan, and Eldar Shafir, "Behavioral Economics and Marketing in Aid of Decision Making among the Poor," *Journal of Public Policy and Marketing*, vol. 25, no. 1 (2006), pp. 8–23.

23. George A. Akerlof and Rachel E. Kranton, "Economics and Identity," *Quarterly Journal of Economics*, vol. 115, no. 3 (2000), pp. 715–53.

24. George Loewenstein and Ted O'Donoghue, "Animal Spirits: Affective and Deliberative Processes in Human Behavior," working paper, Department of Social and Decision Sciences, Carnegie Mellon University, 2004.

25. Baba Shiv and Alexander Fedorikhin, "Heart and Mind in Conflict: The Interplay of Affect and Cognition in Consumer Decision Making," *Journal of Consumer Research*, vol. 26, no. 3 (1999), pp. 278–92; Saul Shiffman and Andrew J. Waters, "Negative Affect and Smoking Lapses: A Prospective Analysis," *Journal of Consulting and Clinical Psychology*, vol. 72, no. 2 (2004), pp. 192–201.

26. Lisa Gennetian, Sendhil Mullainathan, and Eldar Shafir, "Economic Instability, Mental Resources, and Poverty Traps," in *The Behavioral Foundations of Policy*, edited by Eldar Shafir (New York: Russell Sage Foundation, forthcoming).

27. Arthur Okun, *Equality and Efficiency: The Big Trade-Off* (Brookings, 1975).

28. Hanming Fang and Dan Silverman, "Time-Inconsistency and Welfare Program Participation: Evidence from the NLSY," *International Economic Review*, vol. 50, no. 4 (2009), pp. 1043–77.

29. Hanming Fang and Dan Silverman, "On the Compassion of Time-Limited Welfare Programs," *Journal of Public Economics*, vol. 88, no. 7–8 (2004), pp. 1445–70.

30. James A. Mirrlees, "An Exploration in the Theory of Optimal Income Taxation," *Review of Economic Studies*, vol. 38, no. 114 (1971), pp. 175–208.

31. George A. Akerlof, "The Economics of 'Tagging' as Applied to the Optimal Income Tax, Welfare Programs, and Manpower Planning," *American Economic Review*, vol. 68, no. 1 (1978), pp. 8–19; Albert L. Nichols and Richard J. Zeckhauser, "Targeting Transfers through Restrictions on Recipients," *American Economic Review*, vol. 72, no. 2 (1982), pp. 372–77.

32. Joshua Leftin and Kari Wolkwitz, *Trends in Supplemental Nutrition Assistance Program Participation Rates: 2000–2007* (Washington: Mathematica Policy Research, June 2009).

33. Dean Plueger, "Earned Income Tax Credit Participation Rate for Tax Year 2005," in *IRS Research Bulletin: Recent Research on Tax Administration and Compliance* (Internal Revenue Service, 2009), pp. 151–95.

34. Robert Moffitt, "An Economic Model of Welfare Stigma," *American Economic Review*, vol. 73, no. 5 (December 1983), pp. 1023–35.

35. Donald Nichols, Eugene Smolensky, and T. Nicolaus Tideman, "Discrimination in Waiting Time in Merit Goods," *American Economic Review*, vol. 61, no. 2 (1971), pp. 312–23; Nichols and Zeckhauser, "Targeting Transfers through Restrictions on Recipients."

36. Bertrand, Mullainathan, and Shafir, "Behavioral Economics and Marketing in Aid of Decision Making among the Poor."

37. Dahlia K. Remler and Sherry A. Glied, "What Other Programs Can Teach Us: Increasing Participation in Health Insurance Programs," *American Journal of Public Health*, vol. 93, no. 1 (2003), pp. 67–74; Janet Currie, "The Take-Up of Social Benefits," in *Public Policy and the Income Distribution,* edited by Alan J. Auerbach, David Card, and John M. Quigley (New York: Russell Sage Foundation, 2006), pp. 80–148.

38. Janet Currie and Jeffrey Grogger, "Explaining Recent Declines in Food Stamp Program Participation," *Brookings-Wharton Papers on Urban Affairs* (2001), pp. 203–44; Caroline Ratcliffe, Signe-Mary McKernan, and Kenneth Finegold, "The Effect of State Food Stamp and TANF Policies on Food Stamp Program Participation" (Washington: Urban Institute, March 2007).

39. Rebecca M. Blank and Patricia Ruggles, "When Do Women Use Aid to Families with Dependent Children and Food Stamps? The Dynamics of Eligibility versus Participation," *Journal of Human Resources*, vol. 31, no. 1 (1996), pp. 57–89; Bowen Garrett and Sherry Glied, "Does State AFDC Generosity Affect Child SSI Participation?" *Journal of Policy Analysis and Management*, vol. 19, no. 2 (Spring 2000), pp. 275–95.

40. Susan Bartlett, Nancy Burstein, and William Hamilton, "Food Stamp Program Access Study: Final Report," Report to the U.S. Department of Agriculture, Economic Research Service (Cambridge, Mass.: Abt Associates, 2004).

41. Ratcliffe, McKernan, and Finegold, "The Effect of State Food Stamp and TANF Policies on Food Stamp Program Participation."

42. Marcia K. Meyers and Theresa Heintze, "The Performance of the Child-Care Subsidy System: Target Efficiency, Coverage Adequacy, and Equity," *Social Service Review*, vol. 73, no. 1 (1999), pp. 34–64.

43. Beth Osborne Daponte, Seth Sanders, and Lowell Taylor, "Why Do Low-Income Households *Not* Use Food Stamps? Evidence from an Experiment," *Journal of Human Resources,* vol. 34, no. 3 (1999), pp. 612–28.

44. Esther Duflo and others, "Saving Incentives for Low- and Middle-Income Families: Evidence from a Field Experiment with H&R Block," *Quarterly Journal of Economics,* vol. 121, no. 4 (2006), pp. 1311–46.

45. Emmanuel Saez, "Details Matter: The Impact of Presentation and Information on the Take-up of Financial Incentives for Retirement Saving," *American Economic Journal: Economic Policy,* vol. 1, no. 1 (2009), pp. 204–28.

46. Kurt Lewin, *Field Theory in Social Science* (New York: Harper, 1951).

47. Brigitte C. Madrian and Dennis F. Shea, "The Power of Suggestion: Inertia in 401(k) Participation and Savings Behavior," *Quarterly Journal of Economics,* vol. 116, no. 4 (2001), pp. 1149–87.

48. William J. Reeder, "The Benefits and Costs of the Section 8 Existing Housing Program," *Journal of Public Economics,* vol. 26, no. 3 (1985), pp. 349–77.

49. Hugo Benítez-Silva, Moshe Buchinsky, and John Rust, "How Large Are the Classification Errors in the Social Security Disability Award Process?" Working Paper 10219 (Cambridge, Mass.: National Bureau of Economic Research, February 2004).

50. Paula Diehr and others, "Will Uninsured People Volunteer for Voluntary Health Insurance? Experience from Washington State," *American Journal of Public Health,* vol. 86, no. 4 (1996), pp. 529–32.

51. Henrik Jacobson Kleven and Wojciech Kopczuk, "Transfer Program Complexity and the Take Up of Social Benefits," Working Paper 14301 (Cambridge, Mass.: National Bureau of Economic Research, September 2008).

52. Susan M. Dynarski and Judith E. Scott-Clayton, "The Cost of Complexity in Federal Student Aid: Lessons from Optimal Tax Theory and Behavioral Economics," *National Tax Journal,* vol. 59, no. 2 (2006), pp. 319–56; Susan M. Dynarski and Judith E. Scott-Clayton, "Complexity and Targeting in Federal Student Aid: A Quantitative Analysis," in *Tax Policy and the Economy,* vol. 22, edited by James M. Poterba (University of Chicago Press, 2008), pp. 109–50.

53. Susan M. Dynarski and Judith E. Scott-Clayton, "College Grants on a Postcard: A Proposal for Simple and Predictable Federal Student Aid," Hamilton Project Discussion Paper 2007-01 (Brookings, 2007).

54. Stan Dorn and others, "Nine in Ten: Using the Tax System to Enroll Eligible, Uninsured Children into Medicaid and SCHIP," Urban Institute working paper (Washington: Urban Institute, January 2009).

55. Anna Aizer, "Public Health Insurance, Program Take-Up, and Child Health," *Review of Economics and Statistics,* vol. 89, no. 3 (2007), pp. 400–15; Mark G. Duggan, "Hospital Ownership and Public Medical Spending," *Quarterly Journal of Economics,* vol. 115, no. 4 (2000), pp. 1343–73.

56. Wojciech Kopczuk and Cristian Pop-Eleches, "Electronic Filing, Tax Preparers, and Participation in the Earned Income Tax Credit," *Journal of Public Economics,* vol. 91, no. 7–8 (2007), pp. 1351–67.

57. Eric P. Bettinger and others, "The Role of Simplification and Information in College Decisions: Results from the H&R Block FAFSA Experiment," Working Paper 15361 (Cambridge, Mass.: National Bureau of Economic Research, September 2009).

58. Jesse M. Shapiro, "Is There a Daily Discount Rate? Evidence from the Food Stamp Nutrition Cycle," *Journal of Public Economics,* vol. 89, no. 2-3 (2005), pp. 303–25.

59. Parke E. Wilde and Christine K. Ranney, "The Monthly Food Stamp Cycle: Shopping Frequency and Food Intake Decisions in an Endogenous Switching Regression Framework," *American Journal of Agricultural Economics* (February 2000), pp. 200–13.

60. Jeffrey B. Liebman and Richard J. Zeckhauser, "Schmeduling," unpublished working paper, Harvard University, 2004.

61. Diane Whitmore, "What Are Food Stamps Worth?" Princeton University Industrial Relations Section Working Paper 468 (2002).

62. Shapiro, "Is There a Daily Discount Rate? Evidence from the Food Stamp Nutrition Cycle."

63. Justine Hastings and Ebonya Washington, "The First of the Month Effect: Consumer Behavior and Store Responses," *American Economic Journal: Economic Policy*, vol. 2, no. 2 (2010), pp. 142–62.

64. Daniel Read and Barbara van Leeuwen, "Predicting Hunger: The Effects of Appetite and Delay on Choice," *Organizational Behavior and Human Decision Processes*," vol. 76, no. 2 (1998), pp. 189–205.

65. Melvin Stephens Jr., "'3rd of the Month': Do Social Security Recipients Smooth Consumption between Checks?" *American Economic Review*, vol. 93, no. 1 (2003), pp. 406–22; Giovanni Mastrobuoni and Matthew Weinberg, "Heterogeneity in Intra-Monthly Consumption Patterns, Self-Control, and Savings at Retirement," *American Economic Journal: Economic Policy*, vol. 1, no. 2 (2009), pp. 163–89.

66. Melvin Stephens Jr. and Takashi Unayama, "Can Governments Help Households Smooth Consumption? Evidence from Japanese Public Pension Benefits," unpublished working paper, May 2008.

67. Thomas M. Fraker and others, "The Effects of Cashing Out Food Stamps on Household Food Use and the Cost of Issuing Benefits," *Journal of Policy Analysis and Management*, vol. 14, no. 3 (1995), pp. 372–92; Hilary W. Hoynes and Diane Whitmore Schanzenbach, "Consumption Responses to In-Kind Transfers: Evidence from the Introduction of the Food Stamp Program," *American Economic Journal: Applied Economics*, vol. 1, no. 4 (2009), pp. 109–39.

68. Stephen D. Holt, *Periodic Payment of the Earned Income Tax Credit* (Brookings Institution Metropolitan Policy Program, June 2008).

69. Government Accountability Office, *Advanced Earned Income Tax Credit: Low Use and Small Dollars Paid Impede IRS's Efforts to Reduce High Noncompliance*, GAO-07-1110 (August 2007).

70. General Accounting Office, *Earned Income Tax Credit: Advance Payment Option Is Not Widely Known or Understood by the Public*, GAO/GGD-92-26 (February 1992).

71. Damon Jones, "Information, Preferences, and Public Benefit Participation: Experimental Evidence from the Advance EITC and 401(k) Savings," *American Economic Journal: Applied Economics*, vol. 2, no. 2 (2010), pp. 147–63.

72. Timothy M. Smeeding, Katherin Ross Phillips, and Michael O'Connor, "The EITC: Expectation, Knowledge, Use, and Economic and Social Mobility," *National Tax Journal*, vol. 53, no. 4 (2000), pp. 1187–1210.

73. Michael S. Barr and Jane K. Dokko, "Tax Filing Experiences and Withholding Preferences of Low- and Moderate-Income Households: Preliminary Evidence from a New Survey," *IRS Research Bulletin: Recent Research on Tax Administration and Compliance*, Publication 1500 (2006), pp. 193–210.

74. Jennifer L. Romich and Thomas Weisner, "How Families View and Use the EITC: Advance Payment versus Lump Sum Delivery," *National Tax Journal*, vol. 53, no. 4 (2000),

pp. 1245–66; Ruby Mendenhall and others, "The Role of Earned Income Tax Credit in the Budgets of Low-Income Families," National Poverty Center Working Paper 2010-5 (Ann Arbor, Mich.: National Poverty Center, June 2010).

75. Lisa Barrow and Leslie McGranahan, "The Effects of the Earned Income Credit on the Seasonality of Household Expenditures," *National Tax Journal,* vol. 53, no. 4 (2000), pp. 1211–44.

76. Office of Management and Budget, *Budget of the United States Government, Fiscal Year 2011* (2010).

77. Sherrie L. W. Rhine and others, "Householder Response to the Earned Income Tax Credit: Path of Sustenance or Road to Asset Building," *Proceedings,* Federal Reserve Bank of Chicago (April 2005); Sondra Beverly and others, "Low-Cost Bank Accounts and the EITC," in *Inclusion in the American Dream: Assets, Poverty, and Public Policy,* edited by Michael Sherraden (Oxford University Press, 2005), pp. 167–84.

78. Timothy M. Smeeding, "The EITC and USAs/IDAs: Maybe a Marriage Made in Heaven?" in *Inclusion in the American Dream,* edited by Sherraden, pp. 323–47.

79. Carlos Dobkin and Steven L. Puller, "The Effects of Government Transfers on Monthly Cycles in Drug Abuse, Hospitalization, and Mortality," *Journal of Public Economics,* vol. 91, no. 11–12 (2007), pp. 2137–57.

80. Peter Kooreman, "The Labeling Effect of a Child Benefit System," *American Economic Review,* vol. 90, no. 3 (2000), pp. 571–83.

81. Johannes Abeler and Felix Marklein, "Fungibility, Labels, and Consumption," IZA Discussion Paper 3500 (Bonn, Germany: Institute for the Study of Labor, May 2008).

82. Robert Cherry and Max Sawicky, "Giving Tax Credit Where Credit Is Due: A 'Universal Unified Child Credit' That Expands the EITC and Cuts Taxes for Working Families" (Washington: Economic Policy Institute, 2000); David T. Ellwood and Jeffrey B. Liebman, "The Middle-Class Parent Penalty: Child Benefits in the U.S. Tax Code," in *Tax Policy and the Economy,* vol. 15, edited by James M. Poterba (MIT Press), pp. 1–40.

83. Ron Haskins, *Work over Welfare: The Inside Story of the 1996 Welfare Reform Law* (Brookings, 2006).

84. Robert A. Moffitt, "The Temporary Assistance for Needy Families Program," in *Means-Tested Transfer Programs in the United States,* edited by Robert A. Moffitt (University of Chicago Press, 2003), pp. 291–364.

85. Christopher A. Swann, "Welfare Reform When Recipients Are Forward-Looking," *Journal of Human Resources,* vol. 40, no. 1 (2005), pp. 31–56.

86. Jeffrey Grogger, "The Behavioral Effects of Welfare Time Limits," *American Economic Review,* vol. 92, no. 2 (May 2002), pp. 385–89; Jeffrey Grogger, "The Effects of Time Limits, the EITC, and Other Policy Changes on Welfare Use, Work, and Income among Female-Headed Families," *Review of Economics and Statistics,* vol. 85, no. 2 (May 2003), pp. 394–408.

87. Fang and Silverman, "Time-Inconsistency and Welfare Program Participation."

88. Fang and Silverman, "On the Compassion of Time-Limited Welfare Programs."

89. Fang and Silverman, "On the Compassion of Time-Limited Welfare Programs."

90. V. Joseph Hotz and John Karl Sholz, "The Earned Income Tax Credit," in *Means-Tested Transfer Programs in the United States,* edited by Moffitt, pp. 141–98.

91. Nada Eissa and Jeffrey B. Liebman, "Labor Supply Response to the Earned Income Tax Credit," *Quarterly Journal of Economics,* vol. 111, no. 2 (1996), pp. 605–37; Bruce D. Meyer and Dan T. Rosenbaum, "Welfare, the Earned Income Tax Credit, and the Labor Supply of Single Mothers," *Quarterly Journal of Economics,* vol. 116, no. 3 (2001), pp. 1063–1114.

92. Bruce D. Meyer, "Labor Supply at the Extensive and Intensive Margins: The EITC, Welfare, and Hours Worked," *American Economic Review*, vol. 92, no. 2 (2002), pp. 373–79; Nada Eissa and Hilary W. Hoynes, "Behavioral Responses to Taxes: Lessons from the EITC and Labor Supply," in *Tax Policy and the Economy*, vol. 20, edited by James M. Poterba (MIT Press, 2006), pp. 73–110.

93. Romich and Weisner, "How Families View and Use the EITC."

94. Raj Chetty and Emmanuel Saez, "Teaching the Tax Code: Earnings Responses to an Experiment with EITC Recipients," Working Paper 14836 (Cambridge, Mass.: National Bureau of Economic Research, April 2009).

95. Liebman and Zeckhauser, "Schmeduling."

96. Emmanuel Saez, "Do Taxpayers Bunch at Kink Points?" *American Economic Journal: Economic Policy*, vol. 2, no. 3 (2010), pp. 180–212.

97. Jennifer L. Romich, "Difficult Calculations: Low-Income Workers and Marginal Tax Rates," *Social Service Review* (March 2006), pp. 27–66.

98. Assar Lindbeck, "Incentives and Social Norms in Household Behavior," *American Economic Review*, vol. 87, no. 2 (1997), pp. 370–77; Assar Lindbeck, Sten Nyberg, and Jorgen Weibull, "Social Norms and Economic Incentives in the Welfare State," *Quarterly Journal of Economics*, vol. 114, no. 1 (1999), pp. 1–35.

Chapter Seven

1. Congressional Budget Office, *The Budget and Economic Outlook: Fiscal Years 2010 to 2020* (Washington: January 2010).

2. U.S. Census Bureau, *2008 Annual Survey of Government Finances* (Washington: July 2010), table 1.

3. Tax Policy Center, "Sales Tax Rates, State and Local, 2004–2010," in *Tax Facts*, March 3, 2010 (www.taxpolicycenter.org/taxfacts/displayafact.cfm?Docid=492), based on information from the Federation of Tax Administrators and the Sales Tax Institute.

4. Laurence J. Kotlikoff and David Rapson, "Does It Pay, at the Margin, to Work and Save? Measuring Effective Marginal Taxes on Americans' Labor Supply and Savings," in *Tax Policy and the Economy*, vol. 21, edited by James M. Poterba (MIT Press, 2007).

5. James A. Mirlees, "An Exploration in the Theory of Optimal Income Taxation," *Review of Economic Studies*, vol. 38, no. 114 (1971), pp. 175–208.

6. Frank P. Ramsey, "A Contribution to the Theory of Taxation," *Economic Journal*, vol. 37, no. 145 (March 1927), pp. 47–61.

7. Raj Chetty, Adam Looney, and Kory Kroft, "Salience and Taxation: Theory and Evidence," *American Economic Review*, vol. 99, no. 4 (2009), pp. 1145–77.

8. Amy Finkelstein, "*E-ZTax*: Tax Salience and Tax Rates," *Quarterly Journal of Economics*, vol. 124, no. 3 (2009), pp. 969–1010.

9. Aradhna Krishna and Joel Slemrod, "Behavioral Public Finance: Tax Design as Price Presentation," *International Tax and Public Finance*, vol. 10, no. 2 (2003), pp. 189–203.

10. Robert M. Schindler and Patrick N. Kirby, "Patterns of Rightmost Digits Used in Advertised Prices: Implications for Nine-Ending Effects," *Journal of Consumer Research*, vol. 24, no. 2 (1997), pp. 192–201; Eric T. Anderson and Duncan I. Simester, "Effects of $9 Price Endings on Retail Sales: Evidence from Field Experiments," *Quantitative Marketing and Economics*, vol. 1, no. 1 (2003), pp. 93–110.

11. Tanjim Hossain and John Morgan, "… Plus Shipping and Handling: Revenue (Non) Equivalence in Field Experiments on eBay," *Advances in Economic Analysis and Policy*, vol. 6, no. 2 (2006), article 3.

12. Emmanuel Saez, "Do Tax Filers Bunch at Kink Points?" *American Economic Journal: Economic Policy*, vol. 2, no. 3 (2010), pp. 180–212.

13. Claudia R. Sahm, Matthew D. Shapiro, and Joel Slemrod, "Check in the Mail or More in the Paycheck: Does the Effectiveness of Fiscal Stimulus Depend on How It Is Delivered?" Working Paper 16246 (Cambridge, Mass.: National Bureau of Economic Research, July 2010).

14. Matthew D. Shapiro and Joel Slemrod, "Consumer Response to the Timing of Income: Evidence from a Change in Tax Withholding," *American Economic Review*, vol. 85, no. 1 (1995), pp. 274–83; Naomi E. Feldman, "Mental Accounting Effects of Income Tax Shifting," *Review of Economics and Statistics*, vol. 92, no. 1 (2010), pp. 70–86.

15. Valerie Chambers and Marilyn Spencer, "Does Changing the Timing of a Yearly Individual Tax Refund Change the Amount Spent vs. Saved?" *Journal of Economic Psychology*, vol. 29, no. 6 (2008), pp. 856–62.

16. Jeffrey B. Liebman and Richard J. Zeckhauser, "Schmeduling," unpublished working paper, Harvard University, 2004.

17. Charles A. M. de Bartolome, "Which Tax Rate Do People Use: Average or Marginal?" *Journal of Public Economics*, vol. 56, no. 1 (1995), pp. 79–96.

18. Tomer Blumkin, Bradley J. Ruffle, and Yosef Ganun, "Are Income and Consumption Taxes Ever Really Equivalent? Evidence from a Real-Effort Experiment with Real Goods," unpublished working paper, January 2008.

19. Harvey S. Rosen, "Taxes in a Labor Supply Model with Joint Wage-Hours Determination," *Econometrica*, vol. 44, no. 3 (1976), pp. 485–507; Edwin T. Fujii and Clifford B. Hawley, "On the Accuracy of Tax Perceptions," *Review of Economics and Statistics*, vol. 70, no. 2 (1988), pp. 344–47.

20. Jennifer L. Romich and Thomas Weisner, "How Families View and Use the EITC: Advance Payment versus Lump Sum Delivery," *National Tax Journal*, vol. 53, no. 4 (2000), pp. 1245–66.

21. Raj Chetty and Emmanuel Saez, "Teaching the Tax Code: Earnings Responses to an Experiment with EITC Recipients," Working Paper 14836 (Cambridge, Mass.: National Bureau of Economic Research, April 2009).

22. Naomi E. Feldman and Peter Katuscak, "Effects of Predictable Tax Liability Variation on Household Labor Income," unpublished working paper, May 17, 2010.

23. Esther Duflo and others, "Saving Incentives for Low- and Middle-Income Families: Evidence from a Field Experiment with H&R Block," *Quarterly Journal of Economics,* vol. 121, no. 4 (2006), pp. 1311–46.

24. Mark M. Pitt and Joel Slemrod, "The Compliance Costs of Itemizing Deductions: Evidence from Individual Tax Returns," *American Economic Review*, vol. 79, no. 5 (1989), pp. 1224–32; General Accounting Office, *Tax Deductions: Further Estimates of Taxpayers Who May Have Overpaid Federal Taxes by Not Itemizing*, GAO-02-509 (March 2002).

25. Nicholas Epley, Dennis Mak, and Lorraine Chen Idson, "Bonus or Rebate? The Impact of Income Framing on Spending and Saving," *Journal of Behavioral Decision Making*, vol. 19, no. 3 (2006), pp. 213–27.

26. Andrew Leigh, "How Much Did the 2009 Fiscal Stimulus Boost Spending? Evidence from a Household Survey," unpublished working paper, 2009.

27. Alan J. Auerbach, "The Theory of Excess Burden and Optimal Taxation," in *Handbook of Public Economics,* vol. 1, edited by Alan J. Auerbach and Martin S. Feldstein (Amsterdam: Elsevier Science Publishers, 1985), pp. 61–127.

28. Chetty, Looney, and Kroft, "Salience and Taxation"; Raj Chetty, "The Simple Economics of Salience and Taxation," Working Paper 15246 (Cambridge, Mass.: National Bureau of Economic Research, August 2009).

29. Liebman and Zeckhauser, "Schmeduling."

30. Lawrence H. Summers, "Some Simple Economics of Mandated Benefits," *American Economic Review,* vol. 79, no. 2 (May 1989), pp. 177–83.

31. Liebman and Zeckhauser, "Schmeduling."

32. Ravi Kanbur, Jukka Pirttila, and Matti Tuomala, "Non-Welfarist Optimal Taxation and Behavioural Public Economics," *Journal of Economic Surveys,* vol. 20, no. 5 (December 2006), pp. 849–68.

33. Laurence J. Kotlikoff and Lawrence H. Summers, "Tax Incidence," in *Handbook of Public Economics,* vol. 2, edited by Auerbach and Feldstein, pp. 1043–92.

34. Chetty, Looney, and Kroft, "Salience and Taxation."

35. Rudolf Kerschbamer and Georg Kirchsteiger, "Theoretically Robust but Empirically Invalid? An Experimental Investigation into Tax Equivalence," *Economic Theory,* vol. 16, no. 3 (2000), pp. 719–34.

36. Michael G. Allingham and Agnar Sandmo, "Income Tax Evasion: A Theoretical Analysis," *Journal of Public Economics,* vol. 1, no. 3–4 (1972), pp. 323–38.

37. Erich Kirchler, *The Economic Psychology of Tax Behavior* (Cambridge University Press, 2007).

38. James Andreoni, Brian Erard, and Jonathan Feinstein, "Tax Compliance," *Journal of Economic Literature,* vol. 36, no. 2 (1998), pp. 818–60; Joel Slemrod, "Cheating Ourselves: The Economics of Tax Evasion," *Journal of Economic Perspectives,* vol. 21, no. 1 (2007), pp. 25–48.

39. Sanjit Dhami and Ali al-Nowaihi, "Why Do People Pay Taxes? Prospect Theory versus Expected Utility Theory," *Journal of Economic Behavior and Organization,* vol. 64, no. 1 (2007), pp. 171–92; Sanjit Dhami and Ali al-Nowaihi, "Optimal Income Taxation in the Presence of Tax Evasion: Expected Utility versus Prospect Theory," *Journal of Economic Behavior and Organization,* vol. 75, no. 2 (2010), pp. 313–37.

40. Michael W. Spicer and Lee A. Becker, "Fiscal Inequity and Tax Evasion: An Experimental Approach," *National Tax Journal,* vol. 33, no. 2 (1980), pp. 171–75; James Alm, Betty R. Jackson, and Michael McKee, "Estimating the Determinants of Taxpayer Compliance with Experimental Data," *National Tax Journal,* vol. 45, no. 1 (1992), pp. 107–14; James Alm, Betty R. Jackson, and Michael McKee, "Fiscal Exchange, Collective Decision Institutions, and Tax Compliance," *Journal of Economic Behavior and Organization,* vol. 22, no. 3 (1993), pp. 285–303.

41. Joel Slemrod, "Trust in Public Finance," in *Public Finance and Public Policy in the New Century,* edited by Sijbren Cnossen and Hans-Werner Sinn (MIT Press, 2003), pp. 49–88.

42. Bruno S. Frey and Benno Torgler, "Tax Morale and Conditional Cooperation," *Journal of Comparative Economics,* vol. 35, no. 1 (2007), pp. 136–59.

43. Joel Slemrod, Marsha Blumenthal, and Charles Christian, "Taxpayer Response to an Increased Probability of Audit: Evidence from a Controlled Experiment in Minnesota," *Journal of Public Economics,* vol. 79, no. 3 (2001), pp. 455–83; Benno Torgler, "Moral Suasion: An Alternative Tax Policy Strategy," *Economics of Governance,* vol. 5, no. 3 (2004), pp. 235–53.

44. Bruno S. Frey, *Not Just for the Money: An Economic Theory of Personal Motivation* (Cheltenham, U.K.: Edward Elgar, 1997); Uri Gneezy and Aldo Rustichini, "A Fine Is a Price," *Journal of Legal Studies*, vol. 29, no. 1 (2000), pp. 1–17.

45. Joel Slemrod and Wojciech Kopczuk, "The Optimal Elasticity of Taxable Income," *Journal of Public Economics*, vol. 84, no. 1 (April 2002), pp. 91–112.

46. Raj Chetty, "Is the Taxable Income Elasticity Sufficient to Calculate Deadweight Loss? The Implications of Evasion and Avoidance," *American Economic Journal: Economic Policy*, vol. 1, no. 2 (2009), pp. 31–52.

47. Raj Chetty and others, "Adjustment Costs, Firm Responses, and Labor Supply Elasticities: Evidence from Danish Tax Records," working paper, March 2010.

48. Wojciech Kopczuk, "Economics of Estate Taxation: A Brief Review of Theory and Evidence," Working Paper 15741 (Cambridge, Mass.: National Bureau of Economic Research, February 2010).

Appendix A

1. Richard H. Thaler and Cass R. Sunstein, *Nudge: Improving Decisions about Health, Wealth, and Happiness* (Yale University Press, 2008).

2. Richard H. Thaler and H. M. Shefrin, "An Economic Theory of Self-Control," *Journal of Political Economy*, vol. 89, no. 2 (1981), pp. 392–406; Daniel Kahneman, Peter P. Wakker, and Rakesh Sarin, "Back to Bentham? Explorations of Experienced Utility," *Quarterly Journal of Economics*, vol. 112, no. 2 (1997), pp. 375–405; John Beshears and others, "How Are Preferences Revealed?" *Journal of Public Economics*, vol. 92, no. 8-9 (2008), pp. 1787–94.

Index

CPSIA information can be obtained
at www.ICGtesting.com
Printed in the USA
BVHW031219120219
540065BV00003B/376/P

9 780815 722588